'While all of t  ιs
peculiar.' What 's
of Ross-shire m n
who led and shaped the nineteenth century Free Church
of Scotland. They were all excellent – excellent Christians,
churchmen, intellectuals and orators. But they all had their
own peculiarities, as Professor Finlayson demonstrates in
this new collection of memoirs. From the administrative
genius of Thomas Chalmers to the confessional radicalism
of Kennedy himself, the men featured in this book were all
endowed with qualities singularly suited to their respective
callings. Where there is a love for the gospel in Scotland,
their story deserves to be told, and Sandy Finlayson has
told it well. A highly commended volume.

REV DR IAIN D CAMPBELL
Free Church of Scotland, Isle of Lewis, UK

Sandy Finlayson's study of the nineteenth century leaders of the Free Church of Scotland is neither hagiography
nor iconoclasm; rather, it is the thoughtful reflection of a
committed presbyterian on the men who helped shape the
Scottish church through their commitment to orthodoxy,
evangelism, and social action. The attractive churchman-
ship which these church leaders represented is all too rare
today; and I hope this work will do something to restore it
to its rightful place in the wider Christian landscape.

DR CARL TRUEMAN
Westminster Theological Seminary, Philadelphia

At this moment in church history the people of God sorely
need to be reminded that following Christ means being
willing to part with cherished denominational identities
and connections, church buildings, and even houses and

secure salaries. This welcome book includes a photograph of each of these founding fathers of the Free Church of Scotland and —to a man—they all look as sober as hot, black coffee in a styrofoam cup. As we are in no danger of overdoing their earnestness, spending a few hours with such steely-eyed men can safely serve to remind us of what it means to stake one's life and livelihood on the lordship of Jesus Christ. Sandy Finlayson has written a clear, lively book that concedes when these churchmen were wrong without thereby obscuring their passionate stand for the Gospel.

DR TIMOTHY LARSEN,
McManis Professor of Christian Thought,
Wheaton College,Wheaton, Illinois

Unity and Diversity

The Founders of the Free Church of Scotland

•

Alexander (Sandy) Finlayson

For my parents
Cameron Finlayson, 1916–94
Ruth Finlayson, née Campbell, 1916–94

Alexander (Sandy) Finlayson is Library Director and Professor of Theological Bibliography at Westminster Theological Seminary in Philadelphia. Sandy holds degrees from the University of Toronto and Tyndale Theological Seminary in Canada, where he was also Library Director for eleven years. Sandy served as an elder in the Toronto congregation of the Free Church of Scotland for ten years. He is married to Linda, who writes books for children, and they have one son.

ISBN 978-1-84550-550-9

© Alexander (Sandy) Finlayson 2010

10 9 8 7 6 5 4 3 2 1

Published in 2010
by
Christian Focus Publications, Ltd,
Geanies House, Fearn, Ross-shire,
IV20 1TW, Great Britain.

www.christianfocus.com

Cover design by Moose77.com

Printed by Bell & Bain, Glasgow

Mixed Sources
Product group from well-managed forests and other controlled sources
www.fsc.org Cert no. TT-COC-002769
© 1996 Forest Stewardship Council
FSC

TABLE OF CONTENTS

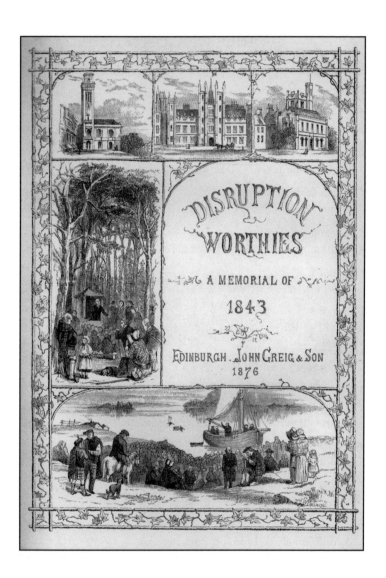

DISRUPTION
WORTHIES

A MEMORIAL OF

1843

EDINBURGH. JOHN GREIG & SON
1876

PREFACE

IN 1876, on the thirty-third anniversary of the first General Assembly of the Free Church of Scotland, the Assembly authorised 'the publication of the *Annals of the Disruption*', which was intended to present the official history of the founding of the Free Church.[1] In the same year John Greig and Son, the Edinburgh publishers, released an elaborate volume entitled *Disruption Worthies: A Memorial of 1843*. Dedicated to the 'Ministers, Office-Bearers and Members of the Free Church of Scotland', it lovingly paid tribute to forty-eight ministers and laymen who played a significant role in the creation of the Free Church. In the 'prefatory note', the publishers stated that the purpose of the book was 'to aid in perpetuating the remembrance of the great event of 1843 which called the Free Church of Scotland into existence'.[2] What followed were brief, highly stylised and worshipful biographies.

Ten years later, another publisher released a volume which expanded the scope of the project to include those ministers who had served exclusively in Highland congregations. The biographies of the twenty-nine ministers included

---

[1] Thomas Brown, *Annals of the Disruption: with extracts from the narratives of Ministers who left the Scottish establishment in 1843* (Edinburgh: Macnivan and Wallace, 1890), p. vii.

[2] *Disruption Worthies: A Memorial of 1843* (Edinburgh: J. Greig & Son, 1876), p. ii.

in *Disruption Worthies of the Highlands, a Memorial of 1843* were presented in such a way as to demonstrate the

> ... character and services of those devoted Ministers of the Gospel who were largely instrumental in bringing about so important a result as the almost unanimous adherence of the Highland population to the Free Church of Scotland.[3]

These volumes, along with the second and much expanded edition of the original *Disruption Worthies*, became standard sources for Free Church history and held pride of place in the homes of those who belonged to the church.

These books also had an ideological purpose. In addition to the biographical sketches, they included introductory essays which attempted to place the Free Church in historical context and to show how the church was a worthy heir of the Reformation. This impulse was even more in evidence in the second edition published in 1881. This edition was released when debate about the future of the Free Church was still very much alive, particularly as it related to the issue of union with other Presbyterian churches in Scotland.[4] It is important to note here that the *Disruption Worthies* volumes were never intended as objective treatments of their subjects. Rather, their purpose was to keep alive the memories of some of the

---

[3] *Disruption Worthies of the Highlands, a Memorial of 1843* (Edinburgh: John Grant, 1886), p. iv.

[4] The inclusion in this volume of Robert Rainy is particularly noteworthy. He is included as a 'Free Church Worthy' and is depicted as an heir to Thomas Chalmers and the other leaders of the Disruption. This, despite the fact that he spent much of his career deemphasising much of what the Free Church had originally stood for, and working hard to unite the Free Church with other Presbyterian bodies who allowed a much looser subscription to the *Westminster Confession of Faith*.

leading figures in the church, so that their lives might be emulated.

The origins and history of the Free Church have been examined by some contemporary scholars. Thomas Chalmers, the undisputed leader and first Moderator of the Church, and Hugh Miller, the geologist and journalist, have both received careful study. However, many of the other ministers and laymen who were featured in the *Free Church Worthies* have been largely ignored in recent years.

The work which follows will look at the life and ministry of ten figures in the Disruption era Free Church. My intent is to present as objective an account as possible of their lives, with an emphasis on why they mattered in their time and what they still have to say to us in the twenty-first century. The men chosen represent a cross-section of the Free Church, starting with Thomas Chalmers, who led the church at its beginning, and concluding with John Kennedy, who represented the Highland part of the church. All of these men shared a commitment to the reformed expression of the Christian faith. Yet while they had much in common, there was also diversity in how they lived out their faith and conducted their ministries. They were imperfect men who nonetheless were greatly used by God. All of the book's subjects deserve a much longer treatment than was possible here, but I hope these brief glimpses will be helpful to the reader.

There are a number of people I would like to thank for making the publication of this book possible. I'm particularly grateful to Willie Mackenzie, Malcolm Maclean and the staff of Christian Focus who willingly took on this project and who have seen it through to publication.

A number of colleagues and friends at Westminster Theological Seminary, Philadelphia, have played an important role in this project and without whom it would not have been completed. I am grateful to the Board of Trustees for their generous allowance of a semester of leave in 2009, when the book was written. I am also very grateful to the staff of the Montgomery Library: Grace Mullen, Marsha Blake, Donna Campbell and Karla Grafton. They have taken a lively interest in the book, as well as keeping the Library running very smoothly during my absence. I would also like to thank the Rev. Dr Carl R. Trueman, Academic Dean at Westminster, my boss and, more importantly, my friend. Carl has encouraged me throughout this project, pointed me in the direction of important sources and listened patiently while the book has evolved. His expert knowledge of Hugh Miller and his excellent library have also been of great assistance.

In addition to Carl's help with Hugh Miller, there are a number of other people who drew my attention to important resources and also provided feedback on parts of the book. The Rev. Dr A. Donald MacLeod, Research Professor of Church History at Tyndale Seminary in Toronto, drew my attention to *The Scotsman Digital Archive* which has been a goldmine of information. Don also alerted me to the existence of Charles Cowan, paper-maker, politician and Free Church elder, who was both eyewitness to, and actively involved in, the early years of the Free Church. The Rev. Dr Iain D. Campbell, minister of Point Free Church, read and provided helpful insight on the chapter on John Kennedy. I'm grateful to the Rev. Dr Mike Honeycutt for providing me with a copy of his excellent dissertation on William

Cunningham. Thanks are due to my sister Cathie Morton, who supplied me with information on Thomas Guthrie and the Ragged Schools movement. I would also like to thank Lorna Young, Manager, Bibliographic Services at Oakville Public Library, who searched *The Globe* newspaper archives and provided me with material on Alexander Duff's visit to Toronto.

Finally, I would like to express my gratitude to my wife Linda Finlayson and my colleague Marsha Blake, for reading and editing the manuscript and helping to smooth out my prose. Their contribution has made the book better than it otherwise would have been, but I remain wholly responsible for the opinions expressed and for the blemishes that remain. I am also indebted to Linda for allowing me to visit the nineteenth century for the last several months. I have been even less attentive than usual to the realities of twenty-first-century life over the last few months and she has been very supportive and patient!

Unity and Diversity: the Founders of the Free Church of Scotland is affectionately dedicated to the memory of my parents Cameron and Ruth Finlayson, who quietly modelled love for Christ and His church.

Oreland, Pennsylvania

November, 2009

Tanfield Hall, Canonmills.—First General Assembly, 1843.

Picture Credits

THE title page from the first edition of the *Disruption Worthies* and the picture of the First General Assembly of the Church of Scotland are taken from *Disruption Worthies: A Memorial of 1843*, Edinburgh: J. Greig & Son, 1876. The title page from the *Disruption Worthies of the Highlands* and the portrait of John Kennedy are from *Disruption Worthies of the Highlands, a Memorial of 1843*, Edinburgh: John Grant, 1886.

The remainder of the portraits and the title page from the expanded second edition of *Disruption Worthies* are from James B. Gillies, *Disruption Worthies: A Memorial of 1843; with a Historical Sketch of the Free Church of Scotland from 1843 Down to the Present Time*, Edinburgh: T.C. Jack, 1881.

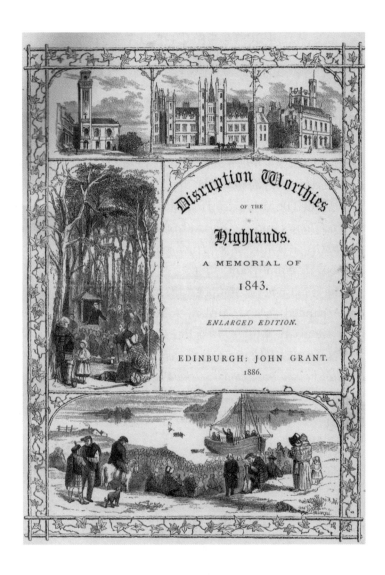

Disruption Worthies

OF THE

Highlands.

A MEMORIAL OF

1843.

ENLARGED EDITION.

EDINBURGH: JOHN GRANT.
1886.

1

SETTING THE SCENE

The Disruption of the Church of Scotland ... has ...
proved a mighty blessing, not only to Scotland, but also
in the noble example to Christendom which has been
set by the Free Church, and the wonderful blessing
which has followed her various enterprises both at
home and abroad.[1]

ENTERING Presbytery Hall in the offices of the Free
Church of Scotland in Edinburgh, the eye is drawn
to a massive picture hanging at one end of the room.
Painted by David Octavius Hill over a period of twenty-
three years, the picture is entitled *The First General
Assembly of the Free Church of Scotland; signing the Act
of Separation and Deed of Demission*. It captures the
images of 457 people out of the 1,500 who were present
at the opening of first Free Church General Assembly in
Edinburgh on 18 May 1843.

This picture is famous because of its place in photo-
graphic history, Hill having used a camera to take photo-
graphic images of many of the people depicted before
they were then painted. But it is even more important for
what it commemorates, the founding of the Free Church
of Scotland. In the picture are many of the eminent men

---

[1] Charles Cowan, *Reminiscences* (Edinburgh: Printed for private circulation, 1878), p. 313.

and women of nineteenth-century Scotland as well as other important figures from much further afield.

> Dr Lyman Beecher, the father of Harriet Beecher Stowe, who wrote *Uncle Tom's Cabin*; Dr Merle D'Aubigne of Geneva, who wrote *The History of the Reformation*; Dr Adolphe Sydow, Chaplain to the King of Prussia who reported on the Assembly to Queen Victoria [and] ... Dr James McCosh who became President of Princeton University ...[2]

The Free Church would become an influential force in the ecclesiastical life of Scotland and beyond. As the nineteenth century progressed, the Free Church had to contend with the issues of confessional orthodoxy during a time when the winds of theological change were blowing. The church also evidenced a desire to inculcate evangelical piety in the lives of its members and to put the gospel into action in the world. Its ministers, office bearers and organisations would show genuine concern for the social conditions of the poor in Scotland. Lest it be thought that this was a parochial church, it should be noted that it would be responsible for mission work in a number of parts of the world. The achievements of the Free Church have been described in the following terms: 'New Churches and manses were built, theological colleges were opened, an extensive educational system developed,

---

[2] William S. Anderson, *A guide to the Free Church of Scotland College and Offices* (Edinburgh: Knox Press, 1994), p. 22. Anderson notes that there are a number of anachronisms in the painting in that some of the subjects were painted as they appeared later in life and others are included who were not actually present at the Assembly. For example, John Duncan, Hebrew scholar, missionary and professor, and Alexander Duff, the pioneer missionary to India (both of whom will be featured later in this book), are shown but were not actually present.

and thriving missions opened overseas.'[3] A number of key figures led the church during this period and it is their contributions that we will be focusing on in this book. But before we can examine their lives and their impact, we must first briefly sketch how the Free Church came into being.

At the very simplest of levels it has been asserted that the Free Church of Scotland came into existence as a result of a 'protest against what [was] perceived as state efforts to undermine the church's spiritual independence and integrity'. [4] Since we live in a day when most Christians take for granted that the church may regulate its own affairs, it sounds odd to modern ears that this should be a cause for major division in the church. But this is what happened in Scotland in the nineteenth century. In order to understand how this happened, we need to look back into Scottish church history.

CHURCH AND STATE IN SCOTLAND

The events of May 1843 had their immediate genesis in a ten-year conflict within the Church of Scotland. The chief issue in question was the nature of the relationship between the church and the state. More particularly, did the civil magistrate have any jurisdiction over how ministers were appointed to parish churches? All parties firmly believed in an established church and in the 'establishment principle',

---

[3] Maurice Grant, 'The heirs of the Disruption in crisis and recovery 1893–1920', in C. Graham, *Crown Him Lord of All: essays on the life and witness of the Free Church of Scotland* (Edinburgh: Knox Press, 1993), p. 1.

[4] S.J. Brown, 'The Disruption and the dream: the making of New College 1843–61', in D.F. Wright and G. D. Badcock (eds), *Disruption to Diversity: Edinburgh Divinity 1846–1996* (Edinburgh: T & T Clark, 1996), p. 29.

but there was significant disagreement as to what this meant and how it was to be implemented.

The establishment principle states that there is a link between the church of Christ and the state. Both institutions have been created by God and are to support and further the work of the other. Therefore a religious establishment

> ... involves making legal provision for the expense of religious ministrations – in other words, a nation stating its specific preference for supplying Christian teaching by providing a church or churches with the legal sanction and financial resources to carry out this task.[5]

This view was firmly rooted in the history of the church in Scotland and in fact traced its origins back to the *Westminster Confession of Faith*. The *Confession* describes how the relationship between the church and the state ought to work in chapter twenty-three, section three.

> The civil magistrate may not assume to himself the administration of the word and sacraments, or the power of the keys of the kingdom of heaven; yet he hath authority, and it is his duty, to take order, that unity and peace be preserved in the church, that the truth of God be kept pure and entire, that all blasphemies and heresies be suppressed, all corruptions and abuses in worship and discipline prevented or reformed, and all the ordinances of God duly settled, administered and observed. For the better effecting whereof, he hath power to call synods,

---

[5] William M. Mackay, 'Thomas Chalmers and His Vision Of The Church Of Scotland'. *Free Church of Scotland*, http://www.freechurch. org/resources/history/chalmers2.htm (accessed 15 November 2008).

to be present at them, and to provide that whatsoever is transacted in them be according to the mind of God.[6]

So how did the manner of the appointment of clergy become the flashpoint in mid-nineteenth-century Scotland? To answer this we must look further back in Scottish church history. Before the Reformation, some landowners had taken upon themselves the right to appoint local parish priests. New ideas of church government that emerged after the Reformation included attempts to do away with this system of patronage and replace it with a system whereby individual parishioners could elect their pastors. However, landowners were unwilling to give up their long-standing rights. As K.R. Ross has pointed out,

> The landowners, who supplied church accommodations and ministerial stipends, retained as a right of property, their positions as patrons. Often the patron, through informal consultation, presented a candidate acceptable to the people, but difficulties arose when the patron was out of sympathy with parochial opinion.[7]

In the seventeenth and eighteenth centuries, a number of pieces of legislation were passed by Parliament in an attempt to settle these issues. The conflicting laws first abolished patronage in 1649, then re-established it in 1662,

---

[6] 'Westminster Confession of Faith', *Free Church of Scotland*, http://www.freechurch.org/resources/confessions/westminster.htm (accessed 15 November 2008). In 1788 the Presbyterian Church in the United States made significant revisions to this chapter of the *Confession* which effectively removed the establishment principle.

[7] N.R. Needham, 'Patron, Patronage, Patronage Acts', in D.C. Lachman, D.E. Meek (eds), *Dictionary of Scottish Church History and Theology* (Downers Grove Ill: InterVarsity Press, 1993), p. 649.

abolished it again 1690 only to have it re-established in the *Patronage Act* of 1712. This act was

> ... patently aimed at advancing Episcopalian opinion within the Church ... The General Assembly deplored it as 'grievous and prejudicial to this Church' and called for its repeal ...[8]

Thus the later part of the eighteenth and early part of the nineteenth centuries saw significant conflict within the Church of Scotland regarding who had the right to call ministers.

It may well be wondered how it is that those who were faithful to the reformation vision of a church that was free to preach the gospel could possibly tolerate this situation? There were those who were willing to accept the status quo for at least two reasons. Some accepted it because it was, after all, the law of the land and they were reluctant to disobey the civil authorities. There were also those who believed that pastoral charges would be better served if their ministers were carefully chosen by the patron, who would be in the best position to better judge their education and giftedness, rather than by an open call by male heads of families in the parish. There was also a hope that suitable ministers could be chosen if there was adequate consultation between patrons and individual congregations.[9]

There were some who did publicly state their opposition to the situation in the Church of Scotland. In 1733, four ministers left the church because of what they perceived

---

[8] Ibid.

[9] Needham, 'Patron, Patronage, Patronage Acts', *Dictionary of Scottish Church History and Theology*, p. 649.

as doctrinal laxity, the usurping of Presbyterial powers of ordination by the General Assembly and the General Assembly's refusal to receive their protests. Then in 1761 there was another secession when Thomas Gillespie and five other ministers presented a petition to the General Assembly which protested against the imposition of ministers on parishes. Gillespie was ultimately deposed and formed the Presbytery of Relief 'for Christians oppressed in their church privileges'. [10]

As the Church of Scotland entered the nineteenth century, it was clear that the status quo was becoming increasingly unworkable. Evangelicals within the Church of Scotland were expressing real concern that the spiritual independence of the church was being compromised. Pointing back to the *Westminster Confession*, they argued that the church had the sole right to decide matters which had to do with worship and discipline. And surely, the choice and selection of pastors for local congregations ought not to be imposed.

Another contributing factor to the events leading up to the Disruption was a popular movement for democratic reform that was beginning to exert more influence in British political life. This movement emphasised representative government and equality of opportunity through the extension of popular education. These two movements, the one grounded in evangelical piety and the second based on political ideology, combined to create forces which would bring about the creation of the Free Church.

---

[10] For more information on the Secession Churches see K.R. Ross, 'Secessions', in *Dictionary of Scottish Church History and Theology*, pp. 764–5, and D.C. Lachman, 'Associate Presbytery', in *Dictionary of Scottish Church History and Theology*, pp. 35–6.

THE TEN YEARS CONFLICT

In 1834 the Church of Scotland General Assembly passed *The Veto Act*. The purpose of this act was to restrict the power of patronage by giving to male heads of families the right to veto the parish patron's appointment of the local minister. Dr Thomas Chalmers, the leader of the Evangelical party in the Church of Scotland, maintained that 'the common sense of parishioners ... could be trusted to guard against improper appointments'. [11] Charles Cowan, paper-maker, politician and elder at St George's Church, Edinburgh, described the rationale behind *The Veto Act* in these terms:

> The object and desire of Dr Chalmers and his friends ... was not to abolish the right of presentation to vacant benefices, but merely to interpose the ancient and constitutional check upon its capricious or arbitrary exercise, by reviving the ancient right of congregations ... to exercise the 'call' in the appointment of their pastor.[12]

The passage of this act opened a period of intense conflict which culminated in the events of May 1843.

The first test of the *Veto Act* occurred in 1834 in the parish of Auchterarder, Perthshire, where out of a total of 336 heads of families, only 2 of them were prepared to sign a call to the laird's preferred candidate Robert Young. When the call was not then acted upon, Young sued, thus beginning a long legal wrangle. Essentially the Veto Act was viewed by the gentry as 'the stuff of

---

[11] Brown, 'The Disruption and the dream: the making of New College 1843–61', p. 31.

[12] Cowan, *Reminiscences*, p. 295.

bloody revolution' [13] and they were not prepared to allow the election of pastors by any sort of democratic vote.

Also in 1834, the Church of Scotland passed *The Chapels Act*. This Act gave official recognition to *Chapels of Ease*[14] granting them similar status as parish churches. They would have

> ... kirk-sessions with disciplinary authority, and their clergy and elders were granted full membership on the presbytery, synod and General Assembly courts. Further, the new churches received territorial parish boundaries recognized by the Church. The new parishes were termed, *quoad sacra*,[15] to distinguish them from the existing *quoad civilia* parishes which were defined by the civil law.[16]

With the passage of *The Chapels Act*, the Church of Scotland began an aggressive church extension programme which would see the building of many churches and schools in Scotland. Rather than asking for full government financial support for this expansion programme, the Church of Scotland decided to fund this effort largely through private contributions. They only looked to the government to provide a partial endowment in those areas where poverty was

---

[13] John MacLeod, *Banner in the West: A Spiritual History of Lewis and Harris* (Edinburgh: Birlinn, 2008), p. 168.

[14] Chapels of Ease had been established toward the end of the eighteenth century in response to the national church's inability to create fully endowed parishes to meet the needs of the growing population. Initially these Chapels did not have elders and enjoyed the right of popularly electing their ministers.

[15] A Latin term meaning 'in respect of sacred things'. These parishes were subdivided from larger parishes so that their residents would be properly served.

[16] Stewart J. Brown, *Thomas Chalmers and the Godly Commonwealth in Scotland* (Oxford: Oxford University Press, 1982), p. 234.

so great that parish residents could not afford to pay the stipends of the local school-master and minister. It is important to note here that

> Private giving to the Church's educational, philanthropic and evangelical work increased fourteen-fold between 1834 and 1839, and some two hundred new churches were built or begun.[17]

Nineteenth-century Scotland saw significant population growth which brought with it growing social problems. It might be thought that the societal benefit of new schools and churches would therefore have brought with it the favour of the government, but this was not the case. As events progressed it became clear that there was little or no interest in changing the patronage system that most parliamentarians believed was working well.

In 1837, a series of events began in the Banffshire parish of Marnoch which would have far-reaching implications. This case, which would drag on until 1841, perhaps more than any other, highlighted the issues of whether or not the civil courts had any business in ecclesiastical matters. When the parish became vacant, John Edwards was presented as the next minister. Of all the male heads of families only the local innkeeper signed the call and, as a result, the Presbytery sought advice from the Church's Commission of Assembly who told them to reject the nomination, which they initially did. While the patron accepted this decision, Mr Edwards did not, and he took the Presbytery to court. The Presbytery responded to the court

---

[17] Brown, 'The Disruption and the dream: the making of New College 1843–61', p. 31.

action by stating that they would await the result of the court action before making a final decision on whether or not to proceed with the call and ordination. Ultimately, the Court of Session instructed the Presbytery to proceed and the Church's Commission of Assembly told them not to. Faced with the dilemma of having to choose between obedience to the state or the church, the Presbytery met and agreed by a vote of seven to four to sustain Edwards' ordination. The 'Stathbogie Seven', as they came to be known, were subsequently deposed for disobeying the church, and the minority were called upon to announce the sentence. As for the vacant parish, 'on a bleak January day five ministers appeared at Marnoch and amid scenes of considerable uproar and unhappiness, Edwards was admitted as minister of the parish'. The seven suspended ministers then constituted themselves as *the* Presbytery and sought court protection to keep those who opposed them out of the area.[18]

In 1838 and 1839 two significant events took place. First, the British government announced that they would not support the work of the church in the poorer areas where the partial endowments had been sought. Secondly, the Court of Session in Scotland ruled that *The Veto Act* which had been passed by the Church of Scotland General Assembly was illegal, since it infringed on the long established property rights of patrons. A sense of just how strongly the Scottish legal establishment viewed these matters may be seen from the following statement by Lord Hope, who wrote:

---

[18] A. Herron, 'Stathbogie Case', in *Dictionary of Scottish Church History and Theology*, pp. 801–2.

> That our Saviour is the Head of the Kirk in Scotland in any temporal or legislative, or judicial sense, is a position which I can signify by no other name than absurdity. The Parliament is the Head of the Church, from whose Acts, and whose Acts alone, it exists as the National Church, and from which alone it derives all its powers. Who ... gave the Church Courts any jurisdiction? The law and law alone, gave it, and the law defines what it is has so given.[19]

After they announced their decision, the Court of Session began to instruct Presbyteries to ordain and induct ministers who had been chosen by patrons even if parishioners did not want the appointee inducted. Some Presbyteries went along with the Court's ruling, but others did not. Matters further escalated when the Courts began to threaten Presbyteries with fines and imprisonment if they did not induct ministers appointed by parish patrons. In another key decision, the Court also decided that the Church of Scotland did not have the legal right to establish new parishes without the consent and financial support of local landowners, thus effectively blocking the church's extension plans. The most notorious example of this was the 'Stewarton Case' which began in 1839. A congregation was received into the Church of Scotland, parish boundaries established and the minister granted a seat on Presbytery. Local landowners complained to the Court that this was illegal and judgment was given against the Church of Scotland.[20]

---

[19] Norman L. Walker, *Chapters from the History of the Free Church of Scotland* (Edinburgh: Oliphant, Anderson and Ferrier,1895), p. 13.

[20] For more details see, A. Heron 'Stewarton Case', in *Dictionary of Scottish Church History and Theology*, p. 796.

Despite repeated appeals to the Courts, it became increasingly clear that the situation was not going to change. Therefore, a growing number of evangelicals reluctantly came to the conclusion that in order for the spiritual independence of the church to be maintained, they would have to clearly protest at what was taking place and if these protests failed, to leave the Church of Scotland. The clearest statement of concern was embodied in *The Claim Declaration and Protest anent the Encroachments of the Court of Session* that was passed by the 1842 General Assembly. While the *Claim* acknowledged that the civil courts had absolute jurisdiction over the temporalities conferred by the state on the church, it totally rejected court and state jurisdiction over matters relating to spiritual matters which included the appointment of ministers and the creation of new parishes. It has been rightly argued that the

> ... framing of the Claim ... crystallized the issues at stake, and set the church on a course which inevitably, as the Claim itself anticipated, led to the Disruption of 1843.[21]

In November of 1842, Dr Thomas Chalmers called for a meeting of ministers of the Evangelical party to meet in Edinburgh to discuss the growing crisis. After much debate, the 'convocation' (which was made up of 374 ministers) agreed that they would leave the established Church of Scotland if their claim for the spiritual independence of the church was not recognised by the courts in Scotland

---

[21] P.E.H. Hair, 'Claim of Right', in *Dictionary of Scottish Church History and Theology*, p. 188.

and by Parliament in London.[22] It must be remembered that in taking this stand, these men were prepared to give up their stipends, churches and manses with no guarantees that they would be able to continue to provide for their needs and those of their families.

In March of 1843, a final attempt was made to have the British government resolve the crisis in favour of the Evangelical party in the Church of Scotland. A motion was brought to the House of Commons in London which, if it had passed, would have set up a select committee. This committee would

> ... have moved an address to the Crown, praying 'That a Declaratory Act be passed, to the effect of better defining the subject matter of the jurisdiction of the Church, and confirming her jurisdiction within her own province.' [23]

The motion was defeated by a vote of 211 to 76. One contemporary observer noted, with some bitterness, that although the majority of Scottish members voted in favour of it, the proposal failed because as

> ... is usual in the House of Commons, in ecclesiastical and particularly in Scotch questions, probably not above one out of ten members who voted had heard a word of the debate, nor, had they been asked seriatim, could they have given any intelligible explanation of the question before the House.[24]

By May of 1843, the Church of Scotland had come through a period of intense stress and strain. The battles of the

---

[22] K.R. Ross, 'Convocation', in *Dictionary of Scottish Church History and Theology*, p. 210.

[23] Cowan, *Reminiscences*, p. 298.

[24] Ibid.

'Ten Years Conflict' had been played out between two groups in the Church of Scotland, the Moderate party and the Evangelicals. The Moderates were willing to live with the status quo, which confirmed a patron's right to appoint ministers and gave to the state the right to determine where parishes could be erected. The Evangelicals, on the other hand, were discontent with what came to be seen as civil interference in ecclesiastical matters and were determined to defend the spiritual independence of the church. Both groups firmly believed that they were the true heirs of the Reformation church in Scotland and both claimed that they were pursuing the best interests of the church and people of Scotland. The issue of the day was what direction the Church of Scotland would take after a period of intense political and ecclesiastical struggle. Would the church survive as one body or would it divide and go in different directions?

THE DISRUPTION

On 18 May 1843, a large crowd assembled in Edinburgh outside of St Andrew's Church. Inside, the General Assembly of the Church of Scotland was about to convene. Contemporary accounts of the events describe the sense of expectation and tension. The streets of Edinburgh were full of '... masses of eager spectators while inside the church the dense crowd, after long hours of suspense, were intently waiting for the issue'.[25] The events which followed have been called 'probably the most important event in the history of nineteenth-century Scotland and a major episode in the

[25] Brown, *Annals of the Disruption: with extracts from the narratives of Ministers who left the Scottish establishment in 1843*, p. 69.

history of the modern western church'. [26] Hugh Miller, geologist, journalist and elder in the church, vividly described the scene as it unfolded.

> Never before was there seen so crowded a General Assembly: the number of members had been increased beyond all precedent by the double returns; and almost every member was in his place. The Moderator opened the proceedings by deeply impressive prayer; but though the silence within was complete, a Babel of tumultuary sounds outside, and at the closed doors, expressive of the intense anxiety of the excluded multitude, had the effect of rendering him scarcely audible in the more distant parts of the building. There stood beside the chair, though on opposite sides, the meet representatives of the belligerent parties. On the right we marked Principal M'Farlan of Glasgow. ... On his left stood Thomas Chalmers, the man through whose indomitable energy and Christian zeal two hundred churches were added to the Establishment in little more than ten years.
>
> The Moderator rose and addressed the House in a few impressive sentences. There had been an infringement, he said, on the constitution of the Church, — an infringement so great, that they could not constitute its General Assembly without a violation of the union between Church and State, as now authoritatively defined and declared. He was therefore compelled, he added, to protest against proceeding further; and, unfolding a document which he held in his hand, he read, in a slow and emphatic manner, the protest of the Church. For the first few seconds, the extreme anxiety to hear defeated its object, — the universal hush, hush,

---

[26] Brown, 'The Disruption and the dream: the making of New College 1843–61', p. 30.

occasioned considerably more noise than it allayed; but the momentary confusion was succeeded by the most unbroken silence; and the reader went on till the impressive close of the document, when he flung it down on the table of the House, and solemnly departed. He was followed, at a pace's distance, by Dr Chalmers; Dr Gordon and Dr Patrick M'Farlan immediately succeeded; and then the numerous sitters on the thickly occupied benches behind filed after them, in a long unbroken line, which for several minutes together continued to thread the passage to the eastern door, till at length only a blank space remained. As the well-known faces and forms of some of the ablest and most eminent men that ever adorned the Church of Scotland glided along in the current, to disappear from the courts of the State institution for ever, there rose a cheer from the galleries, and an impatient cry of 'Out, out', from the ministers and elders not members of Assembly, now engaged in sallying forth, to join with them, from the railed area behind.[27]

The ministers and elders who left St Andrew's Church proceeded to Tanfield Hall which had been prepared in advance for this first General Assembly of the Free Church of Scotland.[28] The proceedings were opened by the retiring Modera-

---

[27] Hugh Miller, 'The Disruption', *Headship of Christ and the Rights of the Christian People* (Boston: Gould and Lincoln, 1863), pp. 478–9.

[28] G.N.M. Collins has noted that there was some discussion as to what the new church should be called. While Chalmers and other leaders in the church were determined to maintain that those who had withdrawn from the established church were still by right *THE* Church of Scotland, there was recognition that this would be challenged and lost in the civil courts. Some argued that the new body should be called The Free Protesting Church of Scotland or the Free Presbyterian Church of Scotland, but by the time of the second General Assembly later in 1843, the church was called The Free Church of Scotland. See G.N.M. Collins, *The Heritage of Our Fathers* (Edinburgh: Knox Press, 1976), pp. 62–3.

tor Dr Welsh, and then Dr Thomas Chalmers was immediately appointed the first Moderator. In his prepared remarks, Chalmers set the tone for the new church when he said this:

> Reverend fathers and brethren, it is well that you should have been strengthened by your Master in Heaven to make the surrender you have done, of everything that is dear to nature; casting aside all your earthly dependence rather than offend conscience, or incur the guilt of sinful compliance by thwarting your own sense of duty, and running counter to the Bible, our Great Church Directory and Statute Book. It is well that you have made, for the present, a clean escape from this condemnation — and that in the issue of the contest between a sacrifice of principle and a sacrifice of your worldly possessions, you have resolved upon the latter; and while to the eye of sense you are without a provision and a home, embarked upon a wide ocean of uncertainty, save that great and generous certainty which is apprehended by the eye of faith — that God reigneth, and that He will not forsake the families of the faithful.[29]

As the Assembly began its work, 470 ministers signed the *Act of Separation and Deed of Demission* which stated that they were separating from the ecclesiastical establishment in Scotland and were also renouncing 'all rights and emoluments pertaining to them in virtue thereof'.[30] In addition to the ministers who joined the new church, 192 probationary ministers also aligned themselves with

[29] William Hanna, *Memoirs of the Life and Writings of Thomas Chalmers*, v. 2 (Edinburgh: Edmonston and Douglas, 1867), pp. 645–6. While originally published in four volumes, references in this book are to the two volume edition.

[30] Brown, *Thomas Chalmers and the Godly Commonwealth in Scotland*, p. 334.

the new body and in a remarkable display of solidarity, all of the Church of Scotland's oversees missionaries joined the Free Church of Scotland. While no definite number may be asserted, it is estimated that 40 per cent of the church's lay membership withdrew from the established church.[31]

In the days and months to come, the newly founded Free Church of Scotland would face significant challenges as it struggled to provide for the spiritual and educational needs of the people who had affiliated themselves with the new church. There were major sacrifices that would have to be made by both ministers and people. Whole congregations were forced out of church buildings and many ministers and their families lost their manses. The church would need to undertake a massive rebuilding programme and as this work began, it did so under the watchful eye of Thomas Chalmers.

A glance at David Octavius Hill's famous picture shows Thomas Chalmers at the centre, presiding over the Assembly. One senses both his charisma and the respect in which he was held by so many people in Scotland. It was

> ... the presence of Chalmers at the head of the procession out [of the Church of Scotland], a man who, for all his weaknesses, remained the greatest Scottish churchman of his day, was sufficient guarantee for many that it was indeed the true Church that was abandoning the State connection.[32]

It is therefore appropriate that we now turn our attention to Thomas Chalmers and survey his life and work.

---

[31] Ibid., p. 336.

[32] Ibid.

THOMAS CHALMERS, D.D. LL.D.

Home & Macdonald.

2

THOMAS CHALMERS
VISIONARY PASTOR

> It is not often that the world sees men like Thomas
> Chalmers; nor can the world afford to forget them, or in
> its most careless mood be willing to do it, when they do
> appear, in whatever guise that be. Probably the time is
> coming when it will be more apparent than it now is to
> every one that *here* intrinsically was the chief Scottish
> man of his Time.[1]

THOMAS Chalmers was born on 17 March 1780. Over
the next sixty-seven years, he would lead a very
public life as pastor, university professor, visionary social
reformer and leader in the church, punctuated by significant successes and disappointments. In his own time he
was viewed as a hero by many in Scotland and sneered
at by Karl Marx as 'the arch-parson'. [2] A complex man,
Chalmers had a major impact on the church and society
of his day.

---

[1] Thomas Carlyle, 'Letter to William Hanna 7 June 1852', *The Carlyle
Letters Online*, http://carlyleletters.dukejournals.org/cgi/content/full/27/1/
lt-18520607-TC-WH-01? (accessed 10 January 2009). Emphasis is in the
original. It should be noted that Carlyle was not always as complementary
as this in describing Chalmers. He once described him as being '... a man
essentially of little culture of narrow sphere all his life'. For Carlyle's full
description, see R.B. Johnson, *Pen portraits by Thomas Carlyle, found in
his works and correspondence*, (London: 1896), pp. 12–13.

[2] Karl Marx, *Capital: A Critique of Political Economy* (New York:
Modern Library, 1936), p. 676.

EARLY LIFE AND EDUCATION
1780–1802

Thomas Chalmers was the sixth child in a family of fourteen. His father, John Chalmers, was a businessman in the town of Anstruther on the Fife coast. The family business included ship owning and the management of the local thread and dye works. By the beginning of the nineteenth century, the family business had suffered a number of setbacks and John Chalmers finished his days as the proprietor of a small retail wool shop. Despite the downturn in business, John Chalmers has been described as 'an affable man who was devoted to his family and community'. [3] Both John and Elizabeth Chalmers were very active in their community. John became a magistrate in Anstruther and Elizabeth devoted some of her time to working with paupers in the parish. This concern for those less fortunate was passed on to their son Thomas. As Calvinists they were anxious 'that their family should grow up to view Christianity from that position', but it was not until 1811 at the age of thirty-one that Thomas Chalmers came to fully embrace the faith of his parents for himself.[4] Chalmers was educated at the local parish school where he was remembered more for his physical strength and warm-heartedness than he was for academic attainment. He completed his elementary education by the age of eleven and then moved on to St Andrews University where he completed the arts course. He then entered the Divinity Faculty 'largely at

[3] Brown, *Thomas Chalmers and the Godly Commonwealth*, p. 116.

[4] William M. Mackay, *Thomas Chalmers: A Short Appreciation* (Edinburgh: Knox Press, 1980), p. 7.

the insistence of his father'.[5] Although Chalmers had grown up in a home that was strictly Calvinistic in its theology, this came to be challenged at St Andrew's. While he was intellectually stimulated at the university, he was at the same time drawn away from the faith. In later life he described the religious climate in which he found himself in this way:

> St Andrews was at this time overrun with Moderatism, under the chilling influences of which we inhaled not a distaste only, but a positive contempt for all that is properly and peculiarly gospel, insomuch that our confidence was nearly as entire in the sufficiency of natural theology as in the sufficiency of natural science.[6]

Chalmers completed his theological course at the age of nineteen and was licensed to preach on 31 July 1799, then in 1802 he was presented to the parish of Kilmany in Fife.

PASTORAL MINISTRY IN KILMANY 1802–14

The first years of ministry at Kilmany were not marked by much zeal or concern for the church to which he had been appointed. In fact, quite the opposite was the case. It has been noted that

---

[5] Stewart J. Brown, 'Chalmers, Thomas', in *Oxford Dictionary of National Biography,* v. 10 (Oxford: Oxford University Press, 2004), p. 879.

[6] Hanna, *Memoirs of the Life and Writings of Thomas Chalmers,* v. 1, p. 11. William Hanna was Thomas Chalmers' son-in-law and published these *Memoirs* between 1849 and 1852. While they are laudatory in tone, they are also an important source of information on Chalmers since they contain many lengthy extracts from his diaries, letters and other primary sources.

When Chalmers was presented to that parish by the Senatus of St Andrews, its chief merit in his eyes was that its location enabled him to hold simultaneously an assistantship in Mathematics at the University.[7]

In a letter to his father dated 18 October 1803 Chalmers indicated his desire to teach mathematics and chemistry classes at the university and attempted to justify this by saying:

> ... my chief anxiety is to reconcile you to the idea of not confining my whole attention to my ministerial employment. The fact is that no minister finds that necessary.[8]

While his lectures at the university were well received they attracted the displeasure of his Presbytery. At a meeting held on 4 September 1804, the Presbytery minuted their opinion that '... Mr Chalmers giving lectures in chemistry is improper and ought to be discontinued'.[9] Chalmers chafed against the Presbytery's directive and took the step of writing to the Moderator, concluding his strenuous argument by saying 'to the last sigh of my breath I will struggle for independence, and eye with proud disdain the man who presumes to invade it'.[10] This determination in the face of opposition would be a characteristic which would be displayed time and again in Chalmers' life. The Presbytery censure did little to change Chalmers' approach to his

---

[7] Ian Henderson, 'Thomas Chalmers: Famous Church Leader and Orator', *The Scotsman Digital Archive, May 30, 1947,* http://archive.scotsman.com/ (accessed 31 January 2009).

[8] Hanna, *Memoirs of the Life and Writings of Thomas Chalmers,* v. 1, p. 50.

[9] Ibid., p. 61.

[10] Ibid., p. 63.

work and in 1807 he travelled to London and spent three months there with his brother George.

At the beginning of the nineteenth century, Britain was under significant threat of invasion as a result of the growing power of Napoleonic France. Even if there was no military invasion, there were real strains on the British economy. During his time in London, Chalmers became very interested in the economic and political questions of the day, which prompted the publication of his first book, *An Inquiry into the Extent and Stability of Natural Resources*. *An Inquiry* looked at the issue of what would happen if British imports to the continent were blocked as a result of the Napoleonic wars. In the book Chalmers argued that Britain's economy could survive this threat and he also suggested that

> ... foreign trade only encouraged the growth of 'surplus' population supported precariously by commerce and man-ufacturers. [He would also argue that it] would be better to tax the surplus agricultural wealth used to finance foreign trade and transfer the surplus population ... to the service of the state in an enlarged military and educational establishment.[11]

His first venture into print was not successful. It received very poor reviews and, much to Chalmers' distress, was largely ignored by those he most wanted to impress. Despite the adverse criticism, his pamphlet was a sign of things to come, as Chalmers would display genuine concern for socio-political issues all his life. Chalmers'

---

[11] Brown, 'Thomas Chalmers', in *Oxford Dictionary of National Biography*, v. 10, p. 880.

return to Kilmany did not bring him much satisfaction either, as over the course of the next two years he saw declining church attendance. While his sermons were competent enough, they 'lacked deep spiritual concern for those amongst whom he ministered'. [12]

Between 1809 and 1811 a series of events took place which would have a major impact upon him. From viewing his pastoral ministry as a means to preferment and a way of receiving recognition, Chalmers' priorities began to change. Up to this point he had reflected the moderate views he had learned at St Andrews, but Chalmers would soon undergo a real change of heart that altered his life.

In 1809, Chalmers came into contact with and under the influence of a number of young evangelicals in the Church of Scotland. One of these men, David Brewster, invited Chalmers to contribute a series of scientific articles to a forthcoming encyclopaedia. As *The Edinburgh Encyclopaedia* developed, Chalmers was also offered the article on Christianity, which he took on with considerable enthusiasm promising that he would conduct 'a careful scientific inquiry into the historical evidence for the Christian revelation'. Thus he also began a period of 'serious study of the Bible and of the early church fathers'.[13]

In early June 1809, Chalmers became very ill with consumption. The disease had already claimed the lives of his sister Barbara and his brother George. He had been close to his siblings and their deaths caused him 'to reflect more seriously about a dimension of life which, by his own confession

---

[12] Mackay, *Thomas Chalmers: A Short Appreciation,* p. 13.

[13] Brown, *Thomas Chalmers and the Godly Commonwealth,* p. 51.

he had not fully considered'. [14] During the summer his condition steadily worsened, until there was very real concern for his life. During his illness he wrote to a friend that:

> My confinement has fixed on my heart a very strong impression of the insignificance of time – an impression which I trust will not abandon me though I again reach the heyday of health and vigour ... I have been reading Pascal's *Thoughts on Religion* ... [it is written by] a man who could stop short in the brilliant career of discovery, who could resign all the splendours of literary reputation, who could renounce without a sigh all the distinctions which are conferred upon genius, and resolve to devote every talent and every hour to the defence and illustration of the Gospel.[15]

By April 1810, Chalmers was sufficiently recovered from his illness that he was able to return to the family home in Arnstruther. There he was faced with a series of crises, first when his brief engagement to Anne Rankine came to an end and then when his sister Lucy died of consumption on 23 December 1810. As he dealt with his grief, he began reading William Wilberforce's *Practical View of the Prevailing Religious System of Professed Christians* and in this work he found a warm evangelical piety. In a letter to his brother Alexander dated 14 February 1820 he looked back on this period of his life and he wrote:

> ... as I got on in reading it, [I] felt myself on the eve of a great revelation in all my opinions about Christianity ... I am now most thoroughly of the opinion, and it is an

---

[14] Mackay, *Thomas Chalmers: A Short Appreciation*, p. 13.

[15] Hanna, *Memoirs of the Life and Writings of Thomas Chalmers*, v. 1, p. 112.

opinion founded on experience, that on the system of – Do this and live – no peace, and even no true and worthy obedience, can ever be attained. It is Believe in the Lord Jesus Christ and thou shalt be saved. When this belief enters the heart, joy and confidence enter along with it.[16]

Chalmers' religious conversion had an immediate impact on his parish work in Kilmany. He now threw himself into the work. His preaching became much more vigorous and attracted attention from far and wide. He engaged in significantly more pastoral visitation and showed genuine concern for those in his care.

Another significant event took place in August 1812 when he married Grace Pratt to whom he remained happily married for the rest of his life. She is said to have been 'a quiet woman with a practical head for business' and it was she who managed Chalmers' extensive publishing endeavours and acted as his agent with William Collins, the Glasgow publisher. Thomas and Grace raised six daughters to adulthood and there is clear evidence in Chalmers' letters that he enjoyed a happy relationship with his wife and children.[17]

PASTORAL MINISTRY IN GLASGOW
1815–23

Between 1815 and 1823, Thomas Chalmers had two high profile pastorates in the city of Glasgow, serving first in the Tron parish until 1819 and then moving to the newly established parish of St John's. The time he spent in these two

---

[16] Ibid., p. 138.

[17] Brown, 'Thomas Chalmers', in *Oxford Dictionary of National Biography*, v. 10, p. 887.

churches shaped the way in which he viewed the mission of the whole church.

On 25 November 1814, the Town Council of the city of Glasgow elected Chalmers to be the minister of the Tron Parish Church and he began his ministry there on 21 July 1815. It was an event 'celebrated as a major triumph for the Evangelical movement in Scotland'[18] while the city fathers hoped 'that his preaching would fill the church and increase the pew rents which were a main source of income for the city churches'.[19] Chalmers himself had viewed the move to Glasgow with mixed feelings. While the prospect of moving to a city church excited him, he felt genuine affection for the people of Kilmany and struggled for a time as to whether or not he should accept the call.

Once he began the work in Glasgow, he did so with great enthusiasm. The Tron parish served an estimated 12,000 to 13,000 people within its boundaries and many of these people were living in conditions of considerable poverty. As Chalmers preached to great acclaim, he developed real concern for the poor and attempted to find ways to reach them both with the gospel and with practical support.

In order to do this, he had to reinvigorate the office of the elder at the Tron. When Chalmers first arrived in the parish, there were only eight elders who could not fully care for the twenty-five districts or proportions. When he ordained twelve younger men in December 1816, he called upon them to revitalise the office of elder and seek to improve conditions within the parish. He gave the new

[18] Brown, *Thomas Chalmers and the Godly Commonwealth*, p. 51.

[19] Brown, 'Chalmers, Thomas', in *Oxford Dictionary of National Biography*, v. 10, p. 880.

elders a threefold charge. First, they were to communicate the good news of the gospel with all those that they visited. Second, they were to actively look for the poor who needed help. Rather than the poor having to apply to the church for assistance, Chalmers wanted to have 'the worthy poor' sought out and aid brought to them. Third, he called upon his elders to challenge the wealthy in the parish to be willing to share with those less fortunate. As this work began, Chalmers stated that:

> I know of nothing which would serve more powerfully to bring and to harmonize into one firm system of social order the various classes of our community.[20]

Another problem that captured his interest was that of illiteracy. While the parish school system was working reasonably well in rural Scotland, the situation in the cities was very different. Chalmers discovered that only a handful of poor children in his parish were attending school. As a result, he created evening Sabbath Schools and within 2 years the attendance grew from 13 children to over 1,200. While he recognised that this was not a full answer to the problem it was a start.

As Chalmers served the Tron church, his preaching and activism attracted considerable acclaim and in 1816 the University of Glasgow conferred on him the degree of Doctor of Divinity.[21] At the same time, he delivered a series of lectures on the interconnection between Christianity and science which attracted huge audiences. When

---

[20] Brown, *Thomas Chalmers and the Godly Commonwealth*, p. 102.

[21] Mackay, *Thomas Chalmers: A Short Appreciation*, p. 17.

these were published as the *Astronomical Discourses*, they sold more than 20,000 copies in 10 months.[22]

By 1819 Chalmers had become firmly convinced that the work being done in the Tron parish was beginning to have an impact, but he wanted an opportunity to put all of his ideas into action in a new parish. He, therefore, persuaded the city government to appoint him to the newly created parish of St John's, where he spent the next four years working diligently to bring his vision to reality. His work in the Tron parish had convinced him that the only way to deal with the massive social problems was the development of new communal spirit based on the gospel's call to love one's neighbour. As Stewart Brown has noted, Chalmers believed that

> the only way to preserve the social fabric was to revive... the traditional communal responsibility of Scotland, by which the labouring poor would strive for independence through thrift, delayed marriage, and the limitation of child bearing, while communities would care for the 'worthy poor', the infirm, aged, and orphaned who fell into dependent condition through no fault of their own.[23]

This was to be done under the oversight of the church's elders and deacons through a revitalised parish system. It is tempting to dismiss Chalmers' vision as a utopian dream. However, it was a serious attempt on his part to have the church actively involved in all areas of life. While it didn't work perfectly, Chalmers should not be faulted for

---

[22] Brown, 'Chalmers, Thomas', in *Oxford Dictionary of National Biography*, v. 10, p. 880.

[23] Ibid., p. 881.

trying, and there is significant evidence that it was successful on many levels.

ST ANDREWS UNIVERSITY
1823–8

In November 1823, Chalmers resigned from his parish in
order to take on the position of Professor of Moral Philosophy at St Andrews University. Concerns were expressed
that he was leaving the task in Glasgow unfinished and
others expressed concern that he was leaving the pulpit to
teach secular subjects. There was, however, a logical progression in Chalmers' thinking that led to this move. He
had become increasingly convinced that it was only through
strengthening the religious establishment in Scotland that
the church would grow and economic and social problems
would decrease.

> For Chalmers, the national Establishment encompassed
> not only the Church of Scotland with its parish churches
> and schools, but also the five universities of Scotland ...
> Thus he perceived his move from the parish ministry to
> ... St Andrews University not as a departure from the
> national religious Establishment, but as an elevation to a
> more responsible position within it.[24]

While Chalmers saw his new post as an opportunity to
teach prospective pastors and teachers and instil in them
his vision for an evangelical church that was active in the
society, the university viewed his appointment much more
pragmatically. They were keenly aware of the fact that
they were adding a charismatic and popular pastor to their

---

[24] Brown, *Thomas Chalmers and the Godly Commonwealth*, pp. 162–3.

faculty and hoped his addition to their ranks would swell their enrolment. And the plan worked. New students

> ... came from around Britain in one of the largest intakes the school experienced that century. Students not only were awed by his passionate reconciliation of economics, ethics, philosophy, and theology; they also stimulated one another in Christian vision and commitment to overseas mission.[25]

Chalmers developed strong relationships with many of his students. He was instrumental in inspiring some of them to become actively involved in the church in Scotland and in other parts of the world. Alexander Duff, who gave most of his adult life to missions work in India, commented that Chalmers had been used by God to bring about revival among the students of the university. Perhaps Chalmers' greatest contribution was to inspire his students with a vision 'that all truth was God's truth and the [belief] that Christian faith could and should be actively related to all of society'. [26]

The evangelical fervour displayed by Chalmers was met with increasing resistance. Many of his colleagues on the faculty did not agree with his evangelical views and associated themselves with the Moderate party in the Church of Scotland. They did not resonate with the passion that Chalmers brought to his lectures and did not welcome his involvement in their community. Chalmers also made enemies for himself by pressing for reforms in the univer-

---

[25] John Roxborough, 'The Legacy of Thomas Chalmers', *International Bulletin of Missionary Research,* v. 7, no. 3 (1999), p. 174.

[26] Ibid.

sity's administration and syllabus. He spoke out against those in positions of influence in St Andrews who were more concerned for their own welfare than they were for the university.

In the face of the opposition from his colleagues, Chalmers began to wonder if he should look for another post. Through most of 1827 Chalmers seriously considered an offer to move to the University of London to take their Chair of Moral Philosophy, but when he heard that the Town Council of Edinburgh had elected him to the Chair of Theology at the University of Edinburgh, he decided to remain in his homeland. During his years at St Andrews, Chalmers had remained in contact with the people of Edinburgh and Glasgow through regular preaching in his old parish of St John's and in other locations. It is said that he had 'remained the unrivalled master of Scottish pulpit oratory, inspiring the Edinburgh professional classes with his inspired evangelicalism'.[27]

THE UNIVERSITY OF EDINBURGH AND THE SCOTTISH CHURCH CRISIS 1828–43

As he began his work at the University of Edinburgh in November 1828, Chalmers recognised that now was the opportunity for him to try to implement his ideas surrounding the 'Christian nation'. It was his hope that the principles he had taught and practised during his pastorates in Glasgow might now be put into action on a larger stage. The period from 1828 to 1843 was a tumultuous one for him. In addition to his teaching duties at the University of Edinburgh, he became actively involved in a number of political

---

[27] Brown, *Thomas Chalmers and the Godly Commonwealth*, p. 178.

issues. He also took on increasing leadership responsibilities in the Church of Scotland. As we have already seen in chapter one, he became the person most associated with the Disruption of 1843 and the founding of the Free Church.

One of the most controversial political issues of the day was that of Roman Catholic emancipation. Many evangelicals were unhappy with the notion that Roman Catholics should have the same political and religious freedoms as Protestants, but Chalmers was already on record as being a firm supporter of emancipation. As the Catholic Relief Bill came before Parliament in February of 1829, Chalmers communicated with Sir James Mackintosh, one of the prominent parliamentarians who was in favour of the bill. He wrote,

> I have never had but one sentiment on the subject of the Catholic disabilities, and it is that the Protestant cause has been laid by them under very heavy disadvantage, and that we shall gain prodigiously from the moment that, by the removal of them, the question between us and our opponents is reduced to a pure contest between truth and error.[28]

Chalmers went on to argue in a speech delivered in Edinburgh on 14 March 1829 that the suppression of Catholicism by legal means was unnecessary.

> What other instruments do we read of in the New Testament for the defence and propagation of the faith but the Word of God and the Spirit of God? ... Reason, and Scripture, and prayer – these compose, or ought to compose, the whole armoury of Protestantism.[29]

---

[28] Hanna, *Memoirs of the Life and Writings of Thomas Chalmers*, v. 2, p. 183.

[29] Ibid., pp. 187–8.

Chalmers' support for Catholic emancipation received mixed reviews. Many saw his outspoken support as evidence that he was now 'the most redoubted Champion of Evangelical Liberalism' but it lost him some friends within the church, particularly in the Highlands of Scotland where animosity to Catholicism ran higher than it did in the cities.[30]

One result of Catholic emancipation and the subsequent Reform Act of 1832, which expanded the electoral franchise, was that the old assumptions about the government's duty to support the established church were significantly weakened. As we have seen, Chalmers did not believe that Catholics and nonconformists should be discriminated against for their views, but he still held firmly to the belief that it was the duty of the state to support the work of the church.

In the first part of the nineteenth century, the Evangelical party in the Church of Scotland had gradually gained power and after 1834 they were firmly in the ascendancy. As the Reform Act of 1832 passed into law, the Church of Scotland began a period of major change and revitalisation. Motivated by the desire to evangelise Scotland and concern for its very real social needs, Chalmers threw himself into a massive church extension programme. Beginning in 1834, he and other evangelicals worked tirelessly for the organisation of new parishes so that within 6 years over 200 new churches were opened.[31]

The events leading to the Disruption have already been discussed, but it is important that we understand just how critical Chalmers was to the whole movement. He worked

---

[30] Brown, *Thomas Chalmers and the Godly Commonwealth*, p. 189.

[31] Roxborough, 'The Legacy of Thomas Chalmers', p. 174.

tirelessly as an organiser, leading the church extension movement, while his preaching built popular support for the campaign. He encouraged the development of local church extension societies which were established to document the need for more churches and also to raise funds for the erection of churches and schools in the new parishes. This fundraising targeted both the wealthy and those who could only contribute a few pennies to the cause, and overall it was a considerable success.

While Chalmers showed organisational skills in the church extension campaign, he was much less successful when it came to political negotiation. Over time, he lost the confidence and support of both Whig and Tory politicians in London. He came to recognise that the Whigs would no longer help the church because they did not agree with the establishment principle, which was central to Chalmers' thinking, and the Tories would only do so at the price of interfering in the internal operations of the church.

Chalmers had a formidable temper and when his entreaties addressed to the government fell on deaf ears he expressed 'moral loathing' for what he perceived to be intransigence. As his frustration grew, he waged a vigorous campaign in 1837 against John Lee for the position of Moderator of the Church of Scotland, believing that the Moderate Lee did not have sufficient drive or commitment to prosecute the church extension campaign. While it may be argued that Chalmers had the best interests of the church at heart, some began to believe that he was also motivated by a desire for power and 'unquestioned personal authority'.[32]

[32] Brown, 'Thomas Chalmers', in *Oxford Dictionary of National Biography*, v. 10, p. 885.

As the crisis within the Church of Scotland neared its conclusion, with the Courts decreeing that the Veto Act was illegal and the government refusing additional support for new church endowments, Chalmers reluctantly came to the conclusion that there would have to be a break between the church and the state. At the 1839 General Assembly, he laid out his position in an impassioned three-hour speech. He argued that the church and the state were two independent societies that should be seen as having 'entered into a compact of mutual benefit – the church providing religious and moral instruction to the people and the state providing protection of the church's property'. [33] However, this arrangement did not give the state any jurisdiction over spiritual matters and it was at this precise point that the rights of the church were being infringed.

Between 1839 and 1841, conflict with the civil courts and negotiations with the British government continued with growing tensions on all sides. At the 1841 General Assembly, Chalmers led the charge as seven Moderate ministers of the Presbytery of Strathbogie were deposed for following the instruction of the Court of Session and ordaining a minister over the strenuous opposition of the people of the parish of Marnoch. Whether or not Chalmers was goaded into this action is hard to determine, but what is indisputable is that the possibility of compromise was now gone. The General Assembly of 1842 then passed *The Claim Declaration and Protest anent the Encroachments of the Court of Session*, which explicitly rejected state interference in the appointment of ministers and the creations of new parishes.

---

[33] Ibid.

In the months that followed the 1842 General Assembly, Chalmers would organise and oversee the Convocation where 374 ministers agreed that they would leave the established Church of Scotland if matters were not resolved in their favour. Then in May 1843, Chalmers, who was the obvious choice, was elected the first Moderator of the Free Church of Scotland. In doing this, the church was recognising him as the preeminent leader of the Evangelical movement and the driving force behind the Disruption in the church.

NEW COLLEGE EDINBURGH AND THE FREE CHURCH OF SCOTLAND 1843–7

Having left the established church, Chalmers lost his position as Professor of Divinity at the University of Edinburgh. The new church quickly recognised that they would need their own institutions for training ministers. New College was opened in Edinburgh with Chalmers appointed as the first Principal and Professor of Divinity. When he laid the cornerstone for the New College building, he made it very clear that New College would not be an elitist institution. Rather, its primary purpose was to train ministers who, through the power of the gospel, would reach out to all of society. In his speech he said,

> The youth who frequent our classes will with all earnestness and emphasis be told, that the Christian minister is a man of no rank, because a man of all ranks; and that although he should have an education which might qualify him for holding converse with princes and peers, it is his peculiar glory to be a frequent visitant of the poor man's humble cottage, and to pray by the poor man's dying

bed. Let kings retain their sceptres, and nobles their coronets,—what we want is a more elevated ground-floor for our general population.[34]

The years following the Disruption were active ones for Chalmers. Provision had to be made for the support of poorer churches through the creation of the Sustentation Fund. This fund, which had been conceived by Chalmers before the Disruption, saw wealthier congregations provide funds so that every minister would at least receive a minimum stipend. In the summer months following the Disruption, Chalmers went on a vigorous fundraising campaign and £68,700 was raised for the work of the church. To give an idea of just how successful the Free Church was, we should note that by 1848 over 700 churches, 500 parish schools and 400 manses were built.[35]

Despite his denominational duties, Chalmers still had the energy to continue parish work in the West Port area of Edinburgh. Through this project, Chalmers organised teams of volunteers who worked within the community to build a church, schools, Sunday schools and libraries which, when combined with regular and careful visitation, were intended to bring about moral and material improvement to the area.

Chalmers was also concerned that this be an interdenominational programme that would bring Christians from different backgrounds together. While the project was not an unqualified success, it again pointed to Chalmers' firm belief that the gospel must be put into action.

---

[34] Brown, 'The Making of New College: 1843–6', *New College Bulletin* (2006), p. 3.

[35] Mackay, *Thomas Chalmers: A Short Appreciation*, p. 25.

In May 1847, Chalmers travelled to London in order that he might give testimony before a Select Committee of the House of Commons. It had been set up to investigate Free Church complaints of difficulties finding new sites for churches because wealthy landowners were unwilling to sell property to the church. Chalmers faced vigorous questioning from one member of the committee in particular, who hoped to force Chalmers to say that the Disruption had been wrong. Chalmers held his ground, but this grilling and the travels took a toll on his health. As he returned to Scotland, his family became concerned for his health although he claimed he was fine. He attended church as usual on Sunday, 30 May, but when his housekeeper went to wake him the following morning, he was found dead, the victim of a heart attack.[36]

Chalmers' funeral took place on Friday, June 4 1847, amid scenes of great mourning. The next day, *The Scotsman* newspaper reported that

> The funeral of Dr Chalmers took place yesterday amidst such manifestations of public respect and esteem as became the eminent position and venerated character of the departed. We are not overstating the fact when we say that there never was a larger funeral procession in Edinburgh.[37]

The crowd watching the procession in respectful silence has been numbered as high as 100,000. It is hard to over-estimate the impact of Chalmers' death on the Free Church. His sudden death left a leadership vacuum that was never

---

[36] Brown, *Thomas Chalmers and the Godly Commonwealth*, p. 71.

[37] 'Funeral of Dr Chalmers', *The Scotsman Digital Archive, June 5, 1847*, http://archive.scotsman.com/ (accessed 14 February 2009).

entirely filled and his coherent vision for the church was never entirely emulated by those who followed him.

During his sixty-seven years, Chalmers had risen to national prominence through his preaching, lecturing and writing, and through his involvement in various social and political causes. Ultimately, however, he is remembered for his outstanding leadership in the church. Chalmers was able to inspire people with his vision for the godly common-wealth and his belief that the gospel should make a difference in the world. All of his efforts were animated by a belief that

> Jesus Christ died, the just for the unjust to bring us unto God. This is a truth, which, when all the world shall receive it, all the world will be renovated ... It is this doctrine which is the lone instrument of God for the transformation of our species.[38]

---

[38] Thomas Chalmers, *The Works of Thomas Chalmers,* v. 6 (Glasgow: William Collins, 1836–42), p. 261.

ROBERT S. CANDLISH, D.D.

Home & Macdonald.

3

ROBERT S. CANDLISH
PREACHER AND CHURCHMAN

> Dr Candlish's prominence in the Free Church ... was
> only second to that of Dr Chalmers ... Between Dr
> Chalmers and Dr Candlish the most cordial relations
> existed, and at a meeting of the Free Church General
> Assembly in 1846 the former said, pointing to Dr
> Candlish: 'There goes a very remarkable man – a
> very great and good man – Scotland could not do
> without him'.[1]

WHEN Thomas Chalmers died in May 1847 the Free Church found itself in need of a new leader. While no one could fully assume the mantle of Chalmers, it was clear that visionary leadership would be needed for the church to move forward. Robert Candlish assumed this role. It has been suggested that 'much of the success of the Free Church in its formative years is directly attributable to Candlish's unstinting efforts on its behalf'.[2] During his life Candlish would become one of Scotland's most highly regarded preachers, churchman and theological thinkers. He played a key role in the Disruption that brought the Free Church into being and he was actively involved in the various aspects of the church's life in the thirty years following the Disruption.

---

[1] 'Robert S. Candlish Obituary' *New York Times Oct, 21, 1873*, http://select.nytimes.com/mem/archive (accessed 16 February 2009).

[2] Michael D. McMullen, 'Candlish, Robert S', in *Oxford Dictionary of National Biography*, v. 9 (Oxford: Oxford University Press, 2004), p. 893.

FAMILY BACKGROUND, EARLY LIFE AND EDUCATION 1806–28

Robert Smith Candlish was born in Edinburgh on 23 March 1806, the sixth and youngest child of James Candlish and Jane Smith Candlish. James Candlish began his working career as a teacher although this was 'an occupation for which he had no particular liking'. [3] He did consider training for the pastoral ministry but rejected this idea, since he could not in good conscience embrace all of the doctrines of the Christian faith. Instead, he took up the study of medicine, becoming sufficiently qualified to become a teacher of medicine himself. While there are scant details available about his professional career, he did achieve some success and was 'referred to as an authority twenty years after his death'. [4] James Candlish died, probably from a brain haemorrhage on 29 April 1806, just five weeks after the birth of Robert.

Jane Smith (1768–1854) outlived her husband by almost fifty years. She was remembered as 'a lady of stately and somewhat majestic presence, grave and reserved of manner, although always kindly and courteous'. [5] After the sudden death of her husband she took up residence in Glasgow where she ran a school for young ladies, thus supporting herself and her children. Robert's early education was undertaken at home by his mother, who is said to have taught her children well, instilling in them a firm belief in frugality, 'out of debt, out of danger' [6] being one of her favourite phrases.

[3] William Wilson, *Memorials of Robert Smith Candlish DD* (Edinburgh: Adam and Charles Black, 1880), p. 3.

[4] Ibid., p. 4.

[5] Ibid., p. 5.

[6] Ibid., p. 6.

Young Robert has been described as 'a peculiar, but interesting-looking child, somewhat delicate and rather timid'. [7] His peculiar looks would be commented on in later life when one colleague said of him:

> Dr Candlish, with exceptional occasions due to circum-
> stances, which came like angels' visits, appeared as if, in
> making his toilette, he had mistaken the dress of another for
> his own; or as if he had shot his person into his own dress, not
> caring nor considering whether the articles which composed
> it were put on straight or awry; or whether, when adorned
> after his fashion, his appearance should excite either admira-
> tion or amusement.[8]

Robert Candlish began his studies at the University of Glasgow on 10 October 1818 when he was just thirteen years old. He spent five years there, graduating with an MA in 1823. During his time at university he distinguished himself by winning a number of academic prizes and his contemporaries noted that he also had a serious interest in Christianity. One of his friends would say of him that he demonstrated

> ... a spirituality ... which was so dominant and habitual
> as to be suggestive of its having grown up with him from
> his childhood, and of its being at once indispensable and
> familiar to him as the breath of life.[9]

William Wilson, Candlish's contemporary biographer, offers the opinion that there were three distinct influences that

---

[7] McMullen, 'Candlish', Robert S., p. 891.

[8] Alexander Beith, *A Highland Tour: Three Weeks with Dr Candlish*, second edition (Edinburgh: Adam and Charles Black, 1874), pp. 9–10.

[9] Wilson, *Memorials of Robert Smith Candlish DD*, pp. 19–20.

had a significant impact on the young Robert while he was at university. First, he points to the publication of Thomas M'Crie's biographies of John Knox and Andrew Melville which came off the presses in 1811 and 1819. Both of these books took the opportunity to remind their readers of the glory days of the Scottish reformation, and Wilson suggests they 'were a very effective protest against the Moderatism which had so long cramped and stifled the religious life of Scotland'. [10] Second, Wilson also points to the influence of Andrew Thomson, minister of St George's, Edinburgh, and editor of the popular *Edinburgh Christian Instructor*. Through his preaching, writing and leadership of the Evangelical party in the Church of Scotland Thomson was recognised as one of the leading evangelicals of his day.[11] It was particularly his views on the sufficiency and authority of Scripture that had, according to Wilson, a major impact on Candlish. Third, the growing popularity and prominence of Thomas Chalmers had a significant impact on the young Candlish. Chalmers' work at the Tron and St John's Parish had placed him firmly in the public limelight. Wilson suggests that it was his views on the need for church extension that particularly excited Candlish.[12]

Candlish entered Glasgow Divinity College where he studied from 1823 to 1826. He achieved a number of academic prizes, but also found time for recreational activities and sports. He was extremely well liked by his professors and

---

[10] Ibid., p. 27.

[11] For a brief biography of Thomson, see D.C. Lachman, 'Thomson, Andrew Mitchell', in *Dictionary of Scottish Church history and Theology*, pp. 819–20.

[12] Wilson, *Memorials of Robert Smith Candlish DD*, pp. 28–9.

as a result he was given the honour of being sent to Eton as a Tutor. He accepted this position partly because it was an honour and also because he was required to wait another year before he could be licensed to preach.[13]

His experience at Eton was not a happy one. In a letter dated 8 May 1827, a picture emerges of a young man who is both lonely and underemployed.

> During the first half of my stay here ... you may conceive that among perfect strangers, and without much business, I felt dull enough ... Upon the whole, I cannot avoid preferring that mixture of public instruction and domestic superintendence which forms the system of our [Scottish] Universities.[14]

During the summer vacation of 1828, Candlish was licensed to preach by the Presbytery of Glasgow and accepted his first church position as assistant to Dr Andrew Gibbs at St Andrew's Church, Glasgow.

ASSISTANT MINISTER
1828–34

It may seem a little odd that Candlish was given this position since he held much more evangelical sympathies than those of Dr Gibbs. In fact, he obtained this appointment largely because his father had been a friend of Dr Gibbs while at College and Gibbs was willing to do a favour for the young minister. Candlish was given the opportunity to preach on a regular basis but he found the work difficult. Since the congregation of St Andrew's was used to the

---

[13] 'The rules of the Church [of Scotland] provided that five years must elapse from the time of entering the [Divinity] Hall before the student could be licensed to preach the gospel.' (Wilson, p. 31).

[14] Ibid., pp. 32–33.

Moderate theology of Dr Gibbs they did not fully embrace the preaching of the young assistant. For his part he 'said it hung like a cold blanket about his neck ... his position was a very trying one, and especially to a man who had such a lofty estimate of what sermons ought to be'.[15] Gradually his confidence increased and he began to develop a distinctive preaching style that would mark the rest of his career.

Dr Gibb died in June of 1831. This resulted in the termination of Candlish's appointment and he found himself having to look for another position. Two possibilities presented themselves. First, he was offered the position of teaching assistant to Professor Walker at the University of Glasgow; second, he was also offered the position of assistant minister attached to the parish of Bonhill. Even though the university position paid twice as much, Candlish continued to believe that he had a calling to pastoral ministry and so he accepted the position of assistant to Mr Gregor, minister of Bonhill.

Gregor was less the convinced Moderate than Gibb was, but he wasn't precisely an evangelical either. He viewed his position very pragmatically and attempted to give his congregation what he thought they wanted to hear. After Candlish was appointed, Gregor gave up all preaching duties in his own parish, handing these over to his youthful assistant. When asked why he did this, he replied, 'what is the use of keeping a dog and then barking yourself?'[16] While Candlish worked hard as the assistant and his preaching and pastoral work were well received, he was anxious to be ordained and to take on his own pastoral charge. As he

---

[15] Ibid., p. 38.

[16] Ibid., p. 43.

waited for this to happen, he considered moving to Canada where there was every prospect that he would be ordained and inducted as soon as he could get there. Part of his difficulty was that he had developed a somewhat peculiar pulpit manner. It was said of him that

> ... he had an awkward way of habitually shrugging up one shoulder, which gave him an almost deformed look; his voice often passed into a scream or even a screech, and his gesticulation was sometimes almost extravagant.[17]

In 1834, Candlish discovered that the assistant's position at St George's, Edinburgh was available and through the help of friends he was introduced to the congregation. The appointment was meant to be temporary while the minister Mr Martin recovered from illness. But when Martin died at the end of May, it was decided to offer the parish to Candlish, and he was ordained to the pastoral ministry on 17 August 1834.

MINISTER OF ST GEORGE'S AND THE TEN YEARS CONFLICT 1834–43

Candlish took on this new post with considerable vigour and enthusiasm. His ministry at St George's was described in these terms.

> He had scarcely entered on his labours ere he gave proof that he was the right man in the right place. Into the various departments of parochial work he threw himself heart and soul, and inspired his people to follow his example. By his actions and words they were constrained to duty as they never had been before.[18]

---

[17] Ibid., p. 41.

[18] Andrew Aird, *Glimpses of Old Glasgow* (Glasgow: Aird & Coghill, 1894), p. 275.

It is interesting to note that his distinct pulpit manner seems not to have inhibited his effectiveness as a preacher. His congregation was able to look past his eccentric delivery and focus on the content. Candlish preached his first sermon at St George's on the afternoon of 17 August 1834, from John 4:37: 'And herein is that saying true, One soweth and another reapeth.' In the sermon, Candlish first focused on the work of the Trinity in salvation, then went on to talk about how the church was being built through the faithful labours of God's people and concluded with a humble call for prayer.

> Therefore brethren do ye pray for us that our sufficiency may be of God. Pray that the Spirit of the Lord may be with us in all our private preparations in all our official duties. Pray that we may be enabled to be faithful to remember the commission with which we are charged, to shun all compromise, to declare the whole counsel of God to reprove, rebuke, exhort with all meekness and authority, to comfort the mourner and speak a word in season to him that is weary ... Pray for us brethren, oh pray for us that our own work may not condemn us [and] that after having preached to others we may not ourselves be cast away. Amen.[19]

It has been noted that 'Candlish ... following in the train of [Andrew] Thomson and Chalmers had a profound sense of Scripture being the Word of God, and to preach was above all to preach the Word of God.' [20] This belief shaped his

[19] Robert S. Candlish, *Sermons by the Late Robert S. Candlish. Minister of Free St George's and Principal of the New College, Edinburgh* (Edinburgh: A. & C . Black, 1874), p. 23.

[20] Hughes Oliphint Old, *The Reading and Preaching of the Scriptures in the Worship of the Christian Church*, v. 6 (Grand Rapids: Eerdmans, 1998), p. 636.

preaching, and all of his published sermons that survive are marked by careful exegesis and powerful applications, which pointed his hearers to a living relationship with Christ that would be manifested in their lives.

Five months after beginning his ministry at St George's, Candlish married Janet Brock on 6 January 1835. She was described as having 'a meek and quiet spirit ... and having such a spirit apart from other graces and excellencies, [she] was of unspeakable value to her husband'.[21] Janet and Robert had ten children, many of whom died in childhood.

For the first five years of his ministry at St George's, Candlish focused most of his energies on his parish. However, in 1839 he took on a very public role in the wider church as the conflict which led to the Disruption moved toward a climax. His first speech to the General Assembly was a memorable one in which he argued strenuously for the spiritual independence of the church in the face of state intrusion. Then, at the Commission of Assembly in December of that year, he made an impassioned speech in favour of the suspension of the Strathbogie seven who had defied the General Assembly in the Marnoch case.[22] From this point forward, he would be identified with evangelicals in the Church of Scotland and with the cause of the non-intrusion of Moderate ministers upon evangelical parishes.[23]

Those who were seeking to defend the spiritual independence of the church recognised that they had two tasks.

---

[21] Wilson, *Memorials of Robert Smith Candlish DD*, p. 58.

[22] For a summary of the Marnoch Case, see chapter 1.

[23] J.R. Wolfe, 'Candlish, Robert Smith', in *Dictionary of Scottish Church history and Theology*, p. 134.

One was to seek to persuade legislators that the church had the law of the land on their side. The second element was to rally popular support in favour of their cause. In the summer of 1839 Candlish became aware of the letter written by Hugh Miller of Cromarty entitled *Letter to Lord Broughan,* strenuously attacking the decision of the House of Lords in the Auchterarder Case. This case had determined that members of the Church of Scotland did not have the right to elect their own ministers. Candlish passed the letter on to the church's publishers who issued it as a pamphlet to considerable acclaim. Candlish then played a central role in the appointment of Hugh Miller as the editor of *The Witness,* a newspaper which published its first issue on 15 January 1840.[24]

The year 1841 was an eventful one for Candlish. First, he was nominated for the newly created position of Professor of Biblical Criticism at Edinburgh University. While Candlish was excited about the possibility, he also felt concern about leaving his congregation. He wrote in a letter, 'I fear the prospect of separation from my congregation; but if I can do good to students by devoting myself to this new branch of their studies, I am willing to listen to the call.'[25] But Candlish's increasingly outspoken speeches on behalf of the Evangelical party in the Church of Scotland lost him the favour of the government. He disobeyed the court interdicts issued against preaching within the bounds of the Presbytery of Strathbogie, and

[24] George Rosie, *Hugh Miller: Outrage and Order: a Biography and Selected Writings* (Edinburgh: Mainstream Publishing, 1981), pp. 54–5. Miller and Candlish would have a major 'falling out' after the Disruption. For more details on Hugh Miller and *The Witness,* see chapter 5.

[25] Wilson, *Memorials of Robert Smith Candlish DD,* p. 89.

when this was brought to the attention of the authorities, his appointment was cancelled.

Also in October 1841, Candlish received news of a significant honour from an unexpected source. Princeton University wrote to inform him that they were going to confer on him the title of Doctor of Divinity. After enumerating Candlish's contribution to events taking place in Scotland, the letter concluded by saying that Princeton was taking this action '... to show our estimate of your great services in your controversies, and to manifest to the world where, and on what side, are to be found all our sympathies'. [26] Candlish's biographer goes on to note somewhat caustically that it was not until the year 1865, twenty-four years later, that the University of Edinburgh conferred on Dr Candlish the same degree.[27]

During 1841, Candlish became convinced that a break with the established church was inevitable and he took on an important role in the discussions which led up to the Disruption. Records from the Convocation held in Edinburgh in November 1842 show Candlish taking a key role. When the Convocation ended, 374 ministers had agreed to leave the established Church of Scotland, but arriving at this conclusion had not been straightforward; in fact, at certain points it looked as if agreement might not be reached.[28] As the meeting ended, Candlish announced that he intended to begin preaching more regularly on the matters under discussion. He told the Convocation that 'the great principles, at all events, if not

[26] Ibid., p. 161.

[27] Ibid., p. 162.

[28] K.R. Ross, 'Convocation', in *Dictionary of Scottish Church History and Theology*, p. 210.

the details, should be expounded and pressed upon ...' the people of the church.[29] Candlish took his own advice to heart. In the weeks prior to the 1843 General Assembly, he preached in a number of places stressing how essential it was that the church remain free of interference from the state in spiritual matters. On 17 May 1843, he conducted a prayer meeting in St George's Church which was to be his last in that building. The following Sabbath he preached in a newly erected brick building with almost all of his original congregation moving with him.

CANDLISH THE CHURCHMAN
1843–73

From 1843 until his death thirty years later, Robert Candlish occupied a central place in the life and work of the Free Church. He was an active participant in a number of key debates and many regarded his contributions as being second only to those of Thomas Chalmers.

At the first General Assembly of the Free Church of Scotland, Candlish convened a committee whose purpose was to make sure that church services would be furnished in all places where there was a population that was supportive of the Free Church. In addressing the Assembly, Candlish expressed deep appreciation to those ministers who were willing to make enormous sacrifices in order to maintain the spiritual independence of the church.

From its earliest days, the Free Church looked outward. The first General Assembly devised plans for missionary work, and the Assembly also began to reach out to the wider Christian world. Candlish played a significant role in

---

[29] Wilson, *Memorials of Robert Smith Candlish DD*, p. 258.

this effort. He travelled to England, speaking in a number of locations on the principles of the Free Church. Upon his return, he proposed an overture to the next General Assembly that would provide for regular contact and consultation with other churches. He stated that

> ... the unity in the Christian Church ... was not the unity of immediate incorporation nor yet so much in co-operation as to different schemes of usefulness, but in something more visible than this – a unity of consultation.[30]

Candlish also displayed a concern for social justice issues both in the United Kingdom, and in other parts of the world. At a Commission of Assembly held in September of 1844, he spoke about how the church should respond to the issue of slavery in the United States. He urged that the

> ... Committee cannot but consider it the duty of Christian Churches ... to set themselves against the manifold abuses of slavery, and to aim decidedly at abolition.[31]

In 1845, Candlish undertook an extensive tour of the Highlands of Scotland to examine the situation confronting members of the Free Church who were facing severe difficulties as a result of the refusal of certain landlords to provide sites for churches. The original remit from the Assembly called on the committee to come up with proposals that would 'alleviate the evils under which the Gaelic-speaking population groan, and to promote their spiritual welfare through an adequate supply of the means of grace'.[32]

---

[30] Ibid., p. 333.

[31] Ibid., p. 349.

[32] Alexander Beith, *A Highland Tour: Three Weeks with Dr Candlish*, pp. 1–2.

Candlish offered strenuous criticism of the difficult situation that many members of the Free Church were facing and he was able to bring public pressure to bear on the situation to bring about some improvement.

After the death of Thomas Chalmers in 1847, Candlish's already prominent role in the life and work of the church increased. Despite the protests of St George's Free Church, who wanted to keep their minister, he was appointed Professor of Divinity at New College Edinburgh in the summer of 1847. However, he did not remain long in this post. Before the year was out, his successor at St George's had died suddenly and Candlish asked to be allowed to return to his church.

Three particular honours would be given to Candlish by the Free Church. First, in 1861, he was appointed Moderator of the General Assembly. In the following year, after the death of William Cunningham, he was appointed to the position of Principal of New College. In 1862, a number of his friends undertook to raise money in support of his family as recognition for the work he had done for the church throughout his career. In a circular that was printed to raise funds for the gift, Dr Thomas Guthrie wrote,

> I need not tell you how much the Christian Church in general and the Free Church in particular, owes to the remarkable talents, warm-hearted piety genius, unselfish devotedness, and Herculean labours ... of Dr Candlish.[33]

In the end a total of £5,640 was raised.

Beginning in the 1870s, Candlish began to experience bouts of ill health. Recognising the burdens placed on him

---

[33] Wilson, *Memorials of Robert Smith Candlish DD*, p. 532.

as a result of his work for the wider church, the congregation of Free St George's attempted on several occasions to appoint another minister to help him. Finally, in June of 1870, Rev. Alexander Whyte accepted the position. He eventually succeeded Candlish and served as the church's minister until 1916. Candlish's health deteriorated rapidly during 1873, until in October he was unable to eat at all. When he died on 24 October, *The Scotsman* said of him:

> By men of all parties and of all denominations it will be felt that in Dr Candlish we have lost one of whom his countrymen had some reason to be proud. Whatever opinions may be entertained as to some of the objects to which the life just closed was devoted, none will be found to dispute that it was a life guided by high aims, and in which the injunction to 'work while it is today' received the most conscientious fulfilment.[34]

CANDLISH THE CONTROVERSIALIST

As was alluded to in his obituary, Candlish was no stranger to controversy. In fact, anyone who had been as deeply involved in the events leading up to the Disruption as he had been, had lived through considerable conflict. But there were other issues that Candlish expressed strong opinions on, and to which he devoted considerable energies. These controversies centred around how the church should educate its pastors, how the church should worship and the issue of union with other like-minded churches.

As we have already noted, Candlish was appointed to the position of Professor of Divinity in 1847 after the death

---

[34] 'The Late Dr Candlish', *The Scotsman Digital Archive, October 20, 1873*, http://archive.scotsman.com/ (accessed 26 February 2009).

of Chalmers. The appointment to this position came partly as a result of his deep interest in education, both for the general public but more particularly for prospective ministers. Candlish found himself in the middle of a protracted and sadly personal debate about how the Free Church should deliver theological training.

There was little agreement in the church on how limited financial resources should be spent on theological education. Some, including Candlish, felt strongly that the Free Church needed to place theological colleges in various regions of Scotland. This, they believed, would prevent theological education from being unduly centralised and would allow the widest possible accessibility of theological education for those pursuing a call to the ministry. Others, including William Cunningham, who was Professor of Church History and who became Principal of New College after Chalmers' death, believed that the church would be best served by a central theological college. The opponents of expansion feared that '... college extension threatened the efforts to create a fully-equipped theological college, with a full complement of professors and a comprehensive curriculum'.[35] The debate on the 'college question' raged for many years until those favouring extension eventually triumphed in 1855. As the debate continued, friendships between well-meaning men were damaged. Candlish and Cunningham spoke strenuously and sometimes hurtfully on the issue and for a time their relationship was completely broken. Both of their biographers claim that the personal animosity between them was eventually resolved, but this debate does not show either man at his best.

[35] Stewart J. Brown, 'The Disruption and the Dream: The making of New College 1843–61', p. 45.

Candlish was also involved in the debate in the 1850s and 60s over how the Free Church worshipped. It is important to note here that the Free Church's practice of worship was governed by the sound biblical principle '... that divine warrant or authorisation is required for every element entering into the worship of God'. [36] This is expressed in Chapter XXI Section I of the *Westminster Confession of Faith,* which states that the

> ... acceptable way of worshipping the true God is instituted by himself, and so limited by His own revealed will that He may not be worshipped according to the imaginations and devices of men, or the suggestions of Satan, under any visible representation, or any other way not prescribed in the holy Scripture.[37]

Because there is clear direction in Scripture that the Psalms are to be sung and because it is impossible to find 'divine warrant' for the use of songs of human composition or musical instruments in the New Testament, the Free Church had wisely chosen to follow the biblical pattern and kept its worship simple. In taking this step, the Free Church was following the ancient church's pattern of worship which had been recaptured at the Reformation. As a result, the

---

[36] John Murray and William Young, *Minority Report of the Committee on Song in the Public Worship of God Submitted to the Fourteenth General Assembly of the Orthodox Presbyterian Church,* http://www.opc.org/GA/song.html#Minority (accessed 25 August 2009). This report provides an excellent summary of the biblical support for the 'regulative principle' of worship and for the exclusive use of the Psalms in worship.

[37] *The Confession of Faith Agreed upon by the Assembly of Divines at Westminster: Examined and approved, Anno 1647, by the General Assembly of the Church of Scotland; and ratified by Acts of Parliament 1649 and 1690,* http://www.freechurch.org/resources/confessions/westminster.htm (accessed 25 August 2009).

church in Scotland had confined itself to the use of metrical psalms and paraphrases of other parts of Scripture and had not allowed musical accompaniment in worship.[38]

As the immediate period of the Disruption passed, there were growing calls for liberalising the worship of the Free Church. Some pointed out that other Presbyterian churches were singing hymns and using instrumental music in worship and so they asked, why couldn't the Free Church do the same thing? In response to this, in 1856, Candlish published a book entitled *The Organ Question,* in which he republished two pamphlets that had been presented to the Presbytery of Glasgow in 1808 when a church there had unsuccessfully attempted to get the denomination's approval to allow them to use an organ in their worship. In an extended introduction to the republished pamphlets, Candlish carefully argued that the innovations being proposed should be denied as they would cause disunity and disturbance in the church. In this connection he wrote, 'I dread the agitation of the question in our Presbyterian churches. I dread it because it inevitably tends to schism.'[39]

---

[38] For those who wish to read more on the place of the Psalms in worship, see Rowland S. Ward, *Psalm Singing in Scripture and History* (Victoria, Australia: R.S. Ward, 1985). Also see, Rowland S. Ward, *The Psalms in Christian Worship: A Doctrinal, Historical and Expository Guide* (Melbourne: Presbyterian Church of Eastern Australia, 1992). For an excellent discussion of why instrumental music should not be used in Christian worship, see John Price, *Old Light on New Worship: Musical Instruments and the Worship of God, a Theological, Historical and Psychological Study* (Avinger, Tex: Simpson Pub, 2005).

[39] Robert S. Candlish, *The Organ Question: Statements of Dr Ritchie, and Dr Porteous, for and against the use of the organ in public worship, in the proceedings of the Presbytery of Glasgow 1807–08 with an Introductory notice by Robert S. Candlish, D.D.* (Edinburgh: Johnstone and Hunter, 1856), p. 6.

Two things are striking about the tone and content of Candlish's argument. First, he recognised that to change the way in which the church worshipped over the conscientious objections of those who wished to maintain the historic practice would offend against the very principles of Presbyterianism. Candlish wrote that those

> ... Presbyterians who disapprove, on conscientious and scriptural grounds, of a particular mode of worship, as for instance of the Organ, cannot divest themselves of responsibility by merely excluding it from their own Congregations. They are bound to resist the introduction of it in all the other Congregations of the Church as well as in their own.[40]

Candlish went on to point out that if this change were to take place,

> ... a controversy in the Courts of the Church becomes, in these circumstances, inevitable. And if it is an unnecessary controversy ... it involves more or less the guilt of schism, or at least what tends to schism.[41]

It is also striking that Candlish recognised that those who were seeking change were doing so without the weight of scriptural argument, theology or the history of the Scottish church on their side. In the first two instances, he referred his readers to the second pamphlet in the collection which persuasively made this case. Then he himself argued that the proposed innovations in worship were not part of the history of Scottish Presbyterianism. It does need to be noted that Candlish was not fully consistent on the matter

---

[40] Ibid., pp. 7–8.

[41] Ibid., pp. 8–9.

of changes to worship. By 1870, he was prepared to allow for the use of some hymns in worship, although he remained firmly opposed to the use of instrumental music.[42]

The passage of time indicates that Candlish was correct to worry about this issue. The subsequent history of changes to worship in the church has proven to be controversial and has caused considerable disunity that has distracted the church from its task of preaching the gospel and caring for a needy world.

Candlish was involved in a third major controversy, that of union among Scottish churches. During the eighteenth century there had been a number of church divisions, but after the Disruption in 1843 there was a move toward reunification. At this point there were three main Presbyterian Churches in Scotland: The Church of Scotland, The Free Church and the United Presbyterian Church. In 1863, The United Presbyterian Church set up a committee to examine whether or not union with other churches might be possible, and they invited the Free Church to participate in these discussions.[43] Candlish, who was motivated by a desire to see the church fully equipped to meet the needs of the country, saw the possibility of union in a positive light. His views on church union were forcibly put to the 1863 General Assembly.

But I look forward to the future, not merely as holding out very bright prospects of increased power and increased

---

[42] There is a passing reference to this in the *Memorials of Robert S. Candlish* where William Wilson states that Candlish came to believe that the introduction of some hymns was alright, 'but not so much as to distract the church'. *Memorials of Robert Smith Candlish DD*, p. 544. How this was to be achieved in a non-distracting way is not mentioned.

[43] John McIntosh, 'The Events of 1900', *The Monthly Record of the Free Church of Scotland* (October 2000), p. 224.

influence, but rather as involving very grave responsibilities, in connection with vastly increased ability to promote the glory of God in the salvation of souls. And I would desire all friends of this movement, in anticipating the future, to anticipate it in that spirit. For, if it should please the Lord to make us who have been two separate churches in the land henceforth one, to bring us all together – I hope not a solitary brother on either side left behind, if it should please Him thus to weld us into one, can we doubt that it will be for some great work connected with the glory of His name? [44]

The problem for those like Candlish who desired union with the United Presbyterians was that the two churches were not identical. The United Presbyterian Church did not believe in the establishment principle and were 'Voluntarists', those who rejected any connection between the church and the state. There were also concerns that the United Presbyterians were prepared to allow looser subscription to the *Westminster Confession of Faith*, as well as concerns about the use of hymns and organs in some United Presbyterian churches. Opponents of church union argued that the United Presbyterians did not adhere to the same constitution and were able to forestall union during Candlish's lifetime.[45] It is striking that Candlish, who had argued so strenuously for the Disruption in 1843 on the basis of theological principle, could be found arguing for church union on the basis of its pragmatic value. To be fair to him, it should be noted that he was dead long before church union was finally completed, and it is hard to imagine that he

---

[44] Wilson, *Memorials of Robert Smith Candlish DD*, p. 536.

[45] For other aspects and a more detailed discussion of the church union question, see the chapters on James Begg and John Kennedy.

would ever have agreed to the compromises that had to be made to bring it about.

Candlish the Theologian

No survey of Candlish's life would be complete without reference to his work as a theologian. His commentaries on Genesis, the First Epistle of John and his book *The Atonement* remain in print and are marked by a careful exegesis of the text. But his most significant theological contribution may be found in the Cunningham lectures of 1864. The lectureship had been established to commemorate the life of Dr William Cunningham who had died in 1861. Candlish's lectures, subsequently published as *The Fatherhood of God*, were received with some controversy. In the lectures, Candlish argued that the idea of the universal fatherhood of God was unbiblical. Instead, he argued that the fatherhood of God should be understood as a 'filial relationship and that with believers only and that by adoption'. [46] Candlish went on to argue that what believers receive from Christ in adoption is an entirely new relationship unlike any other. His concern here was to assert that 'the Gospel is doing more than making good the loss brought on our race by sin'.[47] In stating his views, Candlish did not intend to be controversial. In the introduction to the published lectures, he wrote:

> These are not, in my opinion, novel doctrines; I would be
> sorry to think that they were. I may have put some points
> more sharply, and pushed a certain line of thought more

[46] McMullen, 'Candlish, Robert S.', p. 892.

[47] John MacLeod, *Scottish Theology in Relation to Church History Since the Reformation: lectures delivered in Westminster Theological Seminary, Philadelphia, USA* (Edinburgh: Publications Committee of the Free Church of Scotland, 1943), pp. 273–4.

boldly, than some may be quite prepared to approve. I am persuaded that I have really advanced nothing which may not be found, if not categorically asserted, at least fairly implied, in the writings of orthodox and evangelical divines, both of earlier and of later times.[48]

The Cunningham lectures displayed considerable 'dash ... versatility and ... fearlessness', which are good words to use in summing up Candlish's life.[49] He had been a faithful and energetic pastor and a leader in the church. He had been active in controversy, seeking in all of this to live according to his belief in what he called a thorough-going Christianity.

Candlish once concluded a sermon with an impassioned plea to those who had not as yet embraced Christianity. It also stands as testimony to the way in which he lived his life.

Oh you who are yet strangers to the power and practice of the Gospel. We entreat you to understand what sort of Christianity we urge on you; not such as you see in too many professors, – joyless, lifeless, vague, doubtful, undefined. We press a whole Christ and a whole Christianity. It is no half salvation God offers to you. There are no half measures with him; all full, free, unconditional, unreserved. Taste and see. Come be wholly the Lord's. Make fair trial; not half, but whole-heartedly. 'Choose you this day whom ye will serve'.[50]

---

[48] Robert S. Candlish, *The Fatherhood of God: Being the First Course of the Cunningham Lectures Delivered Before the New College, Edinburgh, in March 1864* (Edinburgh: Adam and Charles Black 1865), p. 4.

[49] John MacLeod, *Scottish Theology in Relation to Church History*, p. 275.

[50] Candlish, *Sermons by the Late Robert S. Candlish. Minister of Free St George's and Principal of the New College, Edinburgh*, p. 169.

WILLIAM CUNNINGHAM, D.D.

Home & Macdonald, Li

4

WILLIAM CUNNINGHAM
THEOLOGIAN

In all ... forms of service he upheld our Free Church
principles, our Scottish Calvinism and Presbyterianism,
our common Christianity.[1]

WILLIAM Cunningham has recently been called the
Free Church's 'ablest theologian'. [2] During his lifetime
he served in pastoral ministry for fourteen years, and then for
seventeen years he was first a professor and then Principal of
New College, Edinburgh, the church's first theological institution. He played a prominent role during the Ten Years Conflict
and the Disruption which followed. The Disruption era Free
Church was founded on very definite theological principles
and William Cunningham would be the one to clearly enun-
ciate these. While much of Cunningham's writings were not
published until after his death, he had a major influence on
his own denomination and the broader church.

EARLY LIFE AND EDUCATION
1805–29

William Cunningham was born on 2 October 1805 at
Hamilton, Lanarkshire. His father, Charles Cunningham,

---

[1] Robert Rainy and James Mackenzie, *Life of William Cunningham,
DD* (London: T. Nelson and Sons, 1871), p. 512. Robert Rainy completed
this biography at the request of Cunningham's family. The work had been
begun by Rev. James MacKenzie who left it unfinished at his death.

[2] Macleod, *Banner in the West*, p. 177.

was a merchant who died in 1811 as a result of a fall from a horse. His mother Helen, who would live until 1860, was

> ... a woman of strong independent spirit ... and of much more than ordinary talent and force of character, and trustfully and bravely she set about the heavy task of bringing up her fatherless children.[3]

After some years Helen Cunningham took her children to live with her father on his farm in Lesmahagow. After her father's death, Helen Cunningham was dependent on the generosity of her brother, who was a minister of the Moderate party in the Church of Scotland, and on one of her cousins, who was a very successful businessman, to support her family.

William Cunningham grew up in a family who were descended from the Covenanters, those who had fought for religious freedom in seventeenth-century Scotland. His home was a pious one and his mother made sure that the Bible was read every day. It appears, however, that Cunningham did not display much interest in spiritual things at this stage of his life.

William began his education at the local school where he made a favourable impression on the local schoolmaster, Robert Burns Begg. Begg particularly noted that young William had 'an insatiable thirst for reading...and especially for reading stories of battles'. [4] As well as a love for reading, Cunningham displayed an early love for the classics and he was fortunate that the schoolmaster cultivated and encouraged this. With this encouragement, he

---

[3] Rainy and Mackenzie, *Life of William Cunningham, DD*, p. 12.
[4] Ibid., p. 13.

was able to gain 'the highest place in Classical competition' in the local school, and was well prepared to continue his education at the University of Edinburgh which he began in November of 1820. One writer claims that he did this with the firm intention of becoming a minister, although this was more a career choice than it was a recognition of a particular vocation.[5] It should be noted that the initial interests displayed by Cunningham while at university had more to do with literature and philosophy than theology, and he made an excellent initial impression as a gifted student.

> Only a week after the Session had commenced, Professor Pillans asked the meaning of a hard passage in a difficult Roman author, and William Cunningham was the first out of a large Humanity class who stood up ready to give the translation.[6]

During the course of his university education, Cunningham read omnivorously, working his way through 'five hundred and thirty distinct works besides pamphlets [and] magazines ...'[7]

In the early stages of his college life, Cunningham had little use for the Evangelical party in the Church of Scotland. The early 1820s coincided with the rise of Thomas Chalmers to prominence within the church and it is said that Cunningham 'was honestly convinced

---

[5] John Bonar, 'William Cunningham DD', in James B. Gillies, *Disruption Worthies: A Memorial of 1843; with a Historical Sketch of the Free Church of Scotland from 1843 Down to the Present Time* (Edinburgh: T.C. Jack, 1881), p. 193.

[6] Ibid., p. 194.

[7] Rainy and Mackenzie, *Life of William Cunningham, DD*, p. 23.

Chalmers was not sane'! He also disparaged the burgeon-ing missions movement, believing that 'it would be better were the heathen left alone'. [8] During his fourth term at college his views began to change. Encouraged by a number of his friends, Cunningham began attending the church where Robert Gordon was the minister. Gordon has been called a 'senior statesman of the rising evangeli-cal party in the Church of Scotland'. [9] It was his sermons that were to alter Cunningham's theological orientation. Specifically, a sermon that he heard in 1825 on the subject of regeneration brought about his conversion and

> ...whilst ardent as ever in the accumulation of learning, he [now] took part, with all intense enthusiasm, in every scheme or society within the university which had the progress of the gospel and the glory of Christ for their object.[10]

Cunningham proceeded to the Divinity College without completing a university degree. Now he began to prepare with considerable enthusiasm for his calling to the ministry. In addition to his studies, Cunningham supported himself financially by serving as a tutor to a local family. He was also involved in some controversy. Along with a number of other students he took on the Divinity faculty over how the Divinity Library was being managed. He is said to have

---

[8] William Cunningham (J.J. Bonar ed.), *Sermons from 1825 to 1860* (Edinburgh: T & T Clark, 1872), pp. xiii–xiv.

[9] K.J. Stewart, 'Gordon, Robert', in *Dictionary of Scottish Church history and Theology*, p. 372.

[10] Bonar, 'William Cunningham DD', *Disruption Worthies: A Memorial of 1843; with a Historical Sketch of the Free Church of Scotland from 1843 Down to the Present Time*, p. 195.

remarked that 'controversy would be his life's work', which was to be true, at least in part.[11]

Given Cunningham's early negative opinions of Thomas Chalmers, it is worth noting that, when he had an opportunity to actually meet Chalmers in November of 1828, he had an abrupt change of mind. After his installation as Professor of Divinity at the University of Edinburgh, Chalmers reached out to the young student and set up a meeting with him to talk about the Divinity Library. After the meeting, Cunningham commented that

I have talked a good deal with him, not only about the Library, but also about his plans of teaching; and from all I have seen and heard, both in public and in private, I have no doubt...that he will prove an instrument of almost incalculable usefulness, and that his appointment will form a bright era in the history of our Church.[12]

In December 1828, Cunningham travelled to Dunse to be examined by the Presbytery and to be licensed to preach. His first sermon was preached on 14 December 1828 and he took as his text words from Psalm 23:6: 'Surely goodness and mercy shall follow me all the days of my life; and I shall dwell in the house of the Lord ever.' This sermon, which was entitled 'The Believer's Security and Confidence', focused on the providence of God in the life of the believer. He concluded it with a call to trust in Christ who has 'already done and suffered so much for the salvation of His people and who even now entertains the same feelings

[11] Lionel Alexander Ritchie, 'Cunningham, William', in *Oxford Dictionary of National Biography,* v. 14, p. 704.

[12] Rainy and Mackenzie, *Life of William Cunningham, DD*, p. 36.

and promotes the same objects'. [13] Cunningham's purpose here was to call his hearers to increased faith in Christ as they faced the challenges of life.

PARISH MINISTRY IN GREENOCK
1830–4

William Cunningham was appointed Assistant Minister to Dr John Scott of Middle Parish Church, Greenock, in January of 1830. In the following October he was ordained as Scott's colleague and successor. Scott had served this parish for forty years and had been very popular. He was in failing health and most of the parish duties devolved to Cunningham. They developed a very good relationship and Cunningham would later write, 'I can only say of him ... that I have the greatest veneration of his memory, and that I reckon my knowledge of him among the greatest blessings of my life ...' [14]

The time that Cunningham spent in Greenock would be particularly notable for two events, one ecclesiastical and the other personal. He would not be long in Greenock before he would be called upon to defend orthodoxy in what came to be known as the 'Row Controversy'. John McLeod Campbell, who was minister of the parish of Row, had adopted controversial views on the atonement. Specifically, he argued against the need for penal substitution. He also taught that the death of Christ had secured forgiveness for all in this life and, as a result, it was simply assurance that was essential to salvation. [15] Cunningham made a point of

---

[13] Cunningham, *Sermons from 1825 to 1860* (Edinburgh: 1872), p. 19.

[14] Rainy and Mackenzie, *Life of William Cunningham, DD*, p. 47.

[15] For a fuller discussion of Campbell's views, see 'Campbell, John McLeod', in *Dictionary of Scottish Church History and Theology*, pp.129–30.

going to hear the controversial minister preach and then interacted with some of his followers. In a letter he commented that

> ... some of the Campbellites ... have the boldness to allege that ... Paul misstated the gospel to the jailer, when he said 'Believe on the Lord Jesus Christ, and thou shalt be saved', in place of saying, 'Believe that thou art pardoned, and be saved'.[16]

Campbell was charged with teaching views contrary to the Bible and the *Westminster Confession of Faith* and Cunningham was called to give evidence at his trial. This situation might not have been Cunningham's choice as the best way to be noticed in the wider church, but his attention to detail was noted and the evidence that he gave was significant in establishing the libel. While this issue engaged the interest of the wider church, it also had an immediate impact on the Greenock congregation, because Cunningham had to depose one of the church's elders for agreeing with McLeod Campbell's views.

At this time a much happier personal situation developed when Cunningham was introduced to Janet Denniston. Janet came from 'a family of great Christian worth and of old commercial repute in the town of Greenock'.[17] They were subsequently married on 15 July 1834, and would have a family of five daughters and six sons. Janet outlived her husband by twenty-seven years, dying in 1888.

---

[16] Bonar, 'William Cunningham DD', *Disruption Worthies: A Memorial of 1843; with a Historical Sketch of the Free Church of Scotland from 1843 Down to the Present Time*, p. 196.

[17] Rainy and Mackenzie, *Life of William Cunningham, DD*, p. 72.

Cunningham rose to prominence in the wider church at the 1833 General Assembly. At that Assembly, Thomas Chalmers made a motion to the effect that no minister would be imposed upon a parish if the male heads of families disapproved of the settlement. Although the motion eventually failed, Cunningham gave an impassioned two-hour speech in support of Chalmers that made many of the Moderate party within the church sit up and take notice of the young man from Greenock.

In 1832 approaches were made from two churches in Glasgow to see if Cunningham would be willing to move, but he declined them both. Then late in 1833 he did agree to move and was appointed to Trinity College Church in Edinburgh. He preached his last sermon in Greenock on the first Sabbath in January 1834, which was exactly four years to the day on which he had preached his first sermon there. As Cunningham left Greenock for Edinburgh he noted in his diary, 'the kindness of the Greenock people I can never forget on this side [of] the grave'. [18]

Cunningham's ministry in Greenock must be termed a success. Not only did he confront the problems created by the false teachings of Campbell, but as Michael Honeycutt has pointed out, he did much more.

> To a congregation confused about what they believed, he brought confidence in the doctrines of the Reformation; to a congregation in danger of dividing, he brought the kind of popular appeal that filled the pulpit and gallery stairs and required the construction of additional seats in every available space.[19]

---

[18] Ibid., p. 60.

[19] Michael W. Honeycutt, *William Cunningham: His Life, Thought, and Controversies*, Thesis (Ph. D.) – University of Edinburgh, 2002, p. 306.

MINISTER OF TRINITY COLLEGE PARISH
1834–43

Cunningham began his ministry in Edinburgh with considerable vigour and enthusiasm. Even though he inherited a church that was almost empty he initially enjoyed considerable success. His biographers tell us that from the start of his ministry 'the whole machinery of an evangelical church was set in motion'. [20] Following Chalmers' model, the parish was divided into sections with elders appointed to take care of the spiritual needs of the people. In addition to his regular preaching activities, Cunningham carried out regular visitation and was actively involved in the supervision of the parish schools. Despite his zealousness in parish work, Cunningham never became a popular preacher to rival men like Chalmers and Candlish. The main difficulty was that he chose to read his sermons from a prepared manuscript and this was not well received by many people in his new congregation. Hugh Miller once said of him, 'Oh that Cunningham would *preach* a sermon', [21] referring to that fact that there seemed to be a lack of passion in his delivery. While there are relatively few examples of Cunningham's sermons extant, those that we have are well crafted. It is unfortunate that people were unable to see past the stilted delivery, to what was being said. But if his sermons were not successful, his speeches at Presbytery and the General Assembly were another matter.

Cunningham was involved in a number of public campaigns during this period. One of the most controversial had to do with pointing out the theological errors advanced

[20] Rainy and Mackenzie, *Life of William Cunningham*, p.73.

[21] Ibid., emphasis added.

by the Church of Rome. This campaign was marked with both failure and success. In 1836 he publicly accused the *Encyclopaedia Britannica* of changing their most recent article on Roman Catholicism in response to public pressure and to appease Catholic readers. There was an instant and vociferous response from Catholics and from the editors of the Encyclopaedia. One writer to *The Scotsman* scornfully commented about Cunningham:

> There is no assertion too bold for him to make, no absurdity too incredible for him to swallow. One would suppose that he can scarcely stumble on a correct statement by accident.[22]

When Cunningham's assertions were shown to be false, he had to issue a public retraction on the front page of *The Scotsman*.

> The ... statement which I [made], rested upon authority, which warranted me in believing it at the time ... I am now satisfied; that the information upon which I acted, does not warrant the inference that any concession was made, or any inference injurious to the character of the *Encyclopaedia Britannica*.[23]

Not deterred by his error in judgment, in 1837 he republished Edward Stillingfleet's *The Doctrines and Practices of the Church of Rome*. Cunningham added extensive notes and editorial comments which doubled the length of the

---

[22] J.A. Smith 'Mr Cunningham Again!' *The Scotsman Digital Archive, January 30, 1836*, http://archive.scotsman.com/ (accessed 11 March 2009).

[23] William Cunningham, 'Encyclopaedia Britannica', *The Scotsman Digital Archive, March 16, 1836*, http://archive.scotsman.com/ (accessed 11 March 2009).

work. The work sold well and became a standard work on the subject for many years.

Cunningham's arrival in Edinburgh coincided with the beginning of the 'Ten Years Conflict', which wracked the church and led to the Disruption in 1843. He would come to play an important role in these events. As his involvement increased, he was motivated by the desire to see genuine revival in the church. His biographers state that

> The deepest wish of Cunningham's heart was to see the Church, which he loved with such reverent affection, reanimated to the efficiency of former times. He burned to see her delivered from the corruptions of a hundred years. This was the ruling passion of his heart, and ... the hope of success was as ardent as the desire was deep and strong.[24]

Cunningham would play a role in a number of high profile disputes that took place and so it is appropriate that we briefly sketch his involvement.

It will be remembered that in 1834 the Church of Scotland General Assembly had passed the *Veto Act* which was designed to restrict the power of patronage by giving to male heads of families the right to veto the parish patron's appointment of the local minister. It will also be recalled that in the Marnoch case, seven Moderate ministers of the Presbytery of Strathbogie had been suspended by the church for proceeding with the court-backed ordination and installation of John Edwards. With the significant number of vacancies thus created, the church asked for and received the willing cooperation of other ministers to go and fill the vacant pulpits on a temporary basis and it is said that the

---

[24] Rainy and Mackenzie, *Life of William Cunningham, DD*, p. 100.

'flower of Evangelical preachers from all [over] Scotland were sent to Strathbogie that winter'.[25] When the suspended members of the Strathbogie Presbytery applied for and received a court order, forbidding the use of outside ministers, Cunningham responded. He went into print on the matters under discussion, particularly in response to a work published by another minister of the Church of Scotland.

In October of 1839 the Rev. James Robertson, minister of Elton, had delivered a lengthy speech to the Synod of Aberdeen against the *Veto Act*. The speech which had lasted five hours and twenty minutes was published in March of 1840 in a 'pamphlet' entitled, *Observations on the Veto Act*. If Robertson's Synod speech was long, his pamphlet was even longer! Over the course of nearly 300 pages, he took pains to argue that what the Evangelical party in the church was asking for was neither legal, nor expedient.[26] His *Observations* were published to considerable public acclaim and many in the Moderate party of the Church of Scotland thought that he had achieved a significant victory for their cause.

But Cunningham was unimpressed. A month after Robertson's 'pamphlet' was published, he responded with the first of two pamphlets of his own as well as a letter to Hugh Miller's *Witness* newspaper. Cunningham pointed out how Robertson had consistently misquoted sources and misread church history. He argued that a proper reading of the tradition demonstrated that Protestant

---

[25] Ibid., p. 143.

[26] James Robertson, *Observations on the Veto Act* (Edinburgh: W. Blackwood, 1840), p. 11.

church history approves of, and 'fully sanctions the principle of the popular will in the choice of their pastor'. [27] This publication signalled that Cunningham was a formidable scholarly foe, who knew his church history very well and who was more than capable of developing a cogent argument.

He was also active in the Presbytery of Edinburgh fighting for the church's freedom. At the February 1840 meeting, he presented a motion requesting that the church send a memorial to the government. He told the Presbytery that this would express

> ... anxiety and alarm in regard to the decision of the Court
> of Session as involving an infringement of the rights and
> liberties of the Church of Scotland, as settled at the Revo-
> lution by the *Act of Settlement* and the *Treaty of Union,*
> and urging, upon this ground, an immediate settlement of
> the present unhappy collision.[28]

Cunningham's literary efforts and ecclesiastical activities attracted attention not only in the public press in Scotland, but they were also noticed in America. They were a contributing factor to his being awarded an honorary Doctor of Divinity degree from Princeton in 1842. Princeton's President told him in a letter that the degree was being awarded in

> ... consideration of your attainments in sacred literature
> and theological science, and also of your distinguished
> labours in the cause of Truth and Righteousness, the

---

[27] Rainy and Mackenzie, *Life of William Cunningham, DD,* p. 155.

[28] 'Presbytery of Edinburgh, Wednesday February 26', *The Scotsman Digital Archive, February 29, 1840,* http://archive.scotsman.com/ (accessed 11 March 2009).

Trustees of the College of New Jersey have conferred on you the Degree of Doctor in Divinity.[29]

Cunningham's biographer states that while the newly minted Doctor of Divinity was honoured to receive this letter, he had a

> ... strong liking for the old academic ways, [and] desired to have the old formal diploma. He wrote ... expressing this wish, and the diploma duly engrossed on parchment was sent accordingly.[30]

The last year before the Disruption was a very busy one for Cunningham. As court decisions went against the Evangelical party in the church and as politicians dithered, refusing to take decisive action, it became increasingly clear to him that a break with the established church was now inevitable. He played a role in the Convocation that had taken place in Edinburgh in November 1842 where plans for the Disruption were formalised.[31] After the Convocation, Cunningham went back to his congregation and carefully and persuasively presented the issues to them. Then he undertook a series of public engagements around Scotland to further explain the issues and seek the support of the people for the difficult days ahead.

On Monday, 22 May 1843, Cunningham made an impassioned speech to the first Free Church General Assembly. In the speech 'which was received with loud cheering' he defended the actions of the Evangelical party and ended

---

[29] Rainy and Mackenzie, *Life of William Cunningham, DD*, p. 182.

[30] Ibid.

[31] K.R, Ross, 'Convocation', in *Dictionary of Scottish Church History and Theology*, p. 210.

with the confident expression that if the new church remained faithful to God, it would be blessed. Quoting from George Gillespie's *Aaron's Rod Blossoming*, Cunningham concluded his speech by reminding his hearers that 'they [could rest] ... assured that Christ and his cause shall be victorious for he must reign until all his enemies be made his footstool'. [32]

At the same General Assembly there was discussion about the establishment of a theological college. On 20 May, an Educational Committee was appointed and five days later it made a series of recommendations to the Assembly. These included the appointment of four professors: Thomas Chalmers as Principal and Senior Professor of theology, David Welsh to the chair of church history, and John Duncan to the chair of Hebrew and Old Testament.[33] It was also decided that William Cunningham would be appointed to a junior chair in Theology, but

> as his services will not be required till the session 1844–5, it is with the understanding that he should proceed to the United States, partly with a view of pleading our Church question, and partly that he might have opportunity of witnessing the manner in which education, and particularly theological education, is conducted in the seminaries of the new world.[34]

---

[32] John Baillie (ed.), *Proceedings of the General Assembly of the Free Church of Scotland: With a Sketch of the Proceedings of the Residuary Assembly, 1843* (Edinburgh: W.P. Kennedy, 1843), p. 66.

[33] Brown, 'The Making of New College: 1843–6', p. 1.

[34] Baillie (ed.), *Proceedings of the General Assembly of the Free Church of Scotland: With a Sketch of the Proceedings of the Residuary Assembly, 1843*, p. 77.

The committee concluded its recommendations by wisely calling for the establishment of a library, and that a lecture hall be procured. A second set of recommendations called for a comprehensive Free Church school system that would include, 'primary schools in every parish, grammar schools in every major town and three universities'. [35]

VISIT TO AMERICA
1844

Before Cunningham left for America, he suffered the loss of his four-year-old son Willie, who died from whooping cough on October 16, 1843. Cunningham was still in mourning as he set sail for America in December.

In addition to Cunningham, the deputation to the United States and Canada included Henry Ferguson, a Free Church elder and merchant from Dundee, Rev. William Chalmers, Rev. George Lewis, and Dr Robert Burns.[36] When they arrived in the United States the committee decided that they would divide the work, with some travelling in the southern United States and the other group travelling in the northern States and Canada. Cunningham spent his time in the northern States visiting New York, Boston, Philadelphia, Princeton, Richmond, Baltimore and Washington. The highlight for Cunningham was his visit to Princeton where he stayed with Charles Hodge and struck up a lasting friendship with

---

[35] Brown, 'The Disruption and the Dream: The making of New College 1843–61', p. 33.

[36] Richard W. Vaudry, *The Free Church in Victorian Canada: 1844–61* (Waterloo Ontario: Wilfred Laurier University Press, 1989), p. 30. Robert Burns would return to Canada to serve in Toronto as the Minister of Knox Church and Professor at Knox College.

him. As the deputies travelled the continent, they spoke about the causes for the Disruption and raised funds for the work of the church back in Scotland. They raised $3,500 in the north and as much as $9,000 in the south.[37] The money raised in the southern States came partly from churches who had slave-owning members. This became a matter of public debate when the deputies returned to Scotland. Cunningham reached home in time for the General Assembly in May of 1844 where his reports of his travels were received with great acclaim.

Over the next two years a very public debate was waged within the Free Church and in the press over the donations from slave owners and their churches. The campaign was fuelled by the abolitionist campaigner Frederick Douglass who demanded that the Free Church send back the money. Many outside of the Free Church viewed the debate with considerable amusement as the church struggled valiantly to condemn slavery as such, while at the same time not alienating friends across the Atlantic who had given so generously to the work of the church in Scotland.

On Saturday, 30 May 1846, Cunningham addressed the Assembly on the slavery issue. He began his speech by stating that

> It was perfectly well known that there was not a Minister in the Free Church who did not regard slavery as sinful. The only thing in which he differed ... was ... that he had seen more of the Christians in America, and had been led to form a more favourable estimate of their general character and general principles, and had no hesitation in saying

---

[37] Ibid., p. 31. Equivalent amounts for this would have been in the region of £1,200 and £3,000 respectively.

that there were many amongst them who manifested a very great amount of Christian principles.[38]

The Assembly then passed a resolution which condemned slavery, while at the same time denying that slaveholders were therefore unchristian. The Assembly pledged continued support for all those who were working toward the abolition of slavery in America, but refused to sever connections with slaveholding churches and the monies collected were not returned.

By 1871, when Robert Rainy published his biography of Cunningham, he could write with some truthfulness that by then, the dispute had 'ceased to have practical importance'.[39] It is unfortunate that the trip to America, which had been designed to create goodwill and to support the work of the Free Church, should be remembered for the slavery debate which followed it. While it is not fair to impose twenty-first-century standards of political correctness on this incident, it is fair to note that this whole episode did not display either Cunningham, or the Free Church, to best advantage.

PROFESSOR AND PRINCIPAL OF NEW COLLEGE 1844–61

New College, Edinburgh began operations in purchased rooms in George Street in November of 1843. The College began with a classroom and a library built with 'books donated by well wishers'. In its first term, New College

---

[38] 'General Assembly of the Free Church, Saturday May 30', *The Scotsman Digital Archive, June 3, 1846*, http://archive.scotsman.com/ (accessed 12 March 2009).

[39] Rainy and Mackenzie, *Life of William Cunningham, DD*, p. 221.

had an enrolment of 168 students.[40] William Cunningham began his work as Junior Professor of theology in November of 1844 and was assigned the task of teaching a course on the Evidences of Revealed Religion. A year later, Cunningham was appointed to the Chair of Church History when David Welsh died suddenly. Although this new appointment was received by the majority of the church with enthusiasm, his biographer relates that

> ... on the day of his appointment ... Dr Cunningham met a friend ... who offered her congratulations [to which he replied] 'Well, I'm told that some people are opposed to it on this ground, that I have no imagination. Don't you think a want of imagination is rather a good feature in a historian?' [41]

Whether or not Cunningham was imaginative is an open question, but he certainly had a sense of humour! Even those who have unfairly accused Cunningham of possessing a narrow theology and 'strict theological views' have conceded that he was well liked by students. He is said to have delivered 'clear and forceful lectures, [with] an ability to arouse student interest and a warm manner in personal contacts'. [42]

The early days of New College were exciting ones. A core curriculum was put in place with a logical progression of courses. The faculty was expanded to include permanent chairs of Apologetics, Church History, Systematic Theology,

---

[40] Brown, 'The Making of New College: 1843–6', p. 1.

[41] Rainy and Mackenzie, *Life of William Cunningham, DD*, p. 225.

[42] Brown, 'The Disruption and the Dream: The Making of New College 1843–61', p. 43.

Hebrew and Old Testament, New Testament Exegesis, and Practical Theology. By 1846, an arts curriculum was being delivered by Professors who taught Moral Philosophy, Logic and Natural Sciences. In addition to these achievements, a library of over 13,000 volumes had been collected and an imposing new building was rising on The Mound in Edinburgh.[43] It is also interesting to note that classes were open to all qualified students regardless of their church affiliation. An advertisement in *The Scotsman* dated 26 September 1846 read,

> Admission to the classes of New College is not limited to students qualifying for the Ministry, or connected with the Free Church, but is open to all upon Matriculation.[44]

Tragedy struck the Free Church in 1847 with the sudden death of Thomas Chalmers during the General Assembly of that year. The Assembly moved to replace Chalmers with Dr Robert Gordon, but when he turned down the appointment, Cunningham was offered and accepted the position.

The period of Cunningham's leadership of New College saw both growth and controversy. The greatest achievement in this period was the opening of the new facility on 6 November 1850. Nathaniel Patterson, the Moderator of the General Assembly, preached a sermon from 1 Corinthians 1:17: 'Not with the wisdom of words, lest the cross of Christ should be made of none effect', and then in a separate address to the professors and students he called upon both

---

[43] Brown, 'The Making of New College: 1843–6', pp. 3–4.

[44] 'New College' *The Scotsman Digital Archive, September 26, 1846*, http://archive.scotsman.com/ (accessed 13 March 2009).

the faculty and the students to faithfulness and hard work in their teaching and studies.

> Strength, vigour and happiness increase by virtuous application. Strive to excel: it is not small attainments that will do for these times. The enemies of truth are learned; and you must neither fear them nor meet them with inferior weapons.[45]

In response to the Moderator's charge, Cunningham responded by addressing the important role that the College would have in the life of the Free Church. He concluded his address with an expression of 'earnest desire' that

> ... the church may always continue to watch carefully and strictly over the proceedings of this institution ... [as we] by God's grace, do ... all we can ... to train up a race of men who will be in all respects 'able Ministers of the New Testament'. [46]

In addition to his teaching and administrative duties at New College, Cunningham displayed his scholarship through his editorial work for *The British and Foreign Evangelical Review*. In the pages of this journal, which he edited from 1855 to 1860, Cunningham published some of his own work, which was released in book form after his death. *The Reformers and the Theology of the Reformation* clearly displayed his ability to carefully read texts and place them in their proper historical context, and it is still an important work.

---

[45] Nathaniel Patterson, 'Address to Professors and Students', *Inauguration of the New College of the Free Church, Edinburgh* (Edinburgh: Johnstone and Hunter, 1851), p. 38.

[46] William Cunningham. 'Address Delivered at the Opening of the New College'. *Inauguration of the New College of the Free Church, Edinburgh*, p. 58.

Some controversy would surround Cunningham's tenure as College Principal as the Free Church feverishly debated the issue of whether or not theological education should be offered in Glasgow and Aberdeen as well as Edinburgh. As we noted in the previous chapter, Candlish and Cunningham clashed over this issue. Cunningham firmly believed that the only way that the Free Church could provide quality theological education was by concentrating its resources at New College in Edinburgh. The dispute, which began with a difference of opinion as to how the church would best be served, became intensely personal. Perhaps the darkest moment occurred in April 1855 at a meeting of the Edinburgh Presbytery. As it debated who it should select as members of the next General Assembly, Cunningham made the remarkable statement that he didn't think that the presence of Dr Candlish 'would in any matter be for the good of the Church'. [47] The newspaper account of this meeting goes on to describe the distress on all sides that Cunningham's outburst caused. Cunningham even went so far as to write to Candlish to tell him that their friendship was over.[48]

Ultimately, the Free Church chose to disregard Cunningham's advice on this issue and opened theological colleges in Aberdeen and Glasgow. Whether this was wise is doubtful. Certainly more ministers were trained than might have been possible had the programme remained centralised. However, the question needs to be asked if the

---

[47] 'Free Church Presbytery', *The Scotsman Digital Archive, April 7 1855*, http://archive.scotsman.com/ (accessed 13 March 2009).

[48] Honeycutt, *William Cunningham: His Life, Thought, and Controversies*, p. 262.

decentralisation contributed to the theological drift that plagued the Free Church later in the century. Certainly, the church had a more difficult time watching over her theological institutions in the way that Cunningham had asked them to in his inaugural address of 1850.

In 1858 Cunningham suddenly lost the sight in his right eye. Although he was only fifty-three years old, there was real concern for his health. This medical setback did bring about a rapprochement with Robert Candlish and others in the church that had fallen out over the 'College Question'. Also the church decided to hold a fund-raising campaign for Cunningham and his family as a token of appreciation for all that he had done for the Free Church. In a relatively short space of time the sum of £7,061 was raised. The formal presentation was made to the Cunningham family on 3 January 1859.[49] In the same year, Cunningham was elected as Moderator of the General Assembly and he carried out his duties to great acclaim. He preached his last sermon as 'retiring moderator' at the 1860 General Assembly and from this point his health became increasingly fragile. He died at home on 14 December 1861. At the March 1862 Commission of Assembly, the Commission first extended condolences to the Queen for the loss of Albert, the Prince Consort, and then resolved

> ... in accordance with the universal sense of the Church, to place on their records their deep sense of severe loss which the Church has sustained by the death of Principal Cunningham.[50]

---

[49] Rainy and Mackenzie, *Life of William Cunningham, DD*, pp. 225–6.

[50] 'Free Church Commission', *The Scotsman Digital Archive, March 6 1862*, http://archive.scotsman.com/ (accessed 13 March 2009).

CUNNINGHAM THE THEOLOGIAN

A few hours before he died, Cunningham met with his
literary executors, James Buchanan and James Bannerman, instructing them that '... his whole writings and
manuscripts be used and applied to any purpose they
judged right'. [51] Over the course of the next few years, his
executors published a number of his works including what
has been called 'his *magnum opus*', the two volume *Historical Theology*, a work which is more a systematic theology
than it is an account of church history. [52] It has been noted
that while the

> ... treatment is austere, and the documentation minimal...
> the service performed for the student is immense, as Cun-
> ningham states the issue, summarises the views of the
> various parties, indicates the evidence for the orthodox
> position and finally deals with the objections. The result is
> a superb training in theological method.[53]

In 1939 Principal John Macleod of the Free Church College
delivered a series of lectures at Westminster Theological
Seminary in Philadelphia in which he summarised the
history of Scottish theology since the Reformation. In these
lectures Macleod colourfully described Cunningham's *Historical Theology* in this way:

> This work is like an elaborate and luminous judicial
> charge by a master of his subject addressed from the

---

[51] James Buchanan and James Bannerman, 'Preface', in William
Cunningham, *The Reformers and the Theology of the Reformation*
(Edinburgh: T and T Clark, 1862), p. iii.

[52] Donald Macleod, 'Cunningham, William', in *Dictionary of Scottish
Church History and Theology,* p. 229.

[53] Ibid.

Bench to the jury of Christian students who may well avail themselves of the judgements of so penetrating and comprehensive a mind.[54]

Cunningham's theological output covered a wide range of topics focusing on what he saw as the hierarchy of truth set out in Scripture. He was committed to rooting theology in biblical exegesis and he looked fondly upon the theology of the Reformation and of the *Westminster Confession of Faith.* Donald Macleod has rightly concluded that after Cunningham's death, Scottish theology began to move in a more liberal direction as

> ... Scottish churchmen opted for the theology of the Enlightenment in preference to that of the Reformation. If that situation is ever reversed, people will once again take seriously Cunningham's claim to be considered Scotland's greatest theologian.[55]

---

[54] John MacLeod, *Scottish Theology in Relation to Church History*, p. 269.

[55] Donald Macleod, 'Cunningham, William', in *Dictionary of Scottish Church History and Theology*, p. 231.

HUGH MILLER.

Home & Macdonald, Li

5

HUGH MILLER
JOURNALIST

Hugh Miller of Cromarty was in all respects a
remarkable man. Very rich in natural gifts ... the
stonemason of Cromarty carved out his way in the world
by dint of sharp and sturdy blows ... His contributions
to science ... have given him a claim to the highest
rank and his championship of the Free Church stamps
him as no mean theologian.[1]

HUGH Miller is perhaps the most colourful figure
shown in David Octavius Hill's picture of the first
Free Church General Assembly. He appears in the fore-
ground, just below the Clerk's table, clothed in a tweed
suit with his countryman's wrap draped over his left
shoulder. He is busy writing, using his top hat as a desk,
and there are flowers scattered at his feet. Looking at
his likeness one catches a glimpse of a remarkable man,
which he certainly was.

Over the course of his life he would be a stonemason,
amateur geologist and accomplished journalist and would
have a major impact on the Disruption era Free Church.
He lived a life full of significant incidents and died a tragic
death. He was a larger than life figure who, in his lifetime,
could lay claim to being the voice of the Free Church.

---

[1] 'Hugh Miller Obituary', *New York Times January 14, 1857,* http://
select.nytimes.com/mem/archive (accessed 17 March 2009).

EARLY LIFE AND EDUCATION
1802–19

Hugh Miller was born in Cromarty, north of Inverness, on 10 October 1802. He was the first of three children born to his father Hugh and mother Harriet. According to Miller's nineteenth-century biographer, he made an underwhelming first impression. 'The midwife remarked that the conformation of the head was unusual, and indicated in her sage opinion that the child would turn out an idiot.'[2] Nothing could have been further from the truth!

Hugh Miller's father was a coastal shipmaster who achieved enough success to be able to afford to build a new house, which is still standing in Cromarty. Sadly, Miller senior died at sea in 1807 leaving his widow and young family. In his autobiographical account of his early life, *My Schools and Schoolmasters*, Hugh Miller describes his youthful grief.

> I remember I used to go wandering disconsolately about the harbour ... to examine the vessels that had come in during the night. I [also] used ... to climb ... a grassy protuberance ... immediately behind my mother's house ... to look wistfully out, long after everyone else had ceased to hope.[3]

Miller relates that before his father's death he had been sent to school where he was taught the rudiments of reading by

---

[2] Peter Bayne, *The Life and Letters of Hugh Miller*, v. 1 (London: Strahan & Co., 1871), p. 6. Peter Bayne was selected by Hugh Miller's widow to write his biography and the finished product relied heavily upon input from the Miller family and should therefore be viewed as his 'official biography'.

[3] Hugh Miller, *My Schools and Schoolmasters; or, the Story of my Education* (Edinburgh: William P. Nimmo & Co., 1879), p. 26.

working his way through the Bible and the Shorter Catechism. One gets the impression, however, that any success
he achieved was more a result of his own hard work rather
than the excellence of the teaching.

In the absence of his father, the family turned to two
maternal uncles, James and Alexander, who was known as
Sandy. These two men would play an active part in young
Hugh's education. In fact he would say of them that 'I owed
to them much more of my real education than to any of the
teachers whose schools I ... attended'. [4] His uncles instilled
in him a love of reading. Hugh tells us that with their help
he 'began to collect a library in a box of birch-bark about
nine inches square, which I found quite large enough to
contain a number of immortal works'. [5] Through reading
Miller became aware of his national identity. In his tenth
year, his Uncle James gave him a life of the Scottish hero
William Wallace and the stories of his exploits captured
his imagination. He tells us that he 'longed for war ... that
the wrongs and sufferings of those noble heroes might be
avenged'. [6]

Hugh Miller's scientific interest in the world around him
was cultivated by his Uncle Sandy who took him for long
walks along the shore. It was on these walks that he came
to appreciate creation. He would later comment that there

> ... are professors of Natural History that know less of living
> nature than was known by Uncle Sandy; and I deemed it
> no small matter to have all the various productions of the

[4] Ibid., p. 5.

[5] Ibid., p. 28.

[6] Ibid., p. 41.

sea with which he was acquainted pointed out to me on these walks ...[7]

The Miller family faced another tragedy in 1816 when Hugh's two sisters, Jean and Catherine, both died from a fever. At the same time, by his own admission, Hugh spent most of his time getting into trouble with other boys and resenting discipline at home and school. His mother, in her grief, turned some of her anger and resentment on her son. Hugh's uncles tried to intervene to keep him at his studies, but eventually they had to admit defeat.

In 1819, when Miller was seventeen, his mother married Andrew Williamson. It has been suggested that Hugh did not develop a good relationship with his stepfather and that this contributed to his undisciplined behaviour at school.[8] His formal schooling came to an end after what can only be described as a brawl between Miller and the schoolmaster. Miller admits that he '... was mauled in a way that filled me with aches and bruises for a full month afterwards'. [9]

Not surprisingly his family and, especially his uncles, expressed concern over his behaviour and what he was going to do with his life. Miller himself comments that while many of his friends thought about careers in the law or the church, he felt no such calling and his uncles wisely recognised that it was better to 'be anything honest, however humble, than an uncalled minister'. [10]

---

[7] Ibid., p. 62.

[8] Michael A. Taylor, *Hugh Miller, Stonemason, Geologist, Writer* (Edinburgh: National Museums of Scotland, 2007), p. 24.

[9] Miller, *My Schools and Schoolmasters; or, the Story of my Education*, p. 144.

[10] Ibid., p. 152.

STONEMASON
1820–5

From February of 1820 until November of 1822 Hugh Miller was apprenticed as a stonemason to David Williamson, his mother's brother-in-law. Given his character and his inability to study in a formalised setting, a university education was out of the question. In fact, the opportunity to work at a trade gave Miller what he needed at this stage, a positive channel for his energies.

The work was extremely hard but he found himself enjoying the opportunity it gave him to appreciate and investigate nature. He writes that:

> I soon found that there was much to be enjoyed in a life of labour. A taste for the beauties of the natural scene is of itself a never failing spring of delight; and there was scarce a day in which I wrought in the open air, during this period, in which I did not experience its soothing and exhilarating influence.[11]

In the same passage he goes on to note that the work took a heavy physical and emotional toll on him.

> I became subject ... to frequent fits of extreme depression of spirits, which took almost the form of a walking sleep – results, I believe of excessive fatigue – and during which my absence of mind was so extreme, that I lacked the ability of protecting myself against accident ...[12]

In November of 1822, during a particularly difficult job, he began to cough up blood and experience chest pain. He managed to work through to the end of his apprenticeship,

---

[11] Ibid., p. 156.

[12] Ibid., p. 157.

but had to spend the subsequent winter and spring recovering back home at Cromarty.

When he was able to return to work he did so as an itinerant, travelling wherever he could find employment. Because work was in short supply in the immediate area around Cromarty, he travelled to Edinburgh, arriving there in 1824. There he found himself working with men who would routinely spend significant amounts of their wages on drink. Their main interest outside of their jobs was 'badger-baiting and they harboured deep resentments against their working conditions'. [13] He was somewhat ostracised because he refused to adopt the same lifestyle. It has been said of him that during this period

> ... he learned to distrust the depraved urban workers and detest the radical and Chartist agitators among them, even though he understood the causes of their unrest and bitterness.[14]

This period certainly opened his eyes to the difficult working conditions of labourers in the nineteenth century.

RETURN TO CROMARTY: WRITING, GEOLOGY AND ROMANCE 1825–39

Ill health forced Miller to return to Cromarty in 1825. He was suffering from a relapse of the 'stone cutter's malady', which was in all likelihood a form of either tuberculosis or pneumoconiosis, an occupational lung disease caused by

---

[13] Donald Macleod, 'Macleod on Miller', *The Monthly Record of the Free Church of Scotland*, January, 2003, p. 4.

[14] Elizabeth Sutherland, *Lydia, Wife of Hugh Miller of Cromarty* (East Linton: Tuckwell Press, 2003), p. 4.

the inhalation of dust.[15] While relations with his family had been strained during his teenage years, his mother now took care of him, nursing him back to health. As he slowly regained his strength, he decided to give up cutting stone in the quarries. Instead he became a 'monumental mason', using his skills to carve such things as sundials and gravestones. This work 'was much less dusty than working en mass with other masons'.[16]

At this stage, two people had a significant impact on Hugh: Alexander Stewart, who had been appointed the minister of the parish in 1824, and a childhood friend, John Swanson, who was now training for the ministry. Miller himself concedes that he had been 'a boy-atheist', because he had arrived at the conclusion that he must '... for the sake of peace either do that which was right, or by denying the truth of the Bible to set every action, good and bad, on the same level'.[17] Swanson became a faithful correspondent with Miller, pleading with him to embrace the faith. In a letter dated July 1825 Swanson wrote:

> Oh I pant after that time when I may be fully assured that you are travelling toward Zion. Oh there is much encouragement held out to us in the Scriptures to come to Christ.[18]

Then again in September of the same year Swanson wrote:

> We find [the apostles asking] Dost thou believe? Believe what? That Jesus is the Christ. And I ask you, my dear

---

[15] M.A. Taylor, 'Miller, Hugh', in *Oxford Dictionary of National Biography*, v. 38 (Oxford: Oxford University Press, 2004), p. 202.

[16] Taylor, *Hugh Miller, Stonemason, Geologist, Writer*, p. 34.

[17] Bayne, *The Life and Letters of Hugh Miller*, v. 1, p. 42.

[18] Ibid., p. 173

Hugh, dost thou believe? Do you believe that he lived? That he was sent of God? That he died to save sinners?[19]

While Miller did not respond directly to Swanson's entreaties, he did attend church and was impressed by Alexander Stewart's preaching. Toward the end of 1825, Miller 'settled ... into a lasting commitment' to the Christian faith and to 'Calvinist Presbyterianism'.[20]

Miller had long harboured literary ambitions and had been writing poetry for some time. After he had failed to get his work published in the pages of the *Inverness Courier,* he invested some of his own money to publish *Poems Written in the Leisure Hours of a Journeyman Mason* in 1829. Unfortunately the publication was met with critical scorn. One reviewer wrote 'we are glad to understand that our author has the good sense to rely more on his chisel than on the Muses'. Another said: 'It is our duty to tell this writer, that he will make more in a week with his trowel than in half a century by his pen.'[21]

Two positive results did come from this endeavour. First, it convinced Miller that he should concentrate his energies on the writing of prose rather than on poetry. Second, he was introduced to Robert Carruthers, the editor of the *Inverness Courier,* who hired Miller to be the part-time local correspondent from Cromarty. This gave him an opportunity to write a number of articles on a variety of subjects. His first success came in 1829 when some of his articles were published in a book entitled *Letters on*

---

[19] Ibid.

[20] Taylor, *Hugh Miller, Stonemason, Geologist, Writer,* p. 53.

[21] Rosie, *Hugh Miller: Outrage and Order: A Biography and Selected Writings,* p. 43.

the Herring Industry. These reprints from his *Inverness Courier* articles have been called,

> ... stunning pieces of work. The conjunction of luminous descriptive passages, well-caught dialogue, and real insights into how the herring fisherman worked their trade, makes them minor masterpieces.[22]

During the early 1830s Miller's interest in the world around him developed into the serious study of geology. He did not set out to be a pioneer in the field, but some of his discoveries were groundbreaking. At Cromarty he discovered fish fossils which would later be recognised by the geological community as major finds. His interest in geology would cause him to write a series of remark-able books, *The Old Red Sandstone* (1841), *Footprints of the Creator* (1850) and *The Testimony of the Rocks* (1856), all carefully describing his discoveries. More than simple geology texts, they were a mix of theology, history and science. His writings in this genre have been aptly described as being written by a populariser. And while

> ... the populariser is seldom himself a research pioneer, only someone with an absolute mastery of the science can explain it intelligibly to a lay readership; and only talent bordering on genius can turn descriptions of fossils into masterpieces of creative writing.[23]

Miller was anxious to maintain the place of God in the created order and he had little time for pre-Darwinian

---

[22] Ibid., p. 44.

[23] Donald Macleod, 'Footnotes', *West Highland Free Press*, 26 April 2002, http://www.hughmiller.org/controversies_g.asp (accessed 20 March 2009).

evolutionists. At the same time, he did not read the early chapters of Genesis in a strictly literal sense. His fossil discoveries led him to believe that the earth was of great age and he adopted the view that the days of creation should be viewed as representing long periods of time. He also rejected as unnecessary, the idea of a universal flood in the time of Noah. In the conclusion to his *Testimony of the Rocks* he argued that

> The revelation of Noah, which warned him of a coming Flood, and taught him how to prepare for it, was evidently miraculous: the Flood itself may have been purely providential. But on this part of the subject I need not dwell. I have accomplished my purpose if I have shown, as was attempted of old by divines such as Stillingfleet and Poole, that there 'seems to be no reason why the Deluge should be extended beyond the occasion of it, which was the corruption of man', [The flood] forms, not one of the stumbling-blocks, but one of the evidences, of our faith; and renders the exercise a not unprofitable one, when, according to the poet, –
>
> > *Back through the dusk*
> > *Of ages Contemplation turns her view,*
> > *To mark, as from its infancy, the world*
> > *Peopled again from that mysterious shrine*
> > *That rested on the top of Ararat.*[24]

It is unwise to impose Miller into the Darwinian evolutionary debates, since he died before the publication of the *Origin of the Species*. However, two things are clear. First, Miller would have remained uncomfortable with any theory that removed God from discussions on the origin of the

---

[24] Hugh Miller, *The Testimony of the Rocks* (Boston: Gould and Lincoln, 1857), p. 361.

universe. Second, he would have had no time for modern creationism's attempts to rewrite the scientific record and their treatment of Genesis as a scientific textbook.

The beginning of Hugh Miller's writing career and his growing interest in geology coincided with his meeting his future wife, Lydia Fraser. Lydia was the daughter of a failed merchant from Inverness. After her father died Lydia moved to Cromarty along with her widowed mother. Lydia's mother was unhappy at the prospect of her middle-class daughter marrying the poor stonemason, but eventually in 1833, she agreed to a three-year engagement. When Miller obtained a job as an accountant and clerk at the Commercial Bank in Cromarty he was able to save some money. In the end, he and Lydia were married on 7 January 1837. They were intellectually compatible and enjoyed many of the same interests. Lydia took an active interest in Hugh's writing, was responsible for maintaining his literary legacy and also published a number of successful books of her own.

Hugh and Lydia's first daughter, Elizabeth Logan, was born on 23 November 1837. Not surprisingly her father viewed her as 'a delight and wonder above all wonders'. However, she was not to live long, dying before her second birthday on 25 August 1839. [25]

LETTER TO LORD BROUGHAM
1839

Hugh Miller's life of obscurity came to an end in 1839. He had become increasingly concerned about the struggle that was taking place over the issue of patronage in the Church of Scotland. The final decision in the Auchterarder Case

[25] Sutherland, *Lydia, Wife of Hugh Miller of Cromarty*, p. 52.

roused him to action. In their decision, the House of Lords rejected the claim that parishioners had a say in the selection of their minister, finding rather that the practice of appointment by patrons should continue.

One of the principal authors of the decision was Scotland's own Lord Brougham, and when Miller read the decision he reacted. He tells us that

> It was only when the Church's hour of peril came that I learned to know how much I valued her, and how strong and numerous the associations were that bound her to my affections. I had experienced at least the average amount of interest in political measures whose tendencies and principles I deemed good in the main – such as the Reform Bill, the Catholic Emancipation Act, and the Emancipation of the Negroes; but they had never cost me an hour's sleep. Now, however I felt more deeply; and for at least one night, after reading the speech of Lord Brougham, and the decision of the House of Lords in the Auchterarder Case, I slept none.[26]

Miller was convinced that the people of Scotland needed to be mobilised to protest what was taking place. While there were many ministers in the Church of Scotland who were doing their best to fight against patronage and for spiritual independence, more was needed. He therefore

> ... formed [a] plan of taking up the purely popular side of the question; and in the morning I sat down to state my views to the people, in the form of a letter addressed to Lord Brougham.[27]

---

[26] Miller, *My Schools and Schoolmasters; or, the Story of my Education*, p. 547.

[27] Ibid., p. 549.

It took him about a week to compose his 'letter', which has been called 'probably the most important single piece that Hugh Miller ever wrote'. [28]

The letter begins quietly enough with Miller describing himself as 'a plain working man, in rather humble circumstances, a native of the north of Scotland and a member of the Established Church'. [29] Lord Brougham had previously argued during the debate on the Reform Act that the people of Scotland were worthy of having a say in the government of their land through the election of their politicians. And so, Miller argued that

> ... the people of Scotland are not so changed that but that they know at least as much of the doctrines of the New Testament as of the principles of civil government, and of the requisites of a gospel minister, as of the qualifications of a Member of Parliament! [30]

Miller went on to argue that there was no support for the concept of patronage in Scripture, and that the long history of the reformed church and the Church of Scotland were also against it.

He next aimed even sharper words in the direction of the Moderate party in the Church of Scotland, those who were supporting the *status quo*. Worse than that, Miller accused the Moderates of substituting the true gospel with pagan philosophy and moral platitudes. He claimed that it was these men who were destroying the Church of Scotland, not

---

[28] Rosie, *Hugh Miller: Outrage and Order: A Biography and Selected Writings*, p. 54.

[29] Hugh Miller, 'Letter to Lord Broughan', *Headship of Christ and the Rights of the Christian People*, p. 20.

[30] Ibid., p. 21.

those who longed for the preaching of the gospel by truly called men elected by their congregations. Miller concluded this section with these words:

> We are acquainted with our New Testament, and demand that our ministers give that prominence and space to the ... doctrines of Christianity which we find assigned to them in the epistles of Paul, and of Peter, of James and of John.[31]

Lord Brougham had argued in the House of Lord's decision that the Evangelicals were taking over the church and that their actions were driving the wealthy landowners out. To this Miller replied:

> The Church has offended many of her noblest and wealthiest, it is said, and they are flying from her in crowds. Well, what matters it? – let the chaff fly. We care not though she shake off, in her wholesome exercise, some of the indolent humours which have hung about her so long. The vital principle will act with all the more vigour when they are gone.[32]

Response to the letter was immediate. It quickly went through four printings and it drew the attention of the leadership of the Evangelical party in the Church of Scotland. Previously they had been losing the media battle with none of the major papers taking their side. As a result it was decided that the Evangelicals needed to launch their own paper and who better to edit it than the fiery geologist and bank clerk from Cromarty? Miller was not sure the job was for him, so with some misgivings, he accepted the appointment and moved to Edinburgh in January 1840.

[31] Ibid., p. 31.
[32] Ibid., p. 39.

EDITOR OF THE WITNESS
1840–50

The first issue of *The Witness* was released on 15 January 1840. It has been estimated that between 1840 and 1856 Miller wrote some 10 million words for the paper. Although it began with a modest circulation of about 600, it became a 'must read' and would eventually rival *The Scotsman's* circulation. Peter Bayne, Hugh Miller's official biographer, states that he was

> ... resolved ... that the 'Witness' under his management, should have a high character as an intellectual paper, by no means confining itself to ecclesiastical topics, but making wide incursions into the realms of literature and still more those of science.[33]

Miller's vision for an eclectic paper was carried out, with energy. The very first edition covered topics as diverse as

> ... the opening of the provincial parliament in Upper Canada, fresh riots in Valencia, the draft constitution for the state of Hanover [and] more honours for Prince Albert of Saxe-Coburg. ... The first issue was also liberally peppered with advertisements for ... church meetings ... useful books ... and Mr Thalberg's Third and Farewell Concert.[34]

Miller drew inspiration for the combative and controversial tone of the paper from John Knox who, when he was charged with treason for denouncing Mary Queen of Scots, famously replied: 'I am in the place where I am

---

[33] Peter Bayne, *The Life and Letters of Hugh Miller*, v. 2, p. 254.

[34] Rosie, *Hugh Miller: Outrage and Order: A Biography and Selected Writings*, p. 56.

demanded of conscience to speak the truth, and therefore the truth I speak, impugn it whoso list'. [35] In the three years leading up to the Disruption, Miller would pen thousands of words on the situation facing the church. He took arguments

> which in other hands were dry and abstruse, [but] were translated by him into a style of English so pure, and presented in forms powerfully attractive, they came home at once to the feelings of the people.[36]

When the General Assembly met in Edinburgh in May of 1843, Miller was present, notebook in hand. His article *The Disruption,* which appeared on 20 May 1843, remains the most vivid account of the events of that day.

After the Disruption, Miller turned his attention to the needs of the Free Church and campaigned vigorously for landlords to grant sites for churches and for the continued need to raise funds to support the preaching of the gospel in poor areas. On the issue of sites for churches, he caustically remarked to Lydia that he resented the fact that there were congregations who were forced to meet outdoors when the Moderates had control of empty buildings. Of his home parish of Cromarty he wrote:

> I do begrudge [the Moderates] my father's pew. It bears the date 1741 and has [been] held by the family, through times of poverty and depression, a sort of memorial of better days … But yonder it lies, empty within an empty church, a place for spiders to spin undisturbed, while all who should

---

[35] Taylor, *Hugh Miller, Stonemason, Geologist, Writer*, p. 84.

[36] Brown, *Annals of the Disruption: with extracts from the narratives of Ministers who left the Scottish establishment in 1843*, p. 461.

be occupying it take their places on stools and forms in the factory close.[37]

Miller had begun work at *The Witness* in the capacity of hired editor, but this changed when he became co-proprietor with Robert Fairly. This meant he had financial interest in the paper as well as being responsible for editorial content. The pressures of working on *The Witness* had a negative impact on Miller. His wife noted the

> ... gulf which separated the life after 1840 and that before it was indeed a very wide one. I know not anywhere else an instance of a man being apparently not one individual but two.[38]

This may be an overstatement, but certainly Miller was placed in the midst of conflict. Sadly, the biggest battle he would have to fight would come from within the Free Church as he fought for editorial control of *The Witness*.

Piecing together the exact details of this struggle is inhibited by the fact that the only full description of it that exists is to be found in Miller's own account and in Peter Bayne's sympathetic biography. However, this much is clear. Between 1846 and 1847 conflict arose between Miller and some of the leadership of the Free Church, particularly Robert Candlish. Candlish seems to have wanted *The Witness* to be the official mouthpiece of the Free Church, but Miller wanted to maintain an independent voice.

One area of conflict was on the issue of education. Candlish believed that it was the duty of the Free Church

---

[37] Bayne, *The Life and Letters of Hugh Miller,* v. 2, p. 383.

[38] Sutherland, *Lydia, Wife of Hugh Miller of Cromarty,* p. 71.

to provide for the educational needs of Scotland. In a speech at the 1847 General Assembly he said that

> ... the Free Church of Scotland cannot and dare not abandon the duty which God has laid upon her of providing for the thorough Christian training and godly upbringing of the youth of the land ...[39]

To this end, Candlish and others worked for the creation of a Free Church system of schools that would educate children throughout the country. While Miller was wholeheartedly committed to the teaching of biblical truth as an essential part of education, he did not believe that 'the inculcation of denominational tenets' should be allowed. In fact he argued for 'the exclusion of denominationalism from the machinery of popular education'.[40] Other irritants existed. Miller felt unwelcome pressure from the church to include full reports of Presbytery and other meetings and he found it difficult to balance these demands with his desire to publish a newspaper that would appeal to a broad audience.

As tensions grew, Candlish circulated a memorandum proposing that the paper should be placed under the direction of a Church Committee. He also approached Robert Fairly, *The Witness's* co-owner, and asked him to buy out Miller's share of the newspaper. When Miller heard about this, he was furious and wrote a blistering 10,000 word letter addressed to the 'committee of gentlemen who had from the first interested themselves in the

---

[39] Wilson, *Memorials of Robert Smith Candlish DD*, p. 399.

[40] Bayne, *The Life and Letters of Hugh Miller*, v. 2, p. 341.

paper, repelling the attacks of which he believed himself to be the object'. [41]

The letter was a spirited defence of his editorship of the paper in which Miller made it very clear that he believed he still had work to do for *The Witness*.

> My faults have no doubt been many; but they have not been faults of principle; nor have they lost me the confidence of that portion of the people of Scotland to which I belong and which I represent. And possessing their confidence, I do not now feel myself justified in retiring from my post. Dr Candlish and his ... friends are not the ministers and people of the Free Church of Scotland; nor do I recognize the expression of the doctor's will in this matter as a call to me in Providence to divest myself of my office.[42]

Miller did concede that if the Committee wished him to go, he would accept their judgment. But he wouldn't go quietly.

> Permit me to state further, that if there is to be war between Dr Candlish and me, it must be open war ... The true springs of the undercurrent of 'hinted faults' and 'hesitated dislikes' must be fairly uncovered, should the stream continue to flow. The difference must either close entirely, or the people of Scotland must be made fully acquainted with the grounds on which it rests.[43]

Candlish appears to have recognised quickly that he had been outflanked and withdrew his proposals. His biographer's only comment on the situation is that

---

[41] Ibid., p. 254. The 'committee of gentlemen' included Thomas Chalmers, Robert Candlish and Thomas Guthrie who was Miller's own Minister.

[42] Ibid., p. 290.

[43] Ibid., p. 291.

Doubtless [Candlish] was harassed and vexed ... by the agitation which was being carried on, on the subject of education, and which ultimately led to a painful rupture between him and the editor of *The Witness*. I abstain from saying anything on the merits of the controversy, but it was the occasion of calling forth a very general expression of sympathy with Dr Candlish.[44]

Even though the campaign to remove Miller failed, real damage was done by this incident, and it created distance between Miller, *The Witness* and the Free Church.

Evidence of the distance between Miller and the leadership of the Free Church may be seen in Robert Buchanon's *The Ten Years' Conflict* published in 1852. This otherwise well-researched work makes no reference at all to Hugh Miller and the role that *The Witness* played in the events leading up to the Disruption. Miller's own minister, Thomas Guthrie, said that this omission reminded him of 'the announcement of the play of *Hamlet* without the part of "The Prince of Denmark"'.[45]

THE 1850S

The years from 1850 to 1856 were busy ones for Miller. He had a growing family to support. Harriet had been born in 1839, William in 1842, Bessie in 1845 and Hugh in 1850. He continued his labours on *The Witness* and also found time to publish several books of essays on scientific, literary and other topics. He also received some honours paid to

---

[44] Wilson, *Memorials of Robert Smith Candlish DD*, p. 437. Just how general was the 'expression of sympathy' for Candlish is unclear.

[45] Thomas Guthrie, David Kelly Guthrie, Charles John Guthrie, *Autobiography of Thomas Guthrie. D.D.: And Memoir by His Sons* (Detroit: Craig and Taylor, 1878), p. 344.

him during this period. In 1854 his name was proposed for the vacant chair of Natural History at the University of Edinburgh. Peter Bayne says that it 'was the place which, of all others, Hugh Miller would have been gratified to fill'. [46] Despite widespread enthusiasm for this nomination, the position would eventually be given to another younger man. His lack of formal education has been suggested as the main reason he did not get the appointment, but it is impossible to prove or disprove this.[47]

In 1855 he was offered the position of Distributor of Stamps and Collector of Property Tax for Perthshire. Even though this was a well-paying position which could have lessened his need for work, he turned it down on the grounds that he was too old to learn a new job.

By the mid-1850s the cumulative pressures of work, concern for his wife Lydia's health and his own bouts of illness forced him to take long periods of rest away from *The Witness*. In the last year of his life he suffered from renewed bouts of depression and 'agonizing attacks of inflammation of the lungs'. [48] On the evening of 23 December 1856 Miller spent some time reading to his children, had a bath and went to bed. He was found dead the next morning with a pistol next to his body. The note that he left read:

DEAREST LYDIA,
My brain burns. I *must* have *walked*; and a fearful dream rises upon me. I cannot bear the horrible thought. God

---

[46] Bayne, *The Life and Letters of Hugh Miller*, v. 2, p. 445.

[47] Taylor, *Hugh Miller, Stonemason, Geologist, Writer*, p. 139.

[48] Bayne, *The Life and Letters of Hugh Miller*, v. 2, p. 421.

and Father of the Lord Jesus Christ, have mercy upon me. Dearest Lydia, dear children, farewell. My brain burns as the recollection grows. My dear, dear wife farewell.

Hugh Miller [49]

The post-mortem report makes reference to the fact that he had shot himself and that from '... the diseased appearance found in the brain, taken in connection with the case, we have no doubt that the act was suicidal under the impulse of insanity'. [50] The outpouring of grief and shock at Miller's suicide was considerable. Lydia Miller was flooded with condolences, and the funeral, held in Edinburgh, rivalled that of Thomas Chalmers for the outpouring of grief that it occasioned.

HUGH MILLER'S LEGACY

There are at least three ways in which Hugh Miller still speaks to the present day. First, his belief that the earth and everything in it belongs to God still needs to be heard. The fact that one can have faith in God and also be a person of science should not be seen as mutually exclusive. Like Hugh Miller, there is no need for Christians to fear science that is done for the glory of God.

Second, those who treasure religious freedoms and particularly those in the Presbyterian tradition owe a debt of gratitude to him. In this connection, Donald Macleod has correctly noted that during the Ten Years Conflict

... Chalmers, Cunningham and Candlish could win debates at the Assembly. But it was Miller who took the matter to

[49] Ibid., p. 481.

[50] Ibid., p. 482.

the country. Without him there would have been no Free Church; and without him the wider Presbyterian family ... would not enjoy the spiritual independence it does today.[51]

Lastly, in his death, Miller also has something to say. His suicide, brought on by overwork and ill health, both mental and physical, should be viewed as a tragedy and not as a sign of lack of faith on his part, or that God no longer loved him. Thomas Guthrie, who had been his minister, and who had to break the news of his death to his wife, rightly concluded that he

> ... was a martyr, in his own way, to prodigious efforts in the cause of truth, the cause of patriotism, of the Free Church, of civil and religious liberty and also I will add to the cause of science ...' [52]

[51] Macleod, 'Macleod on Miller', p. 5.

[52] Alexander Richardson, *The Future Church of Scotland by 'Freelance'* (Edinburgh: Maclachlan & Stewart, 1870), p. 103.

THOMAS GUTHRIE, D.D.

Home & Macdonald.

6

THOMAS GUTHRIE
PASTOR AND SOCIAL REFORMER

Thomas Guthrie was the sort of Christian gentleman
Karl Marx could never have imagined.[1]

THE statue of Thomas Guthrie in Princess Street
Gardens, Edinburgh depicts a well-dressed, middle-
aged gentleman holding a Bible in his left hand, while his
right hand rests on the head of a small child who is being
sheltered by his cloak. The inscription on the side of the
statue reads:

> An eloquent preacher of the gospel. Founder of the Edin-
> burgh Original Ragged Industrial Schools, and by tongue
> and pen, the apostle of the movement elsewhere. One of the
> earliest temperance reformers. A friend of the poor and of
> the oppressed.[2]

This stylised description only begins to touch on the
accomplishments of the very full life of a man who is
acknowledged as one of the most eloquent preachers of his
day, and is remembered even more for the active role that
he took in social reform.

---

[1] Old, *The Reading and Preaching of the Scriptures in the Worship of
the Christian Church*, v. 6, p. 643.

[2] 'Guthrie, Thomas 1803–73', *Literate Lifetime*, http://literatelifetime.
com/browse/author/Thomas_Guthrie (accessed 31 March 2009).

Scotland in the nineteenth century was reaping many of the benefits of the industrial revolution. At the same time, it was a society struggling with how to deal with the issues caused by poverty and social deprivation. Thomas Guthrie was committed to the belief that the gospel must impact all areas of life and that the church should be an agent of change in a hurting world. Karl Marx, who as we saw earlier was very dismissive of Chalmers, would have been surprised at Guthrie's ability to transcend social class and enlist the help of the wealthy for the service of the poor.

Upbringing and Education
1803–25

Thomas Guthrie was born at Brechin on 12 July 1803. He was the twelfth of thirteen children and the sixth son of Donald Guthrie and Clemintina Clay. In his autobiography, Guthrie states that his father '... began business in Brechin, and was long the leading merchant, as well as for some years the Provost or Chief Magistrate of the town'. Donald Guthrie's success in business allowed him to provide for the needs of his growing family. More importantly for his son, this was a family that was brought up according to 'the strictest habits of virtue and religion'. [3]

Guthrie was sent, when he was just four years old, to an 'infant's school' where he was taught by Jamie Stewart, an elder in the Secession Church. Stewart augmented his weaver's income by taking in students. He taught them basic

---

[3] Guthrie et.al., *Autobiography of Thomas Guthrie. D.D. and Memoir by His Sons*, p. 15. Thomas Guthrie's autobiography was left unfinished at his death. It was completed by two of his sons and passed through several editions. References in this chapter are taken from the American edition of 1878.

English and mathematical skills. Guthrie learned to read by using the Old Testament *Book of Proverbs* which contained 'quite a repertory of monosyllables and pure Saxon ... English undefiled'. He goes on to comment that there is much to be said for acquiring language skills in this way, since not only were they learning to read but their minds were also being 'stored with the highest moral truths'. [4]

In his autobiography, Guthrie talks about the religious influences in his family. His mother, in particular, was a deeply pious woman who took Thomas and his eldest brother and sister to the local Secession Church. There he heard evangelical preaching from an early age. However, his autobiography is vague on when he embraced Christianity for himself.

Between the ages of four and twelve, Guthrie attended three different schools, all of which had as their goal preparing him for University and a career. By his own admission he was not very interested in his studies, since his ambition was to be the best fighter in his class. This desire was inspired 'by the great war between our country and Napoleon, which occupied the attention of old and young in my early days'. [5]

It appears that Guthrie's parents had hopes that he would become a minister, so in November 1815, he began his studies at the University of Edinburgh at the age of twelve. He says that although his early education had been solid enough, he was 'sent to the University much too soon'. During his first two years in Edinburgh he was frequently

---

[4] Guthrie et.al., *Autobiography of Thomas Guthrie. D.D. and Memoir by His Sons*, p. 23.

[5] Ibid., p. 31.

in trouble with university authorities.[6] He freely admits that his behaviour at university was influenced by the knowledge that after he completed his studies, his hopes for a parish appointment were more dependent on his father's connections than on his own abilities.

> In my early days, and for long years thereafter, the appoint-ment to a parish did not go by merit but by influence; and, by one of the many evils of patronage, there was nothing either to be lost or gained by the candidate being but a raw youth. How often did it come across [to] me, excusing and encouraging idle fits, that my 'getting a living' as it is called, would not turn on my diligence and that, through the influence my father had with those who were patrons of churches, I was sure of an appointment![7]

Despite the early lack of interest, Guthrie did eventually settle down to his studies and finished the courses in arts and theology. Because he was too young to be licensed, he stayed on in Edinburgh, occupying his time studying medicine and science. He hoped to be appointed to a parish as soon as possible and was licensed to preach by the Presby-tery of Brechin on 2 February 1825. He then found himself involved in a nasty case of ecclesiastical politics.

Thanks to his father's political connections, Guthrie was offered a parish with a lucrative living. However, he soon learned that there were strings attached. He was told that before he was 'presented' to the parish he needed to meet with Dr Nicol of St Andrew's who was, at that time, the leader of the Moderate party in the Church of Scotland.

---

[6] Ibid., p. 41.

[7] Ibid., p. 45.

This may seem like an odd request, but it was the practice at the time for those seeking ordination to visit ministers in their manses so that they would be introduced personally to those already in the Presbytery.

Guthrie freely admits that he had 'taken little interest in Church politics, but lived on equally kindly terms with ministers of both parties'. What he says the Moderates were looking for was 'a distinct pledge that ... the Moderate party would have my vote in Church courts'. [8] He candidly concedes that he refused the parish, largely because he was too proud to be told who to support in church politics. He also admits that while he was disappointed by this setback to his career, the parish would have been too much for him and 'would probably have dwarfed and stunted me for life'. [9]

INTERLUDE: PARIS AND BRECHIN
1826–30

With no hope of immediate appointment to a parish, Thomas Guthrie decided to travel. He had enjoyed his scientific and medical studies at the University of Edinburgh and so he chose to pursue these further, at the Sorbonne in Paris. His obituary in *The Scotsman* suggests that he went to Paris in the hope that further medical training might 'stand him in good stead in the prosecution of ministerial work'. [10] While he enjoyed his medical studies, he found the way of life in a largely Roman Catholic country difficult. He found the Sabbath particularly hard. In a letter to his

---

[8] Ibid., p. 54.

[9] Ibid.

[10] 'The Late Dr Thomas Guthrie', *The Scotsman Digital Archive, February 25th, 1873*, http://archive.scotsman.com/ (accessed 3 April 2009).

family, he wrote that the very different environment made him homesick.

> I think of the quiet streets of Brechin; and the stillness of our house is brought sadly to my remembrance, when I hear, in this one, the light song instead of the sacred hymn, and see instead of the Bible, the cards and dominoes upon the table, and the people, instead of repairing to the church, driving off every Sunday night to the playhouse. I confess to you that frequently I am heartily disgusted with Paris, and wish that I were home.[11]

Guthrie returned to Scotland in May 1827. He still had little prospect of being settled in a church and so spent his time at home while taking any preaching engagements that were offered to him. When one of his brothers died suddenly in March 1828, he went to work for his father in the family bank. As his biographers point out, a man who had trained for the ministry was not the most obvious candidate to work in a bank, but he did well and 'was able to play the banker, not only respectably but with credit'. [12]

PARISH MINISTRY IN ARBIRLOT
1830–7

The year 1830 was a notable one for Guthrie. He finally gained the ministerial position he desired when he was appointed to the parish of Arbirlot, located on the eastern coast of Scotland, about sixty miles north of Edinburgh. He was ordained there on 13 May 1830. In October he married Anne Burns of Brechin, who lived from 1810 to

---

[11] Guthrie et.al., *Autobiography of Thomas Guthrie. D.D. and Memoir by His Sons*, p. 231.

[12] Ibid., p. 257.

1899. Over the course of their marriage, they had four daughters and seven sons.[13]

Guthrie's seven-year ministry in Arbirlot is remembered both for his abilities as a preacher and his skills as a pastor to a group of people who were mostly farmers and cottage weavers. When he began his work in the parish, both the church and manse were in a dilapidated condition and he diligently began schemes to improve both. He established a library and savings bank run out of the manse, which allowed him to have daily contact with the people. Guthrie wrote in his autobiography that he had started the bank to encourage the poor people of the parish to save their money. He also encouraged the eleven elders that belonged to his congregation to become more involved in 'household visitations, prayer meetings and superintendence of his flock'. [14]

Guthrie's pastoral ministry began at the same time as the struggles over the spiritual independence of the Church of Scotland. While Chalmers was content with the reform of patronage, Guthrie wanted it abolished. He was warned against becoming involved in the growing controversies, but he ignored these warnings and began holding public meetings to debate the issues. He also took an increasingly active role at Presbytery meetings. He encouraged ruling elders to become more involved in Presbyteries with the result that the Moderate party in the church began to lose their numeric advantage when key votes were taken. While the passage of the Veto Act in 1834 was seen as a step forward by many in

---

[13] Lionel Alexander Ritchie.'Guthrie, Thomas', in *Oxford Dictionary of National Biography,* v. 24 (Oxford: Oxford University Press, 2004), p. 316.

[14] Guthrie et. al., *Autobiography of Thomas Guthrie. D. D. and Memoir by His Sons,* p. 270.

the church, it was not enough for Guthrie. He believed that the whole system of patronage needed to be removed and the selection of ministers placed entirely in the hands of the people.

The passage of the Chapels Act in 1834 marked the beginning of a period of significant church expansion. Guthrie's growing prominence in Presbytery debates drew the attention of several people in Edinburgh. As his popularity grew, many people in the wider church began to think that he should move to Edinburgh and occupy a more prominent pulpit. He had several approaches from churches, but he was initially not interested in moving. In response to one such request he wrote to the inquirer, 'I feel no ambition to be an Edinburgh Minister'. [15]

In 1837, Guthrie was again asked to consider a move. Old Greyfriars Church in Edinburgh, where the National Covenant had been signed in 1638, needed an assistant to help the minister, Mr Sym. While he struggled with his decision, he received a letter from James Begg, the minister of Liberton Church, calling on him to accept the move.

> Of course I know the comforts and advantages of a quiet country parish, and the many reasons which may induce you to remain where you are. But it is of vast importance not merely to Edinburgh, but Scotland – not for the present generation only but for ages – that we should have men of energy and popular talent in Edinburgh.[16]

On 4 July 1837, he learned of his election by the Town Council by a vote of seventeen to thirteen, and with some reluctance he agreed to the move.

---

[15] Ibid., p. 293.

[16] Ibid., p. 296.

ASSISTANT AT GREYFRIARS, EDINBURGH
1837—40

Greyfriars was a prosperous church in a heavily popu-
lated area of Edinburgh which had many pastoral and
social needs. The plan to deal with this was to subdivide
the parish, creating new church extension parishes in the
area. Although Guthrie's appointment was as the Assistant
at the original Greyfriars church, the intention was that he
would eventually take over one of the new congregations.

Guthrie viewed his new responsibilities with some
concern since he was increasingly aware that Greyfriars
was not ministering to the needs of all of the people in the
area.

> From his pulpit each Sunday he looked on an overflow-
> ing congregation, drawn from all quarters of the city, and
> composed chiefly of the middle and upper classes, he saw
> scarce any representatives, alas! of his real parishioners
> from the mean and crowded district hard by.[17] The 'pew
> rents' paid by those who attended Greyfriars went directly
> into the city's coffers, so there was little motivation on the
> part of the Council to change the situation.

During the first three years of his Edinburgh ministry,
Guthrie spent a significant amount of time exploring the
parish. From his home, he was within walking distance
of people who lived in appalling poverty. The area contained many tenements each housing as many as 150
people. Because these people could not afford to pay pew
rents, they were not able to attend the regular worship
services at Greyfriars. In response, Guthrie began con-

[17] Ibid., p. 305.

ducting worship services at the nearby Magdalene Chapel in the Cowgate area of the city. He said that the people who gathered there were '...in some respects, a more interesting congregation' because they were much more needy 'lost sheep of the wilderness'. [18]

ST JOHN'S PARISH CHURCH
1840–3

The church extension programme eventually resulted in the creation of a new parish to which Guthrie was assigned. St John's Parish opened on 19 November 1840 with two unique features. At Guthrie's insistence, the church was planned so that of the 1,000 available seats, 650 were reserved for the poor on the main floor. Wealthy members of the church sat in long galleries on each side and at the back of the church; the pew rents collected from the wealthy made it possible to fund the work of the church. Guthrie also arranged for the construction of a basement under the main auditorium that would serve as a school for the poor children of his parish. He had become convinced that the extreme poverty in Edinburgh would be alleviated by the church providing education for the poor, and attempting to proactively meet the social needs of the area.

Guthrie's reputation in Edinburgh was first built on his preaching. Although his written sermons seem stilted to modern ears, he has been called 'one of the master orators of the Church'. [19] His use of illustration and word pictures

---

[18] Ibid., p. 308.

[19] Old, *The Reading and Preaching of the Scriptures in the Worship of the Christian Church*, v. 6, p. 643.

and his ability to tell stories made his sermons accessible to his hearers. There is a prophetic tone to his messages, which he used both to instruct his congregation and to rally popular support for the various causes that he was passionate about. In his massive study on the history of preaching in the church, Hughes Oliphant Old summarises Guthrie's impact by saying that he

> ... moved the hearts of both the poor and powerful. The poor knew he was their advocate, and many of the causes to which he devoted himself prospered through his support.[20]

With Guthrie's popular preaching, St John's Church was soon full to overflowing and some people went to extraordinary lengths to be able to hear him. They

> ... smuggled planks into the church during the week. Climbing to the open spaces between the suspended ceiling and the true roof, they laid these planks across the ceiling joists; and despite the watchful church officers, many people succeeded in scrambling up into this church attic, where they surrounded the ventilating grilles opening into the church below. This continued for some time, until it reached the ears of the city officials, who prohibited it because they feared ... that the ceiling might give way under the weight of the invisible portion of the congregation.[21]

Like Chalmers in Glasgow, Guthrie depended heavily on the elders and deacons of the parish to carry out the work of the church. The large population of the parish was divided

---

[20] Ibid., p. 644.

[21] Frederick R. Webber, 'Thomas Guthrie, Apostle to the Slums', *Concordia Theological Monthly*, v. 20, no 6 (June 1949), pp. 414–15.

into districts and it was the responsibility of the elders and deacons to seek out those who were not going to church and to do their best to encourage them to start attending. Guthrie's recognition that he could not do everything in the parish was one of the keys to his success. With the support of his elders and deacons and the motivated laity, he was able to achieve a great deal while he was at St John's.

In addition to his parochial duties, Guthrie found himself increasingly involved in the controversies that were plaguing the wider church. Since his days in Arbirlot, he had been an outspoken advocate for the abolition of patronage and the spiritual independence of the church. Remaining committed to these principles, he took on a number of speaking engagements to further the cause. He was one of the ministers who defied the civil courts and preached within the bounds of the Presbytery of Strathbogie. When the interdict was served on him, he told the court official that while he accepted that the court could lawfully forbid him to preach in church buildings and schools that belonged to the state,

> ... when these Lords of Session forbade me to preach my Master's blessed Gospel, and offer salvation to sinners anywhere in that district under the arch of heaven, I put the interdict under my feet and I preached the Gospel.[22]

Looking back on this period, John Kerr said of Guthrie's contribution that

> ... his winged words, with the pen of Hugh Miller, were powerful co-efficients in bringing out the response which the heart of the people gave to the self-sacrifice of the min-

---

[22] Guthrie et. al., *Autobiography of Thomas Guthrie. D. D. and Memoir by His Sons*, p. 357.

isters, and in securing, under God, the success of the Free
Church from the first day of its existence.[23]

As he rallied popular support for the Evangelical party in
the Church of Scotland, Guthrie knew a break within the
church would mean the loss of his church building in Edinburgh. Despite this fact, he continued to work diligently in
his new parish right up to the Disruption.

FREE ST JOHN'S

Following the Disruption, Guthrie's congregation left
their nearly new building and for two years met in a large
Wesleyan Chapel in Nicholson Square. As they did so,
plans were put in motion to begin the construction of a
new building in Johnston Terrace.[24] The congregation
immediately raised £6,000 for the project. While there
was recognition that limited funds ruled out an elaborate exterior, Guthrie was anxious that the architect
should devote his energies 'chiefly on the interior'. When
the building was finally opened on 14 April 1845 he told
his congregation that they should celebrate their attractive new building since 'there is no sin in beauty and no
holiness in ugliness'. [25]

Typical of the man, Guthrie was not only concerned for
the needs of his own congregation, but he exerted consider-

[23] John Kerr, 'Thomas Guthrie D.D.', *Disruption Worthies: A Memorial
of 1843; with a Historical Sketch of the Free Church of Scotland from 1843
Down to the Present Time*, p. 286.

[24] The building was originally designed by Thomas Hamilton and
then underwent renovations in 1908. The building is now the home of
St Columba's Free Church and also serves as the location of the Free
Church of Scotland's General Assembly.

[25] Guthrie et. al., *Autobiography of Thomas Guthrie. D. D. and Memoir
by His Sons*, p. 512.

able energies in a major fund-raising scheme for the Free Church as a whole. Once the new building was opened, he turned his attention to an issue that was facing the whole church. After the Disruption, there was an immediate need for the construction of both church buildings and manses, particularly in rural areas. The ministers who had come out of the established church urgently needed accommodation and so Guthrie travelled extensively on what he called his 'begging tour' raising money for the Free Church Manse Fund. Thanks largely to his efforts the scheme was a major success, with £116,370 collected in just one year.[26]

THE RAGGED SCHOOLS

Guthrie's sons claim that there was a direct link between their father's efforts on behalf of the Manse Fund and his next campaign, which was for the advocacy of the 'Ragged Schools' movement. They say that it was their father's 'compassion' which led him to raise funds for destitute ministers and their families, and it was the same feeling which caused him next to turn his attention to the poor children of the cities.

The Ragged, or Industrial Schools, movement was not Guthrie's invention, although he became its spokesman in Scotland. The movement had been initiated in England by John Pounds of Portsmouth and was then further developed by the London City Mission. These schools were set up to provide free food, clothing, vocational training, education and religious instruction. By the time Pounds died in 1839, over 500 children had been educated. The movement had attracted the notice and support of promi-

[26] Ritchie, 'Thomas Guthrie', p. 316.

nent people like Anthony Ashley Cooper, Lord Shaftsbury, who in 1844 became the President of the Ragged Schools Union, which was the coordinating body for the various schools.[27]

The Ragged School movement in Scotland had begun in Aberdeen in 1841 when Sheriff Watson set up his Industrial Feeding School. It proved successful in keeping children from crime and providing them with the necessities of life. Guthrie originally considered opening a school in the basement of St John's Church, but when some of his elders 'became alarmed' at the prospect of running the school, he decided to go public and so began the search for other premises. A report in *The Scotsman* dated 24 March 1847 also suggests that Guthrie was concerned that his school should not be seen as competing with other church schools in the area.[28]

He therefore began a campaign to raise support for his proposal. Guthrie saw himself as 'following in the footsteps' of Watson's work, but he was able to popularise the movement in such a way that it caught the imagination of the country. The first step was the publication in 1847 of a small pamphlet entitled *A Plea for Ragged Schools*. Published by John Elder and printed by Hugh Miller's *Witness*, the pamphlet very quickly went through several editions. The *Plea* vividly depicted the plight of families who were so poor that they couldn't even provide for the basic needs of their children who were forced onto the streets to beg

[27] Herbert Hewitt Stroup, *Social Welfare Pioneers* (Chicago: Nelson-Hall, 1986), p. 219.

[28] 'Ragged Schools Preliminary Meeting', *The Scotsman Digital Archive, March 24th 1847*, http://archive.scotsman.com/ (accessed 10 April 2009).

for food. Conditions were so difficult that they were forced to scrounge a living through legal or illegal means. Even if there were parish schools that could in theory accommodate them, Guthrie made the point that these children couldn't stay in school because they needed to be working to earn their food. His concern was that without intervention, the poor boy would enter a downward spiral until

> ... a halter closes his unhappy career; or he is passed away to a penal settlement, the victim of a poverty for which he was not to blame, and of neglect on the part of others for which a righteous God will one day call them to judgment.[29]

What is particularly striking about this plea is that it clearly recognised that the plight of the poor was not necessarily their fault and it assumes that Christians had an obligation to help. Even if parents had been indolent or guilty of drunkenness, he argued that it was incumbent on Christians to help the parents so that their children were not 'drawn down into the same gulf with themselves'. [30]

Guthrie's answer to the problem was a simple one. To encourage education, children first needed to be fed. They needed to be attracted into a school by the simple means of providing plain food and so 'remove the obstruction which stands between that poor child, and the schoolmaster and the Bible'.[31] He went on to argue that not only was there a moral obligation to carry out this scheme, it also made economic sense. Guthrie claimed that in Scotland in 1846 a total of £150,045

---

[29] Thomas Guthrie, *A Plea for Ragged Schools or Prevention Better than Cure*, (Edinburgh: John Elder, 1847), p. 13.

[30] Ibid., p. 22.

[31] Ibid., p. 13.

had been spent on criminal prosecution and the maintenance of criminals. He went on to assert that in light of these figures, sensible people would see the value of taking even small steps to prevent further crime. While his scheme to entice children into schools was, in his view, fairly simple he did not expect his proposal to remedy all the wrongs of society, even if it was a success. He wrote in his *Plea* that he did not

> ... entertain the Utopian expectation that, by these schools, or any other means crime can be banished from this guilty world; but certainly institutions which will secure to these children a common and Christian education, and habits of discipline and industry are rich in promise. We know that the returns of autumn fall always short of the promise of summer, that the fruit is never so abundant as the flower; still, however, though we are not so Utopian as to expect that these schools will save all, we have ground, both in reason and Scripture, to expect that they will save many who seem otherwise doomed to ruin.[32]

The *Plea* was received with considerable interest, by many newspapers and magazines. The *Edinburgh Review* began a lengthy review by saying:

> Here is a pamphlet to be had for sixpence and which may be read in half an hour. But, if the reader be worth his salt, the first cost will be but the beginning. Before it has done with *him*, and he with *it*, it will have cost him something more.[33]

After examining Guthrie's proposal the review concluded by saying that

---

[32] Ibid., p. 31.

[33] 'A Plea For Ragged Schools or Prevention Better than Cure', *Edinburgh Review or Critical Journal*, v. 85 (January–April 1847), p. 520.

We heartily wish that as many of our readers as have a spare sixpence, would lay it out upon this pamphlet. They will find it no bad investment. Let them hang its pictures round their chamber of imagery, and sanctify their closets with its thoughts.[34]

Guthrie claimed that the reaction to the pamphlet was 'like a spark among combustibles; it was like a shot fired from the Castle, and it brought me more volunteers to man my boat than she could well carry'. [35] Within a few weeks, the sum of £700 had been raised, a committee formed and premises secured to begin the work. The effort was not solely a Free Church movement. Rather, there was extensive partici- pation from other Protestant churches in Edinburgh. By the end of 1847 three schools had been established: one for boys; another for girls; and one that was for both boys and girls who were under ten years of age. That the schools had an impact cannot be doubted. By 1851 the proportion of children in Edinburgh prisons had dropped from 1 in 20 to 1 in 100.

While the launching of the Ragged Schools must be deemed a success it was not without some controversy. There was some public discussion about whether or not Roman Catholics were being deliberately excluded from the schools. While they were not, it is true that Guthrie was committed to delivering religious education according to his own beliefs. Undoubtedly this did discourage some Roman Catholics from allowing their children to attend one of the Ragged Schools.

---

[34] Ibid., p. 534.

[35] Guthrie et. al., *Autobiography of Thomas Guthrie. D.D.: And Memoir by His Sons*, p. 443.

In the autumn of 1847 Guthrie was diagnosed with a heart condition and his doctors told him that he would need to cut back on his activities if he hoped to survive. For nearly two years he was forced to abandon all public appearances, including preaching. His pulpit at St John's was filled by a succession of ministers from other parts of the church.[36] During his period of rest, Guthrie continued to write, issuing his *Second Plea for Ragged Schools.*

TEMPERANCE

Guthrie was able to return to the pulpit of St John's church in October of 1849. In the same year, he was awarded a Doctor of Divinity Degree by the University of Edinburgh, the first Free Church minister to be so honoured. His preaching ministry continued to great acclaim. This was enhanced by the publication of books of his sermons: *The Gospel in Ezekiel* in 1856, *Christ and the Inheritance of the Saints,* and *The Way to Life* in 1858 and 1862 respectively.

Guthrie's pastoral ministry in Edinburgh had given him an insight into the appalling living conditions that were prevalent in the slums of the city, and he had become convinced that one of the major factors contributing to poverty was alcoholism. Believing that ministers should set an example he became a total abstainer and one of the leaders of the Free Church Temperance Society and of the Scottish Association for the Suppression of Drunkenness.

In 1850 he published a pamphlet entitled *A Plea on behalf of Drunkards and Against Drunkenness* and in 1857

---

[36] One of the people who preached at St John's during this period was William Hanna, who was married to one of Thomas Chalmers' daughters. He was subsequently inducted as Assistant to Guthrie in November of 1850.

the publication *The City Its Sins and Sorrows* displayed his ability to vividly depict the problem of alcoholism and its impact on society. The efforts of Guthrie and others achieved some success with the passage of the *Forbes Mackenzie Act* in 1853. This act reduced the number of hours in which alcohol could legally be sold and totally banned its sale on Sundays. Toward the end of his life Guthrie resumed drinking a small amount of wine each day 'to aid the feeble action of his heart'; but he did not believe that he was compromising his position since he was doing so for medicinal reasons.[37]

In 1862 Guthrie was honoured by the Free Church when he was appointed Moderator of the General Assembly. He used his Moderator's address to plead with the church to provide adequate financial support for ministers and their families. In his address he said 'I would tempt no man to enter the Church by the hope of wealth; but I wish no man to be deferred from it by the certainty of poverty'.[38]

RETIREMENT
1864–73

A reoccurrence of his heart condition forced Guthrie to retire from pastoral duties in May 1864. His doctors told him that if he continued on with his regular pastoral duties, he would in all likelihood drop dead in the pulpit. In paying tribute to him, the *Free Church of Scotland Monthly Record* said that he

---

[37] Guthrie et. al., *Autobiography of Thomas Guthrie. D.D.: And Memoir by His Sons*, p. 583.

[38] Ibid., p. 566.

... will ever be known and remembered in Scotland as one of the four or five men to whom the Free Church owes the most; as the one man, whom next to Chalmers, her Presbyterian people were proud of, and loved best to hear.[39]

In his retirement, his capacity for work was redirected toward various projects largely through his writings. He became the editor of the *Sunday Magazine* which enjoyed a wide circulation. He also continued to speak and write in support of the Ragged Schools and Temperance movements. Although he was no longer actively involved in parish ministry, he continued to accept preaching invitations and he spoke in support of the movement for union with the United Presbyterian Church. This was chiefly motivated by his desire to see a greater unity within the church which he hoped would lead to more concerted social action.

Thomas Guthrie died in Sussex on 24 February 1873. Massive crowds attended his funeral in Edinburgh and *The Scotsman* gave him a glowing tribute.

Dr Guthrie was almost unrivalled as a pastor. ... He devoted himself to unremitting pastoral labour, especially among the poorest, the most wretched ... of the community. ... His name and memory will ever be associated with the system of Ragged Schools ... that have been eminently efficient as a means of juvenile reformation ...[40]

Guthrie's life is a helpful reminder that the church must be concerned with people's physical as well as their spiritual

[39] 'Dr Guthrie', *Free Church of Scotland Monthly Record*, (1 Nov. 1864), p. 662.

[40] 'The Late Dr Thomas Guthrie', *The Scotsman Digital Archive, February 25th, 1873*, http://archive.scotsman.com/ (accessed 31 March 2009).

needs. In a day when some Christians assume that many are poor because they are lazy and others seek to pass off their social obligations onto governments, his call to social action reminds us that we should not be isolating ourselves from the needs of a hurting world. In their recent book, Steve Corbett and Brian Fikkert have accurately described how the church should respond to a needy world.

> We are to embody Jesus Christ by doing what He did and continues to do through us: declare – using both words and deeds – that Jesus is the King of kings and Lord of lords who is bringing in a kingdom of righteousness, justice and peace. And the church needs to do this where Jesus did it, among the blind, the lame, the sick and outcast, and the poor.[41]

This is a sentiment that Thomas Guthrie would have shared.

---

[41] Steve Corbett and Brian Fikkert, *When Helping Hurts: How to Alleviate Poverty Without Hurting the Poor – and Yourself* (Chicago, IL: Moody Press, 2009), p. 42.

JAMES BEGG, D.D.

Home & Macdonald, L

7

JAMES BEGG

SOCIAL REFORMER AND
ECCLESIASTICAL CONSERVATIVE

James Begg [was] a man whose reputation for conten-
tiousness has unfortunately obscured his other (and
more creditable) claims to fame.[1]

JAMES Begg lived a life of contrasts. He was a theological conservative who waged a number of campaigns designed to keep the Free Church close to her
Reformation roots. He was a man who distrusted innovation and was always on the lookout for trends and
movements which he believed would weaken the church.
At the same time, his pastoral ministry was marked
by much social action as he displayed great concern for
the poor and disadvantaged. In more recent times, this
social aspect of his ministry has been ignored, and as
a result, a very one-sided picture of this complex man
has emerged. To redress this balance, we will look at
where he came from, what motivated him, and how his
social concern and ecclesiastical conservatism were both
integral parts of his life and ministry.

---

[1] A.C. Cheyne, *The Transforming of the Kirk: Victorian Scotland's
Religious Revolution* (Edinburgh: Saint Andrew Press, 1983), p. 122.

A SON OF THE MANSE
1808–29

James Begg was born on 31 October 1808 in the manse at New Monkland in Lanarkshire. His father James (1762–1845) was minister of the parish for forty years and his mother Mary (1777–1831) was the daughter of John Matthie, a merchant in Greenock. The Beggs were descended from Covenanter stock and James Begg said of his ancestors that

> ... the very stringency with which they adhered to what they regarded as fixed principles, avoiding ... 'right-hand extremes and left-hand defections', was very remarkable, and a peculiar glory in the race of Scotchmen. I have always felt it to be an honour to have some of this blood running in my veins.[2]

Begg's father was a man of firm evangelical principle whose ministry was known for

> ... preaching, visiting, catechising, managing the poor, attending Presbyteries, assisting at communions, and generally promoting the temporal and spiritual interests of all around.[3]

In later life, Begg would pay tribute to the parish school where he began his education and which gave him a good ground-

---

[2] Thomas Smith, *Memoirs of James Begg: Minister of Newington Free Church, Edinburgh* (Edinburgh: J. Gemmell, 1885), v. 1, p. 5. Thomas Smith's two volume life of Begg includes four autobiographical chapters that cover Begg's life from his birth until his induction as the Minister of Paisley in 1831. Smith's biography makes for turgid reading at best. C.H. Spurgeon once said of it that it was an example of 'a man being buried beneath a pyramid of documents'. C.H. Spurgeon, *Autobiography v. 2: The Full Harvest* (Edinburgh: Banner of Truth, 1973), p. xi.

[3] Smith, *Memoirs of James Begg: Minister of Newington Free Church, Edinburgh*, p. 6.

ing. The local schoolmaster had an excellent track record and managed to send a number of his students directly from the school to university. Begg began his university studies in Glasgow in 1820 at the age of twelve. Like other men who were destined for the ministry, Begg comments that this early enrolment was not the best idea.

> This is one of the defects of our Scotch system for as the curriculum of study for a minister embraces eight years, there is a strong temptation to send boys to college before they can possibly have been grounded in elementary education, so as to secure their being licensed …[4]

His studies included courses in Latin, Greek, logic and moral philosophy. Of the latter he commented:

> Mr Milne taught us Moral Philosophy in a somewhat heathenish style, making man pass through all stages from savage to civilised, insisting on the progress of human nature, even in its primitive state, from worse to better, instead of from better to worse; In short, it was very much philosophy without the fall of man and apart from the Bible.[5]

He completed his arts degree in April 1824 and then moved on to the study of theology.

One professor, Stevenson MacGill, had a significant influence on the young theological student. He was 'pastorally minded', worked hard to improve the standard of theological education prior to the Disruption and was sympathetic to the evangelical movement in the church. In addition to his teaching, McGill was also minister of the Tron Church in Glasgow and had outspoken views on the

[4] Ibid., p. 44.

[5] Ibid., p. 54.

church's role in society. For example, he believed that the French Revolution was wrong and should not be supported by the church. He also instructed his students that they should have a social conscience and that their ministry must reflect this.[6]

In the last year of his theological studies Begg spent a term at the University of Edinburgh, so that he could study under Thomas Chalmers. While he enjoyed his studies with Chalmers, he found himself strenuously disagreeing with him on a matter of public policy. It will be remembered that Chalmers took an influential part in the Catholic emancipation debate and Begg believed this to be wrong. Chalmers had argued that Protestants did not need legal protection from Catholics, that there was nothing to fear from the Church of Rome. Begg disagreed. He believed that those in favour of emancipation were naïve, and that Scotland would be the poorer if this change in policy took place. James W. Campbell has pointed out that from 'the start of his career, therefore, Romanism was seen as a great threat and the nature of the Protestant response to it, a matter of great concern'.[7] What is equally worth noting is that even as a young man, Begg was unafraid of holding minority views if he believed them to be right.

Begg was licensed by the Presbytery of Hamilton on 10 June 1829. Shortly thereafter, he began an assistant-ship to James Buchanan in North Leith, a position he held until May 1830. Buchanan was a popular preacher

---

[6] For a brief biography, see K.J. Stewart, 'MacGill, Stevenson', in *Dictionary of Scottish Church History and Theology*, p. 514.

[7] James W. Campbell, *Trembling for the Ark of God: James Begg and the Free Church of Scotland*, Thesis (Th.M.) – Westminster Theological Seminary, 1980, p. 4.

and his parish was a large one. Begg's responsibilities in the parish included preaching one service a week on Sunday afternoon, conducting a class for young people and pastoral visitation. He found visitation distressing as it brought him into contact with people who were living in conditions of real poverty. He says that this part of the parish

> ... had a very unsavoury reputation, and which gave me a tolerable insight, almost for the first time, into what have since been called the 'lapsed masses' of our towns.[8]

He freely admits that he found working with these people discouraging but, as we shall see in his later ministry much of his energies would become devoted to improving the living conditions of the poor.

MINISTER
1830—83

James Begg was ordained by the Presbytery of Dumfries on 18 May 1830 and he continued in the ministry until his death in 1883. Over those next fifty years, he worked diligently to improve the social conditions of his parishioners. He also found himself embroiled in considerable controversy, as he fought for his vision of the church. Before we look at both his social activism and ecclesiastical conservatism, we will briefly touch on some of the highlights of his ministry in each of the churches that he served.

James Begg's first church was a 'chapel of ease' in Maxwelltown, a suburb of Dunfries. It will be remembered that these chapels had been established in the eighteenth

---

[8] Smith, *Memoirs of James Begg: Minister of Newington Free Church, Edinburgh*, p. 87.

century as a response to the growing population and the church's inability to establish fully endowed parishes. He found his time filled with

> ... various duties, in which I delighted. My plan was to spend the whole of Monday and Tuesday in visiting the people, including the sick. Everywhere I met with the greatest kindness. I had in addition two classes, for young men and women respectively, on the Tuesday evenings. On Wednesday and Thursday I wrote my sermons, and on Friday and Saturday I committed them to memory, and again in retirement prepared myself for my Sabbath work.[9]

His ministry in Maxwelltown met with considerable success. Within a short space of time, many people were attracted to the church so that by the time he left, the church was filled with nearly 1,000 people each week. Begg's time in Maxwelltown was very brief. In December 1830, he accepted a call to be the Assistant Minister and eventual successor to Dr Jones at Lady Glenorchy's Chapel in Edinburgh. This chapel, which could accommodate more than 2,000 people, had been in existence since 1774. While the chapel was a part of the Church of Scotland, it was not given parish boundaries and did not have any voice in the Presbytery or General Assembly. It had a history of evangelical ministers, and as a result Begg felt sure that he was moving to an agreeable situation.

Part of Begg's motivation in accepting this position was that he would have more time for sermon preparation since the preaching duties were shared. He developed a good relationship with the senior minister and his preaching

---

[9] Ibid., p. 101.

attracted the attention of the wider church. But his chief frustration remained that since this was a chapel rather than a parish church, he did not have the right to be involved in the courts of the church.

With the growing agitation in the church spurred on by the increasing strength of the Evangelical party, Begg wanted to be able to play a role in the key debates of the day. So when Begg received a unanimous call to the Middle Parish Church in Paisley he accepted the call. He explained his decision to move in this way:

> The spirit of reform in the Established Church, which had partly begun with the century, but had received an immense impulse from the accession of Dr Chalmers to Glasgow and Dr Thomson to Edinburgh, was beginning to take very definite shape in the Church courts, but chapel ministers were entirely excluded from these courts. And yet I felt strongly that it would be well to have it in my power to take part in the struggle. I had been brought up with very definite views both in regard to the Scriptural lawfulness and practical advantages of Establishments. I had also a strong opinion in regard to the necessity for Church reform; and although most unwilling to leave my present place of comparative ease, great comfort, and many advantages, social and ecclesiastical, yet when called to the full status of a parish minister, in what was at that time one of the most difficult fields in Scotland, I thought it my duty to accept the invitation.[10]

The Middle Parish Church in Paisley had been in existence since 1781 and had a tradition of evangelical preaching. Begg was inducted in November 1831 and he served there

---

[10] Ibid., p. 107.

until January 1835. His pastoral gifts were needed from the moment of his induction, when an outbreak of cholera 'which visited many parts of the country, carried off many of all classes, and produced terror in the hearts of multitudes who escaped its actual attack'.[11] He also had to minister to a parish that was undergoing an economic depression that brought about reduced circumstances for the wealthy and increased hardship for the poor. Begg attended the General Assembly in 1832 which gave him a church-wide platform for the first time.

Begg's ministry in Paisley ended when he was called to the parish of Libberton, just outside of Edinburgh in February 1835. He would remain in this parish until the Disruption in 1843. He then became the minister of the newly established Newington Free Church, which he would serve for the rest of his life.

One significant event that took place while he was minister of Libberton parish was his marriage to Margaret Campbell on 23 September 1835. During the next ten years they had five children, but only three of them survived infancy. Margaret died in October 1845. It is unfortunate that Victorian biographers saw little or no need to say very much about the wives of their subjects. Begg's biographer says this is because 'I believe that she would have sensitively shrunk from the idea of having her life made public'. He does manage to say that the people of the parish saw her as being

> ... all that a minister's wife should be. They [reflected] especially on the assiduity with which she visited the

---

[11] Ibid., p. 212.

sick when ecclesiastical affairs called her husband away, perhaps too frequently, from home.[12]

In December 1845, Begg travelled to North America, spending most of his time in Canada. The purpose of the trip was to visit churches who wished to be more closely associated with the Free Church. While he was sympathetic to the needs of the colonial church, he argued that the best interests of the Canadian church were served by 'the training of an indigenous ministry'.[13] His time in North America also included a visit to the United States. The highlight of this leg of the journey was his invitation to preach before Congress and meet the President.

Begg married for the second time in November of 1846. This time he married Maria Faithful, who was the daughter of Ferdinand Faithful, the rector of Headley in Surrey. They would have six sons and one daughter. Maria outlived her husband by almost ten years.

During Begg's long life, he was the recipient of some significant honours. In 1847, he was awarded the Doctor of Divinity degree by Lafayette College in Pennsylvania. Although his biographer notes that a degree from Princeton would have been a greater honour, 'the Lafayette degree [was] but little inferior to it'.[14] The Free Church conferred her greatest honour on Begg when he was appointed Moderator of the General Assembly in 1865. His nomination was made by Patrick Fairbairn and Lord Dalhousie who complimented Dr Begg on 'the strictness

---

[12] Ibid., p. 315.

[13] Smith, *Memoirs of James Begg: Minister of Newington Free Church, Edinburgh,* v. 2, p. 78.

[14] Ibid., p. 116.

of his Presbyterian sentiments'. [15] This strictness, as we shall see, made him both friends and enemies as he took on several issues dealing with the theology and practice of the Free Church. This nomination was in recognition of his many years of service for the church and all of the work he had done and was doing for the poor and disadvantaged.

SOCIAL REFORMER

During his time at Libberton and then Newington, James Begg devoted some of his energies to a series of causes that marked him out as a social reformer. Despite emigration to Canada, the United States, Australia and New Zealand, Scotland experienced significant population growth during this period. By the end of the nineteenth century, Britain's population would grow to 37 million people.[16] Not surprisingly, the bulk of the population growth took place in the cities. In the case of Edinburgh, rural poverty was cited as one of the causes of the population explosion. The '... implication was that the Church of Scotland and property owners in rural parishes were unwilling to fund and organise parochial relief'. [17] This forced the poor to flee to the cities in search of work. It has been suggested that during

---

[15] 'Opening of the General Assembly of the Free Church', *The Scotsman Digital Archive, May 19, 1865*, http://archive.scotsman.com/ (accessed 25 April 2009).

[16] Iain D. Campbell, 'The Church in Scotland 1840–1940: An Overview. *Quodlibet Journal*, v. 1 no. 8 (December 1999), http://www.quodlibet.net/articles/campbell-scotland.shtml (accessed 21 April 2009).

[17] Richard Rodger, *The Transformation of Edinburgh: Land Property and Trust in the Nineteenth Century* (New York, 2001), p. 362.

> ... the middle years of the [nineteenth] century ...
> churchmen ... still accepted the existing order [and]
> still taught submission as the prime virtue of the dis-
> advantaged. The greater part of Scotland's poverty and
> misery was still ascribed to human failings, moral and
> spiritual.[18]

This is somewhat overstated, since there were those who were writing about the issues and some clergy were taking their social responsibilities seriously. We have already noticed how Chalmers' parochial model of ministry was a serious, though imperfect, attempt to improve living conditions. We have also seen how Guthrie's concern for the education of the poor was beginning to make a difference. James Begg was therefore not the only minister who was working to improve the lives of his parishioners and the wider population. His first tangible step in this direction occurred in 1841 when he became a member of the Edinburgh Association for Improving Lodging Houses of the Working Classes. Within ten years, three developments were built that provided better housing.

Beginning in 1849, he wrote a number of letters in *The Witness* and also issued a series of pamphlets and books which dealt with the social problems of the time. He believed that the church's warrant for engaging in social action was a proper understanding of the Ten Commandments. In the introduction to his *Happy Homes for Working Men and How to get Them,* Begg defended his position using the language of the *Westminster Shorter Catechism.*

---

[18] Cheyne, *The Transforming of the Kirk: Victorian Scotland's Religious Revolution*, p. 118.

The noble breadth of the commentary of our wise ancestors on the Decalogue, – the universal and perpetual standard of moral obligation, – cannot fail to command our admiration: 'The sixth commandment requireth all lawful endeavours to preserve our own life and the life of others'; 'The eighth commandment requireth the lawful procuring and furthering the wealth and outward estate of ourselves and others'; thus placing, in effect our obligation to promote sanitary and social reform on the strongest foundation on which they can rest, *viz.* the direct commandment of God.[19]

In 1850 Begg released a much wider ranging eight-point plan which in modern terms almost reads like an election platform or manifesto. In his 'Charter' he called for

1. Education, improvement of its quantity and quality.
2. Suppression of drunkenness.
3. Better dwellings for working people and the poor.
4. Public washing-houses and bleaching-greens.
5. Reform of the land-laws.
6. Simplification of the transference of land.
7. Treatment of crime and pauperism.
8. Greater justice to Scotland in [the British] Parliament.[20]

This charter displays the breadth of Begg's social concerns; the following highlights indicate some of his involvements.

He gave support for a national system of education in Scotland and, in so doing, disagreed with those in the Free Church who wished the church to retain full control of education. His chief reason for supporting the

---

[19] James Begg, *Happy homes for working men, and how to get them* (London and Edinburgh: Cassell, Petter, & Galpin, 1866), p. iii.

[20] Smith, *Memoirs of James Begg: Minister of Newington Free Church, Edinburgh,* v. 2, p. 144.

national system was that he did not believe that the Free Church had the resources necessary to achieve a truly national scheme that would reach all of the children of Scotland. Begg has been criticised for supporting this, but in fairness to his views, he expected the national school system to maintain, in Robert Candlish's phrase, 'a religious character'. [21]

Along with Thomas Guthrie, Begg was an active campaigner for temperance and he also worked for the reduction of shop hours on Saturdays. His calling for a half-day holiday was partly motivated by a desire to allow people to better prepare for worship the following day.

> Nothing would tend more to 'sweeten the breath of society,' and protect the day of God, than for every minister at present to throw his influence in favour of the Saturday half-holiday, and all similar wholesome movements on the part of the working classes.[22]

Begg's concern for temperance and church attendance did not make him a 'kill joy'. This is demonstrated by his involvement in the setting up of Saturday evening concerts so that people would have a place to go for entertainment and recreation. When these events were criticised, Begg responded by saying that they were

> ... in fact exerting, a powerful influence in elevating the tastes of the people, taking them from the pollution of the dram-shop, and giving them a taste for the ennobling pleasures of literature and science and religion.[23]

---

[21] Wilson, *Memorials of Robert Smith Candlish DD*, p. 436.

[22] Ibid., p. 202.

[23] Ibid., p. 231.

Through his tireless campaigning and pamphleteering, Begg was able to encourage the creation of the Edinburgh Co-operative Building Association whose aim was to assist the working classes to own their own homes. The success of this organisation may be judged by the fact that by 1865 200 houses had been built that provided shelter for over 1,000 people and by 1875 900 homes had been built.[24]

Begg's campaigns not only achieved much for the poor, they also had an impact on the Free Church. Through his persistent advocacy a series of committees were established to investigate and report on issues facing Scotland. In 1858, the 'Committee on Working-Class Housing' was established. This was followed by the 'Committee on Social Evils' in 1859 and the 'Committee on the State of Religion and Morals' in 1860. All of these committees are signs that the Free Church was taking its social responsibilities seriously.

In assessing Begg's work as a social reformer, A.C. Cheyne correctly concluded that his

> ... services to the Church and community...were many. But there can be little doubt that the greatest consisted in reminding his fellow-Christians of the intimate connection between sacred and secular, spiritual and material, and of the dangers threatening any body of men who dared to separate them.[25]

ECCLESIASTICAL CONSERVATIVE

James Begg could lay claim to being social reformer, even a radical one, but this was mixed with a strong strain of

---

[24] Cheyne, *The Transforming of the Kirk: Victorian Scotland's Religious Revolution*, p. 124.

[25] Ibid., p. 126.

ecclesiastical conservatism. He spent some of his considerable energies battling against what he saw as threats to the theology and practice of the Free Church. The most important of these was his campaign to maintain the Free Church's theological principles during discussions over the possible union with other Presbyterian churches in Scotland. The desire for greater unity among churches was not unique to the Scottish scene. As Maurice Grant has noted, this was a time when

> ... several Presbyterian churches in various parts of the world were taking similar measures; and the Free Church, with its liking for being thought enlightened and forward looking, certainly did not wish to be left behind.[26]

Beginning in 1863 and continuing to 1900 there were a series of attempts to bring the disparate Presbyterian churches in Scotland together. Begg was most involved in a debate regarding union with the United Presbyterian Church which took place between 1863 and 1873. He was not against church union *per se*, but if it was going to happen, it needed to take place for the right reasons and without sacrificing key principles. In his opening address to the 1865 Free Church General Assembly, Begg first referred to the divisions brought about by the Disruption and then said this:

> But He who is wonderful in counsel and excellent in working might, after all, be preparing, by that process of breaking to pieces, for a more comprehensive and vital union. Some time and sifting may still be necessary;

---

[26] Grant, 'The heirs of the Disruption in crisis and recovery 1893–1920', p. 6.

but if, in a way thoroughly consistent and honouring to God's truth, without which union is a mere conspiracy against truth, the scattered children of the Covenanters, the sons of Erskine, Gillespie, and Chalmers ... shall be brought to meet around a common centre, and in these days of trouble, and rebuke, and blasphemy, to blend their several protests into one broad standard uplifted on high, and emblazoned with Christ's crown and covenant, Scotland may again become glorious as in the days of old; nay, her latter end may become better than her beginning.[27]

The Free Church principle that Begg was most concerned to preserve was the so-called 'establishment principle', which had been at the heart of the Disruption. While insisting on the spiritual independence of the church, there was nonetheless a very strong link between the church and the state. The key elements of this principle were enunciated by James Bannerman, Professor of Apologetics and Pastoral Theology at New College Edinburgh. In his classic work, *The Church of Christ,* he stated that

... both the state and the Church are to be accounted moral parties responsible to God. Second ... both the Church and state are bound to own and recognize his revealed word. Third ... the state is bound to recognize the true religion, and as far as it is in its power, to promote its interests. Fourth ... the state is bound to advance the interests [of the church]. Fifth ... [it] is the duty of the

---

[27] James Begg, *The Hand of God in the Disruption and the Vital Importance of Free Church Principles. Being an Address delivered at the Opening of the General Assembly of the Free Church of Scotland on the 18th of May 1865,* http://nesher.org.uk/JBS/ebooks/begg_presbyterian-ism/begg_presbyterianism_01.html (accessed 28 April 2009).

state thus to recognize and, in so far as circumstances permit to endow the Church.[28]

Bannerman was not teaching anything new. In fact, he was simply restating what had been taught by the Westminster Assembly and which had been accepted by the majority of the Scottish church since then.

However, as James W. Campbell has noted, this was about to change. By 'the 1860s much had been forgotten in Scotland concerning her own traditions and standards'.[29] The 1860s saw increased calls for the disestablishment of the Church of Scotland. Even though the Free Church was no longer an established church, she had not, at least in theory, given up on the establishment principle. Moreover, a growing number of people in the Free Church were questioning the church's position on this issue. And these divisions would become clear during the debates around a proposed union with the United Presbyterian Church.

In 1863, union talks opened between the United Presbyterian Church and the Free Church and it soon became clear the United Presbyterians had rejected the establishment principle. It also was obvious that for any union to take place, the Free Church would need to agree with this position. Further complicating matters were concerns about what was being taught by some in the United Presbyterian Church regarding the extent of the atonement.[30]

---

[28] James Bannerman, *The Church of Christ* (Edinburgh: Banner of Truth, 1960), v. 1, pp. 126–33.

[29] Campbell, *Trembling for the Ark of God: James Begg and the Free Church of Scotland*, p. 14.

[30] This aspect of the church union debate will be discussed in the chapter on John Kennedy.

In 1867, the Free Church's union committee reported to the General Assembly that 'the differences between the conferring Churches constituted no bar to union between them'. [31] When the Assembly adopted this report, Begg was furious, and he and several other prominent churchmen resigned from the Union Committee. As they did so, they claimed 'that the motion which the Assembly had approved implied an abandonment and subversion of an admittedly constitutional principle of the Free Church of Scotland'. [32] Begg's main point was that the Free Church was bound legally to defend the establishment principle as part of the church's constitution.

As debate over union spread, Begg launched and edited a weekly newspaper called *The Watchword* in which he strenuously advocated for what he believed to be the true principles of the Free Church. Begg's biographer says of this journal that

> ... there was in it little – too little – of the *suaviter in modo*.[33] But the contributors to it honestly believed that their brethren were prepared to sacrifice vital truth; and with this belief they expressed themselves in terms that could not fail to be distasteful to their opponents. The editor did not write much for it; but he never shrank from responsibility for its contents.[34]

Begg's opposition to church union was strengthened by the support of men like Dr John Kennedy of Dingwall. Begg,

---

[31] Collins, *The Heritage of Our Fathers*, p. 72.

[32] Ibid., pp. 72–3.

[33] This phrase has sometimes been translated as 'gentle in manner' and also includes the idea of smooth and persuasive.

[34] Smith, *Memoirs of James Begg: Minister of Newington Free Church, Edinburgh,* v. 2, p. 502.

Kennedy and his Highland supporters, who came to be known as 'The Highland Host', worked tirelessly to try to derail the union talks. Although Begg and his allies were in the minority, the ranks of the anti-unionists or constitutional party were swelled by a 'middle party' in the church. This group were not as opposed to union in principle and some of them were even in favour of disestablishment, but they could not bring themselves to agree with any proposal that would almost certainly bring about a split in the Free Church.

The real possibility of a split became clear when legal opinions were canvassed as to the disposition of property in the event of a break taking place. In addition, 'a building was hired prior to the meeting of the [1873] General Assembly, to which the minority could withdraw to continue their witness and business' [35] if the union proposals were adopted. In the end, and with the assistance and blessing of the Moderator Alexander Duff, a compromise proposal was adopted which allowed for mutual eligibility of ministers between the two churches and required any minister entering the Free Church to 'avow their acceptance of the distinctive position of the denomination to which they sought admission'.[36] Begg's role in advocating for the constitutional party through his tireless speaking and writing cannot be overestimated. Many in the church looked to him for direction, to the extent that had he not accepted the compromise proposals, the unity of the church would almost certainly have been broken.

James Begg brought the same energy to debates over worship in the Free Church that he had brought to the

[35] Collins, *The Heritage of Our Fathers*, p. 73.
[36] Ibid.

issue of church union. In 1865, the issue of whether or not it was permissible to introduce anything other than the Psalms into the public worship of the church was brought to the General Assembly. Because he was Moderator that year, Begg was unable to throw himself as vigorously into the debate as he might have liked, but no one was under any illusions as to his views on this question. He had consistently argued that to introduce 'hymns of human composition' into public worship was unbiblical and bad for the church. He

> ... constantly maintained that the Book of Psalms is given by Divine authority as the hymnal of the Church, and that the use of uninspired compositions is ... a setting aside of a Divine appointment. [37]

He also argued that the introduction of hymns would eventually supplant the use of Psalms in worship. Further, he asserted that hymns could not be introduced in a way that would insure the peace and unity of the church. At the 1870 General Assembly, Begg shifted his position slightly, by stating that he 'was prepared to sing any inspired song'; thus allowing for the use of other parts of Scripture in worship'. [38]

The debate on this issue continued through to the General Assembly of 1872, which finally approved a hymn-book that contained 417 hymns for use in worship. Begg's biographer, who did not object to the change, makes this telling observation.

---

[37] Smith, *Memoirs of James Begg: Minister of Newington Free Church, Edinburgh*, v. 2, p. 408.

[38] Ibid., p. 457.

Looking back over the experience of twenty years, I may be allowed to express the opinion that the use of the hymn-book has not been satisfactory, while I admit that a contrary opinion is held by many. In the first place, the hymn-book has been introduced into some congregations in neglect of or opposition to the caution that it should not be introduced in cases where it would interfere with the peace of the congregation. In other cases members have refrained from opposing its introduction only because they felt that it would be invidious to object, and have considered that they were unfairly treated in being reduced to the alternative of consenting to what they disapproved of, or being regarded as peace-breakers. As to Dr Begg's anticipation that the hymns would gradually supersede the Psalms, I suspect that it is being realised in many cases.[39]

If Begg was concerned about the hymns superseding Psalms in his own day, we can only imagine what he would make of the reformed church in the twenty-first century where the Psalms are largely missing from worship.

Two final points are worth noting. First, even after the church had made up her mind on the issue, Begg did not stop trying to persuade people that the church had gotten it badly wrong. In 1875, he published a pamphlet entitled *Anarchy in Worship or Recent Innovations Contrasted with the Constitution of the Presbyterian Church and the Vows of her Office Bearers*. It was an impassioned plea that the church should return to its reformation roots. Second, Begg did not threaten to leave the Free Church even though he believed it had taken the wrong course of

[39] Ibid., p. 409.

action. His commitment to the unity of the church provides a startling contrast to the fractured nature of the church in our own day.

A third component of Begg's ecclesiastical conservatism was his implacable opposition to Roman Catholicism. He firmly believed that many of the teachings and the polity of the Church of Rome were unbiblical and he was not afraid to state this in the strongest, even intemperate terms. In the 1850s, Begg was one of the driving forces behind the creation of the Scottish Reformation Society whose purpose was to mobilise public opinion against any and all political concessions to Rome. He also edited the Society's journal, *The Bulwark,* for more than twenty years and published a widely read book entitled *A Handbook of Popery,* in 1852. To modern ears, much of Begg's anti-Catholic rhetoric sounds intolerant; however, it needs to be remembered that much of the theology of the Free Church and the Church of Rome was and is incompatible, and he believed that his vows as a minister required him to speak. However, it must be conceded that the tone of much of his rhetoric was unnecessarily strident and it is just possible that he might have been more successful if he had moderated his tone.

Begg was also involved in the controversy surrounding the teachings of the Old Testament scholar William Robertson Smith.[40] Smith had studied theology at New College, Edinburgh as well as in Germany where he studied under Rothe and Ritschl. In 1870, he was elected by the

---

[40] For a brief biography see, N.M. de S. Cameron, 'Smith, William Robertson', in *Dictionary of Scottish Church History and Theology,* p. 782–3.

Free Church General Assembly to the Hebrew Chair in Aberdeen. His lectures and writing attracted the concern of many in the church who came to believe that Smith was undermining 'the authenticity, the historical accuracy, and the inspiration of the Old Testament Scriptures'. [41] Begg's biographer claims that as matters intensified, attempts

> ... were sedulously made to exclude [Begg] and many others of us from the discussion altogether, by represent-ing the question as one of deep scholarship, on which only profound Hebraists were entitled to form a judgment ...[42]

Thankfully, this strategy was unsuccessful and after a pro-tracted trial through the courts of the church, Smith was finally removed from office in 1881. Strangely, the church decided he could keep his ministerial credentials although he would no longer be able to teach theological students. Begg objected to this solution on the sensible grounds that if a man was unworthy to teach theological students, he should not be allowed to preach from the pulpits of the church either.[43]

Begg's activism on various issues made him some implacable enemies in the church. Foremost among these was Robert Rainy, who had been appointed to the Chair of Church History and became Principal of New College after the death of William Cunningham. Rainy was one of the driving forces behind the church union movement

---

[41] Smith, *Memoirs of James Begg: Minister of Newington Free Church, Edinburgh,* v. 2, p. 532.

[42] Ibid., p. 531.

[43] Although Smith's ministerial credentials were not removed, he ceased to function as a Minister of the Free Church and spent the rest of his life occupying a series of academic posts at Cambridge University.

and in the course of those debates he called Begg 'the evil genius of the Free Church'. [44] Rainy went on to say that Begg 'introduced a policy of conspiracy and attempting to carry points by threatening us with law. No man did more to lower the tone of the church and to secularize it'. [45]

To understand the conflict between these two men, it needs to be remembered that Robert Rainy was first and foremost a pragmatist, who could not cope with men like James Begg for whom truth and principle came first. Rainy was also a prime mover in the Free Church's theological drift in the latter part of the nineteenth century. Just how far Rainy had drifted from the biblical and confessional roots of the Free Church may be seen in this statement which he made in 1872:

> We have to deal with the present, not according to past convictions, but according to present convictions; not according to the beliefs of our fathers, but according to our own; we have to convey, in so far as we represent the Church, the message and influence which Christ's Church ought to convey to the men of our time, who inherit the past and are looking forward to the future. For that we would be free of every bond except the regard we owe to Christ's word, and the regard which he has appointed us to have to one another's convictions in shaping our message and our actions.[46]

---

[44] Patrick Carnegie Simpson, *The Life of Principal Rainy* (London: J. Gemmell, 1909), v. 2, p. 50.

[45] Ibid.

[46] Quoted in Alexander Taylor Innes, 'Robert Rainy', *Disruption Worthies: A Memorial of 1843; with a Historical Sketch of the Free Church of Scotland from 1843 Down to the Present Time*, p. 446.

It hardly needs to be said that this kind of thinking contravenes the very essence of confessionalism, and is poisonous when it appears in the church. It is critical that the contemporary church should not embrace Rainy's vision.

Closing Scene

In later life, Begg experienced periods of ill health, suffering as he did from the effects of diabetes. However, he was not someone who could be persuaded to retire. Although he found himself increasingly in the minority in the Free Church, he continued to preach and write up until his final illness. In September 1883, he caught a severe cold and died on 29 September at the age of almost seventy-six. Two thousand people attended his funeral and tributes were paid to him by friends and foes alike. In their obituary, *The Scotsman* aptly summed up his life.

> It would be difficult to measure the loss which the Free Church has sustained by Dr Begg's death. His rugged straightforwardness had little in common with the tactics of the leaders of the present day, but it more truly represented what has been the strength of the church.[47]

James Begg lived his life passionately and never shied away from controversy. Any cause that he took up, he did so with great vigour and it has been rightly said of him that he

> ... was unwilling to allow pragmatic considerations to turn him from his goal. To others, who were unwilling to act in this way, Begg's activities looked like divisiveness, but

[47] 'Dr James Begg', *The Scotsman Digital Archive, 1 October 1883*, http://archive.scotsman.com/ (accessed 30 April 2009).

to one who accepted the principles involved they were the logical conclusion, the necessary consequence, indeed, the only path of Christian conscience.[48]

---

[48] Campbell, *Trembling for the Ark of God: James Begg and the Free Church of Scotland*, p. 107.

ANDREW A. BONAR, D.D.

Home & Macdonald, Lith.

8

Andrew Bonar

Pastor and Evangelist

Bonar was in the front rank of all that was remarkable
about 19th Century Scottish Presbyterianism.[1]

MOST people who have heard of Andrew Bonar
know him through two books: his classic work, *The
Memoirs and Remains of Robert Murray M'Cheyne,* and
The Diary and Letters of Andrew A. Bonar which were
edited by his daughter Marjory. *The Memoirs of M'Cheyne,*
published in 1843, has been called 'the most popular
textbook of Victorian evangelicalism'. [2] Never out of
print, it is a highly romanticised portrait that established
Bonar's literary reputation. If *The Memoirs and Remains*
placed M'Cheyne in the Preacher's Hall of Fame, Bonar's
Diary and Letters, published in 1893, cemented his own
image as a godly pastor. It draws a stylised picture which
shows some aspects of Bonar's life and pastoral ministry.

Andrew Bonar had a succession of successful pastorates in Scotland. He also undertook an eventful trip

---

[1] Colin Dow, 'Andrew Bonar – Joshua of the Disruption', *Streams of
Living Water: Sermons and Writings of Rev. Colin Dow,* http://www.greek-
thomsonchurch.com/dowblog/2007/09/03/andrew-bonar-joshua-of-the-dis-
ruption/ (accessed 5 May 2009).

[2] Crawford Gribben, 'Andrew Bonar and the Scottish Presbyterian
Millennium', in Crawford Gribben and Timothy C.F. Stunt (eds), *Prisoners
of Hope? Aspects of Evangelical Millennialism in Britain and Ireland*
(Carlisle: Paternoster Press, 2004), p. 179.

through Europe and the Middle East in the cause of Jewish missions. Evangelism was the one cause that animated him more than any other. He was passionately committed to the proclamation of the gospel to as many people as he could possibly reach. As we shall see, however, his involvement in the evangelistic crusades of Moody and Sankey proved to be controversial.

EARLY LIFE AND EDUCATION
1810–35

Andrew Alexander Bonar was born in Edinburgh on 29 May 1810, the seventh son of James and Marjory Bonar. James Bonar was Second Solicitor of Excise for Edinburgh. He is said to have been very good at languages and wrote a book entitled *Disquisitions on the Origin and Radical Sense of the Greek Propositions.* In addition to being a founding member of the Astronomical Institute and Edinburgh Sub-scription Library, he also contributed scholarly articles to *The Encyclopaedia Britannica* and to *The Edinburgh Ency-clopaedia.* When James Bonar recorded his son's birth in his diary he wrote that he hoped that his son might 'be spared to be a blessing to his friends and a real member of the Church of Christ'. [3]

The Bonar family was actively involved in the life of the church, attending Lady Glenorchy's Chapel in Edinburgh where James Bonar was an elder. The congregation was made up of firmly committed evangelicals. Dr Jones, the Minister of the Chapel during Andrew Bonar's youth, was an excellent preacher who had a significant influence on Andrew and his approach to ministry.

---

[3] Marjorie Bonar, *Andrew A Bonar, DD, Diary and Letters, transcribed and edited by his daughter* (London: Hodder and Stoughtton, 1894), p. x.

Andrew Bonar's education began at Mr Lindsay's School in Hanover Street, where he showed an early aptitude for languages. At the age of eleven he entered Edinburgh High School and continued to achieve academic success. In 1825, he gained the Dux Gold Medal of the Rector's Class. In this connection, the Rector would say that 'without doubt Andrew Bonar was the best Latin scholar who had ever passed through [my] hands'.[4] Bonar began arts studies at the University of Edinburgh in 1825, where he again excelled as a student, winning the Society of Writers to the Signet's Gold Medal for his work in the Latin class.

He began keeping a diary in 1828 as he contemplated beginning divinity studies; he would maintain it for the rest of his life. The very first entry in the diary for 21 August 1821 explains his motivation for studying for the ministry.

> About this time I thought of marking occasionally my thoughts and God's dealings. It was this week that I resolved to enter upon the study of divinity. My chief motive was the indistinct hope and belief that thereby I should be more likely to find salvation, being much taken up, as I thought I must be, with the pursuit of divine things. For I felt myself unsaved, and felt a secret expectation that in the course of my studies in divinity I might be brought to the truth. My inclination for Biblical Criticism, too, and fondness for languages, had much weight, I suspect in the determination, rather than higher motives.[5]

Two formative influences that appear in the early pages of the diary are Thomas Chalmers and Edward Irving. As an

---

[4] Ibid., p. xi.

[5] Ibid., p. 3.

arts student, Bonar sat in on some of Chalmers' classes. As we noted in chapter two, Chalmers had a major impact on his students, inspiring many of them and providing a model for their future ministries. Bonar notes that Chalmers insisted that his students display love for the gospel in their sermons to the extent that if he found this element lacking, he would insist that the student re-craft their sermon. Chalmers' impact on Bonar is hardly surprising; however, the influence of Edward Irving requires more explanation.

Irving had been licensed to preach by the Church of Scotland in 1815 and served as Chalmers' assistant at St John's Glasgow from 1819 until he was ordained and appointed to one of the Church of Scotland's congregations in London.[6] While serving in London, Irving developed pronounced premillennial views on the second coming of Christ and taught these beliefs with eloquence and enthusiasm. By embracing the view that the second coming of Christ would precede His 1,000 year reign on earth, Irving was breaking with the views held by most people in the Scottish church.[7] Since the Westminster Assembly, the prevailing view had been that expressed in Question 191 of the *Westminster Larger Catechism* which speaks of the conversion of the Jews, and revival among Gentile nations *before* the second coming.[8]

---

[6] For more information see, N.R. Needham 'Irving, Edward', in *Dictionary of Scottish Church History and Theology*, pp. 436–7.

[7] For a discussion of the development of millennial thought, particularly as it relates to the Scottish church, see N.R. Needham, 'Millennialism', in *Dictionary of Scottish Church History and Theology*, pp. 562–4.

[8] Q. 191. *What do we pray for in the second petition?* A. In the second petition (which is, *Thy kingdom come*), acknowledging ourselves and all mankind to be by nature under the dominion of sin and Satan, we pray that the kingdom of sin and Satan may be destroyed, the gospel propa-

It was also at this time that Irving began to teach ideas that would be precursors of the modern Pentecostal movement's stress on the supernatural gifts of the Spirit. Much more alarmingly, he started teaching a faulty view of Christ's incarnation. He believed that Jesus' human nature was exactly like that of all other people, including the fact that it had 'innate sinful propensities'.[9] He would go on to stress that Jesus was completely indwelt by the Holy Spirit from the moment of his conception, which enabled him to live a holy life. Not surprisingly, his critics pointed out that if Jesus had a sinful human nature, he too needed a saviour and thus was in no position to be offered as the perfect atonement for sin. Irving was deposed from the Church of Scotland ministry in 1833 and went on to found the Catholic Apostolic Church.

Irving's views on the millennium had a strong impact on Bonar. In his diary entry for 24 September 1829, Bonar wrote that he had

> ... been hearing Mr Irving's lectures all week, and am persuaded now that his views of the Coming of Christ are

---

gated throughout the world, the Jews called, the fullness of the Gentiles brought in; the church furnished with all gospel officers and ordinances, purged from corruption, countenanced and maintained by the civil magistrate; that the ordinances of Christ may be purely dispensed, and made effectual to the converting of those that are yet in their sins, and the confirming, comforting, and building up of those that are already converted; that Christ would rule in our hearts here, and hasten the time of his second coming, and our reigning with him forever; and that he would be pleased so to exercise the kingdom of his power in all the world, as may best conduce to these ends. *Westminster Larger Catechism*, http://www.reformed.org/documents/index.html?mainframe=http://www.reformed.org/documents/larger1 (accessed 12 May 2009).

[9] Needham 'Irving, Edward', in *Dictionary of Scottish Church History and Theology*, p. 436.

truth. The views of the glory of Christ opened up in his lecture have been very impressive to me.[10]

While Irving's preaching had a major influence on Bonar's thinking, his ideas were not as well received by others in the church. Thomas Chalmers, for example, had a far more negative reaction.[11] Although they had worked together during Irving's tenure as his assistant at St John's parish, Irving's increased interest in prophecy disturbed Chalmers. In his diary, he noted that he found Irving's preaching

> ... quite woeful. There is a power and richness, and gleams of exquisite beauty, but withal a mysticism and an extreme allegorization which I am sure must be pernicious to the general cause.[12]

---

[10] Bonar, *Andrew A Bonar, DD, Diary and Letters, transcribed and edited by his daughter*, p. 5.

[11] Thomas Chalmers' own views on the millennium are the subject of some debate. In the introduction to her father's diary, Marjorie Bonar claimed that 'before his death, Dr Chalmers declared himself on the side of the Pre-Millenarians'. Bonar, *Andrew A. Bonar, DD, Diary and Letters, transcribed and edited by his daughter*, p. xiii. However, evidence for this statement in Chalmers' published works is sketchy at best. In fact, an examination of several of his sermons would seem to point in quite a different direction. It is probably better to take the view of Crawford Gribben, who states that Chalmers' 'published statements... seem to suggest a distinctly apocalyptic philosophy of history combined with firm postmillennialism'. Gribben, 'Andrew Bonar and the Scottish Presbyterian Millennium', p. 185. Those interested in following up on Chalmers' eschatological views should consult his sermons 'The Second Coming of Christ', 'On the New Heavens and the New Earth' and 'Thoughts on Universal Peace', in Thomas Chalmers, *Sermons and Discourses of Thomas Chalmers, D.D., L.L.D., Now Completed by the Introduction of his Posthumous Sermons* (New York: Robert Carter & Brothers, 1853).

[12] Hanna, *Memoirs of the Life and Writings of Thomas Chalmers*, vol. 2, p. 173.

Later in 1829, after he had heard another sermon by Irving, Chalmers wrote to his sister:

> I must just be honest enough and humble enough to acknowledge that I scarcely understood a single word, nor do I comprehend the ground on which he goes in his violent allegorizations, chiefly of the Old Testament.[13]

Andrew Bonar retained a soft spot for Edward Irving even after he was deposed from the ministry of the Church of Scotland for teaching heresy. When Bonar published his life of M'Cheyne, he included M'Cheyne's comment that was made at the time of Irving's death.

> I look upon him with awe, as one of the saints and martyrs of old. A holy man in spite of all his delusions and errors. He is now with his God and Saviour, whom he wronged so much, yet I am persuaded loved so sincerely.[14]

Bonar remained a passionate believer in the premillennial understanding of the second coming of Christ all of his life. Indeed, the need for evangelism implicit in this doctrine had a significant impact on his ministry.

Bonar delayed beginning his formal theological education because he continued to struggle with his faith. Finally, in October 1830, he embraced Christ for himself and began his divinity course in 1831. There are few references to Bonar's theological education in his published diary, although he does mention his growing friendship with M'Cheyne. He completed his studies in March 1835

---

[13] Ibid., p. 174.

[14] Andrew A. Bonar, *Memoir and Remains of Robert Murray M'Cheyne* (Edinburgh: Oliphant, Anderson and Ferrier, n.d.), p. 37.

and was licensed to preach by the Presbytery of Jedburgh in July of the same year.

FIRST YEARS OF MINISTRY
1835–9

Bonar's first experience of parish work was as assistant to John Purves at Jedburgh, where he served for about a year. It was here that Bonar preached his first sermon and began to learn the duties of pastoral ministry. Purves shared Bonar's views on the millennium and it appears that he may have strengthened and confirmed Bonar's belief in this teaching. His time there was to be brief because in November 1836 he was asked by Robert Candlish to serve as his assistant at St George's, Edinburgh. He confided in his diary that he felt that he had not accomplished as much as he would have liked in Jedburgh, but he did feel a call to go to Edinburgh. In the entry for 16 November he wrote that

> ... the district is most needy and destitute. The place is my native town, and full of irreligion, full of lukewarm-ness also, which thing, it seems to me, God might make me useful in testifying against.[15]

While Bonar worked faithfully as a missionary in Candlish's St George's parish, he yearned to be called to a church of his own, which would allow him to be ordained to the ministry. As he waited somewhat impatiently for a call, he recognised that his millennial views were a barrier. In his diary for 9 September 1837, he wrote that he was

---

[15] Bonar, *Andrew A Bonar, DD, Diary and Letters, transcribed and edited by his daughter,* p. 43.

... greatly cast down by the circumstances of my being kept out of several appointments on account of my millenarianism chiefly. I had prayed about the matter in the full conviction that bearing testimony to this and other truths was the way of duty.[16]

Finally, in September of 1838, Bonar was called to the parish of Collace and was ordained on 20 September 1838, with Robert Candlish preaching at the ordination service. One of the things that is demonstrated again and again in Bonar's diary is his deep piety. In the entry for 26 September he wrote that he was going to

... go earlier to bed and rise at six; and spend from six to eight in prayer for myself, my parish and the cause of God through the world. Oh, if I could do this all the days of my life while I have health, for I have never yet succeeded in such resolutions, and never yet have I given much time to prayer daily. Neither cold nor darkness need hinder me. I may just rise and at once begin communion with God, and my soul's fervour will heat the body. O, Lord, grant me the power.[17]

Subsequent references indicate that Bonar did follow through on this resolution and that throughout his life he spent a great deal of time in prayer and personal devotion.

A MISSION OF DISCOVERY
1839

One of the important features of Scottish church life was a concern for the Jewish people which had existed since

[16] Ibid., p. 55. It should also be noted here that Bonar also rejected the view that the Pope was the Antichrist which was taught in the *Westminster Confession of Faith*.

[17] Ibid., p. 71.

the Reformation. This was rooted in the belief that the Jews would one day be converted to Christianity, a belief that can be traced to some of the foundational works of the Reformation. The *Geneva Bible*, published in 1560, said in a marginal note on Romans 11:15 that 'it will come to pass that when the Jews come to the Gospel, the world will as it were come to life again, and rise up from death to life'.[18] *The Directory for the Public Worship of God,* the first document produced by the Westminster Assembly, instructed ministers to pray

> ... for the propagation of the gospel and kingdom of Christ to all nations; for the conversion of the Jews, the fullness of the Gentiles, the fall of Antichrist, and the hastening of the second coming of our Lord.[19]

These views had been perpetuated and developed by a number of the Puritans and was further maintained by evangelical ministers in the Church of Scotland up to and including the nineteenth century. It has also been suggested that

> ... concern for Israel seems to have been heightened by the arrival in Scotland of quite a number of Jewish people in the early part of [the nineteenth] century ... and as the theme of revival was coming to the fore, so also as an accompaniment came a desire to reach out to the Jews with the Gospel.[20]

---

[18] *Geneva Bible Notes,* http://www.reformedreader.org/gbn/gbnromans. htm (accessed 12 May 2009).

[19] *The Directory for the Public Worship of God,* http://www.reformed. org/documents/wcf_standards/index.html?mainframe=/documents/wcf_ standards/p369-direct_pub_worship.html (accessed 12 May 2009).

[20] Allan M. Harman, 'Introduction', in Andrew A Bonar and Robert

In 1838, no less than sixteen petitions were sent by various Synods and Presbyteries to the Church of Scotland's General Assembly on the subject of Jewish mission work. The Assembly passed an act which acknowledged

> ... the high importance of using means for the conversion of God's ancient people, and recommend the object to the attention of the Church, and that the Ministers, in their preaching and public prayers, more frequently avail themselves of opportunities of noticing the claims of the Jews ...[21]

The committee that was set up at this Assembly decided that before they could establish clear strategies for Jewish evangelism, they needed more information. As a result, they decided to send out a 'Commission of Enquiry' to eastern and central Europe and Palestine. The membership of the commission was Dr Alexander Keith, minister of St Cyrus in Kincardineshire; Dr Alexander Black, Professor of Theology at Marischal College, Aberdeen; Andrew Bonar; and Robert Murray M'Cheyne. M'Cheyne was chosen by Robert Candlish who felt that the trip would help him recuperate from the ill health he had been experiencing. When Bonar informed his congregation that he was being sent to Palestine, one elderly member of his church is reported to have 'held up her hands and exclaimed, "Oh, then, we'll no see him again for forty years!"' [22]

Murray McCheyne, *Mission of Discovery* (Fearn, Ross-shire: Christian Focus, 1996), p. 5.

[21] *A Course of Lectures on the Jews by Ministers of the Established Church in Glasgow* (Philadelphia: Presbyterian Board of Publication, 1840), p. 1.

[22] Bonar, *Andrew A Bonar, DD, Diary and Letters, transcribed and edited by his daughter*, p. 78.

This expedition has been called 'perhaps the most influential missionary journey undertaken by representatives of the Scottish churches in the nineteenth century'.[23] The written account of the journey, entitled *Narrative of a Mission of Inquiry to the Jews from the Church of Scotland in 1839,* was co-authored by Bonar and M'Cheyne. The book was released in 1842 and went through several editions on both sides of the Atlantic. In their introduction, Bonar and M'Cheyne stated that the purpose of their journey was 'to see the real condition and character of God's ancient people, and to observe whatever might contribute to interest others in their cause'.[24]

The travellers departed from Dover on 12 April 1839 and made their first stop at Boulogne. Over the course of the next six months, they travelled through France, Italy, Malta, Greece, Egypt and Palestine. They stopped in Jerusalem, and then on the way home they travelled through Moldavia, Austrian Poland and Prussia before reaching Scotland. The book contains moments of drama as they faced the confiscation of some of their belongings and even threats of death. Although the trip had been designed to include the four ministers selected by the church, Doctors Keith and Black experienced ill health during their travels and had to abandon the trip when they reached Beirut, leaving Bonar and M'Cheyne to complete the mission.

The trip was supposed to be largely for investigative purposes and the *Narrative* does contain a great deal of detail

---

[23] Gribben, 'Andrew Bonar and the Scottish Presbyterian Millennium', p. 186.

[24] Andrew Bonar and Robert Murray M'Cheyne, *Narrative of a Mission of Inquiry to the Jews from the Church of Scotland in 1839* (Philadelphia: Presbyterian Board of Publication, 1842), p. 1.

about what they discovered. The most emotional description was reserved for when they approached Jerusalem.

> At that moment we were impressed chiefly by the fact that we were now among 'the mountains that are round about Jerusalem' ... The nearer we came to the city the more we felt it a solemn thing to be where 'God manifest in the flesh' had walked.[25]

In addition to the description of how the Jewish people lived in the various places they visited, the narrative is rich in detail on the evangelistic opportunities that the visit afforded. It is also noticeable that the *Narrative* places almost as much stress on the evangelisation of Roman Catholics as it does on the Jews.

Bonar and M'Cheyne arrived back in Scotland in November 1839. They immediately reported to the committee of the church who had sent them. When they published their account, they stated that God

> ... had blessed this undertaking from the beginning to the end. Both in the towns and rural parishes of Scotland, a deep and we trust Scriptural interest has been excited in behalf of Israel; an interest which has penetrated to the very poorest of our people.[26]

Their return coincided with a revival of interest in religion that had begun in M'Cheyne's own church in Dundee. As far as Bonar and M'Cheyne were concerned, this was abiding proof that God was blessing the interest in Jewish mission work.

---

[25] Ibid., p. 126.

[26] Ibid., p. 519.

In light of Andrew Bonar's lifelong enthusiasm for Jewish missionary work, Colin Dow has recently challenged the church to reconsider its own commitment to this type of mission. Pointing to the prevailing amillennial approach to eschatology in most reformed churches, he notes that a view that does not expect a conversion of the Jews to Christianity before the second coming of Christ reduces the impetus for evangelism among Jews. In contrast, Dow notes that Andrew Bonar was convinced that

> ... the evangelism of the Jews was Biblical. In Acts 1:8 our risen Lord [told] His disciples that after the Spirit came upon them *'you will be my witnesses in Jerusalem and in all Judea and Samaria, and to the ends of the earth'*. We tend to read that passage through a redemptive historical matrix, but for Bonar, nothing has changed about the Lord's call to his church. The Gospel must first and always be preached in Jerusalem. Bonar differentiated between Jewish and Gentile mission and saw the foundation for blessing in Gentile mission as being in the faithful pursuit of Jewish mission. His reading of Scripture also led him to believe that *'there is a day coming when God will bless the Jews more than he has done the Gentiles'*. [27]

PASTORAL MINISTRY
1839–92

As Andrew Bonar returned to his parish, the crisis leading to the Disruption continued around him. He was among those ministers who preached in the Presbytery of Strathbogie and attended the Commission of Assembly, where agreement was reached on the need to leave the

---

[27] Dow, 'Andrew Bonar – Joshua of the Disruption', *Streams of Living Water: Sermons and Writings of Rev. Colin Dow*.(accessed 5 May 2009)

established church. He recorded his feelings about this meeting in his diary.

> *Thursday Aug 26th* – Yesterday attended the great meeting in Edinburgh in defence of the Church. An immense assembly of ministers and elders, the numbers beyond anything known hitherto since our fathers' days. Both the Commission and the meeting in the evening very solemn. We have now looked our danger fully in the face, and it is wonderful how many are standing fast. I feel, however, too little concern, too little anxious or excited to pray.[28]

After the November 1842 Convocation he wrote in his diary that it

> ... has been a very remarkable time; much prayer. Very great unity among the brethren. There was a spirit, too, of brotherly love and Christian feeling that was quite unusual. Often our discussions ended with unanimity, although previously there seemed complete opposition of views.[29] There was a solemnity, too, over all, for we felt the circumstances were imminent to the land. Of those present upon Tuesday evening, 340 resolved to leave the Church in event of no response being obtained from Government, after our remonstrance and application had been laid before them.[30]

Two events in 1843 effected Bonar deeply. First, on 25 March he heard news of the death of Robert Murray M'Cheyne at the age of twenty-nine. The two men had developed a deep

---

[28] Bonar, *Andrew A Bonar, DD, Diary and Letters, transcribed and edited by his daughter*, p. 93.

[29] While Bonar is correct that the Convocation ended with agreement on the way forward, he does downplay some of the disagreements that took place during the meeting.

[30] Ibid., p. 100.

friendship while at university, which had been cemented during their foreign travels. The death of his friend devastated Bonar.

> *Saturday 25th* – This afternoon about five o'clock, a message has just come to tell me of Robert M'Cheyne's death. Never, never yet in all my life have I felt anything like this. It is a blow to myself, to his people, to the Church of Christ in Scotland ... It makes me feel death near myself now. Life has lost half its joys, were it not the hope of saving souls. There was no friend whom I loved like him ... [His death] startles me. It is as if God were striking myself. Perhaps He may be taking me next. The same fever may come to me now, but the time at any rate is short.[31]

The second major event of 1843 took place on 18 May when Bonar was in Edinburgh for the General Assembly of the Church of Scotland and the first General Assembly of the Free Church. His diary entries reflect his pride in the stand taken by his brethren in the church and the firm belief that God would honour the witness of the Free Church. Like other ministers who left the Church of Scotland, Bonar's congregation lost the use of their building and initially they were forced to meet in the open air. However, a new building was erected quickly in the village of Kinrossie and was opened for worship on 12 October 1843.

During 1845, Bonar devoted a significant portion of his time to the preparation of *A Commentary on Leviticus*. It has been correctly noted that in this work Bonar

> ... interpreted the Old Testament's ancient liturgical details through an evangelical and pre-millennial paradigm ... The

---

[31] Ibid., p. 101.

commentary was explicitly aimed at convincing a Jewish readership of the propriety of regarding Jesus Christ as the Messiah.[32]

Bonar had what can only be described as a mystical approach to writing. In looking over his life of M'Cheyne, he wrote in his diary that

> I have often felt things in study so plainly *given* me, not at all like the products of my own skill, that this is the way in which I account for them. The Lord sends them because of people praying for me.[33]

In April 1848, Bonar married Isabella Dickson. On his wedding day, he wrote his brother that if "...ever I have true affection for any, it is for her, and yet I still feel that 'Christ is chief among ten thousand". [34]. They would have two sons and four daughters.

Bonar would continue serving the Free Church in this area until he was called in 1856 to be minister of Finnieston Free Church in Glasgow. The call to the city church interested Bonar because of the opportunities for evangelism. In a letter to a friend he wrote that

> I am much pressed to consider the subject of Glasgow evangelisation – in short, to agree to be called to a district and church about to be erected in Finnieston in Glasgow. I have prayed, considered, and in every way reviewed the matter as impartially as I could, and the result is I am feeling my

---

[32] Gribben, 'Andrew Bonar and the Scottish Presbyterian Millennium', pp. 193–4.

[33] Bonar, *Andrew A Bonar, DD, Diary and Letters, transcribed and edited by his daughter*, p. 128.

[34] Ibid., p. 136.

way toward it. The thousands in that part of Glasgow ... made me yearn; so few to care for them and every day more homes built, and more souls arriving, richer and poorer... To leave Collace...would be like Abraham leaving Ur of the Chaldees – that is, nothing but the clear call of God of glory would effect it; but this seems to me like His call.[35]

Ultimately, he accepted the call and remained as the pastor of Finnieston Free Church for the rest of his life.

Bonar's pastorate was noted for his tireless preaching and evangelistic work. In contrast to men like Guthrie and Begg, he does not seem to have been particularly interested in the social questions of his day. While he had genuine concern for the poor people to whom he ministered, he was more agitated by their spiritual needs rather than their living conditions. While some of his ministerial brethren were actively campaigning for improved living conditions, Bonar was busy preaching, teaching and evangelizing. It has been suggested that it was a 'concern for personal religion' that animated him and certainly this theme is deeply imbedded in his diaries and sermons.[36] It is also clear that his confident expectation that the second coming of Christ was imminent made him more concerned for evangelistic outreach than he was about social reform. Bonar's parish work received public acclaim during his lifetime. He was awarded an honorary Doctor of Divinity degree by the University of Glasgow in 1874 and served as Moderator of the Free Church in 1878, a role which he accepted with considerable reluctance.

---

[35] Marjorie Bonar, *Reminiscences of Andrew A. Bonar, DD* (London: Hodder & Stoughton 1895), pp. 30–1.

[36] K.R. Ross. 'Bonar, Andrew', in *Dictionary of Scottish Church History and Theology*, p. 84.

THE MOODY AND SANKEY CAMPAIGNS

In November 1873, the American evangelist Dwight L. Moody and his musical companion Ira D. Sankey arrived in Scotland.[37] They had previously toured England in 1867 where their mission had met with considerable success and had received the blessing of the English Baptist pastor C.H. Spurgeon. Moody and Sankey's mission in Scotland had an almost instant impact. They drew huge crowds to their evangelistic meetings and Moody was invited to preach at Andrew Bonar's church in Glasgow. This was the beginning of a friendship and partnership which would last for the rest of Bonar's life. Bonar was attracted by Moody's eloquence and by his ability to draw large crowds to hear the gospel preached. While Bonar's Finnieston congregation had been enjoying steady growth, he recognised that Moody was reaching many more people with his message. As a result, Andrew and his brother Horatius quickly became two of Moody and Sankey's strongest supporters in Scotland. Looking back on the campaign, Bonar stated that those

> ... in Glasgow who have watched this movement and taken part in it, are aware that our testimony cannot have much influence on those to whom we are strangers, but to any of those who will listen we should like to testify to the permanence of the work among us, and any who will come and see for themselves will at once discover how extensive and sincere this work has been. Personally I can say, and many of my brethren are prepared to make the same statement, that the fruit of last year has been as satisfactory

[37] For a brief biography of Moody, see L.W. Dorsett, 'Moody, Dwight Lyman' in Timothy Larsen (ed.), *Biographical Dictionary of Evangelicals* (Leicester:InterVarsity Press, 2003), pp. 433–40.

in every way as at any period in my ministry, while it has also had some new features of special interest. There have indeed been cases of backsliding, but what of that? Is not the parable of the sower true in all ages? [38]

While Bonar's views were shared by some Free Church ministers, there were dissenting voices. Chief among these was Dr John Kennedy, Minister of Dingwall Free Church. Kennedy, in the days before blogging and as was the custom of the age, launched an attack in print, publishing a pamphlet entitled *Hyper-Evangelism 'Another Gospel' Though a Mighty Power: A Review of the Recent Religious Movement in Scotland*.[39]

In the pamphlet, Kennedy outlined a number of concerns about Moody's underlying Arminian theology as well as his style of evangelism. He believed that the success of the campaigns were more apparent than real. He feared that the enthusiasm caused by these meetings would cause people to make emotional decisions to follow Christ, but which would not result in genuinely changed lives that were characterised by holy living. Rather, Kennedy believed that real change could only be brought about by the power of the Holy Spirit through the regular and consistent preaching of the Word of God in the context of the local church. As we shall see in chapter eleven, Kennedy's own ministry in Dingwall had been blessed over the course of his long ministry there, so he was speaking from considerable experience.

---

[38] William Revell Moody, *The Life of Dwight L. Moody* (New York: Fleming H. Revell, 1900), p. 202.

[39] John Kennedy, *Hyper-Evangelism 'Another Gospel' Though a Mighty Power: A Review of the Recent Religious Movements in Scotland* (Edinburgh: Duncan Grant & Co, 1874).

Kennedy was also concerned that Moody's style of evangelism placed a greater influence on humanity's ability to respond to the gospel than on the sovereignty of God. Equally telling, he critiqued Moody for what sometimes appeared to be a formula-based method of conversion.

> Men, anxious to secure a certain result, and determined to produce it, do not like to think of a controlling will, to whose sovereign behests they must submit, and of the necessity of almighty power being at work, whose action must be regulated by another will than theirs. Certain processes must lead to certain results. This selfish earnestness, this proud resolve to make a manageable business of conversion work, is intolerant of any recognition of the sovereignty of God. 'Go to the street', said the great American evangelist to a group of young ladies who were seated before him, 'and lay your hand on the shoulder of every drunkard you meet, and tell him that God loves him, and that Christ died for him; and if you do so, I see no reason why there should be an unconverted drunkard in Edinburgh for forty-eight hours'.[40]

Kennedy went on to critique Moody and Sankey's use of hymns and instrumental music in worship, fearing that if these became accepted in the setting of evangelistic campaigns, they would soon make their way into the church. In this regard, his fears proved to be correct.

Andrew Bonar's brother Horatius, who was also a Free Church minister, published a vigorous response to Kennedy in the same year. In *The Old Gospel: Not 'Another Gospel' but the Power of God Unto Salvation. A Reply to Dr Kennedy's Pamphlet 'Hyper-Evangelism'*, Horatius Bonar argued that conversions could and did happen when, where

[40] Ibid., p. 13.

and how God chose and that looking back through the pages of history, God had used many different preachers to bring people to Christ. 'He wrought not only by the Calvinist Whitefield, but the Arminian Wesley'. [41] Andrew Bonar was not persuaded by Kennedy's critique of Moody and Sankey and would subsequently travel to America to speak at conferences with Moody. He also helped the evangelist on future tours of Scotland, and continued to maintain that Moody's contribution to the advance of the gospel had been a positive one.

Kenneth R. Ross has suggested that the very different contexts in which Kennedy and the Bonar brothers were working helps to explain their different responses to Moody's revivalism. In Kennedy's case, he was ministering in a rural parish where the church was still very much at the heart of the community and where the vast majority of the population attended worship services on a weekly basis. In the case of the Bonars, they were working in city churches which were only reaching a fraction of the population, and as a result, the 'paramount need of the day ... was for missionary work which would lead to the recovery of the "lapsed masses"'. [42]

Ross has also argued that this '... disagreement proved to be a marker in the parting of the ways between the Highland Calvinism and Lowland Evangelicalism which had been united in the Free Church at the Disruption'. [43] While

---

[41] Horatius Bonar, *The Old Gospel: Not 'Another Gospel' but the Power of God Unto Salvation. A Reply to Dr Kennedy's Pamphlet 'Hyper-Evangelism'* (London: Andrew Elliot, 1874), p. 10.

[42] Kenneth R. Ross, 'Calvinists in Controversy: John Kennedy, Horatius Bonar and the Moody Mission of 1873–4', in *Scottish Bulletin of Evangelical Theology*, v. 9, no. 1 (Spring 1991), p. 54.

[43] Ibid., p. 52.

Bonar's rejection of the idea that the Pope was the Antichrist, his embracing of Moody and Sankey revivalism, and his passionate premillennial views were all departures from the teachings of the *Westminster Standards*, we should be careful not to push Ross's argument too far. On some issues Andrew Bonar fell strictly in line with more conventional Free Church beliefs. Surveying all of his life, he ultimately resisted union with the United Presbyterian Church and expressed real concerns over liberal views on the nature of Scripture during the Robertson Smith case. It is also important to note that there were some ministers in the Highlands who embraced the Bonars' broader evangelicalism, and, equally, there were ministers in the south who shared the Highland and more confessional vision of the Free Church.

ANDREW BONAR AND THE FREE CHURCH

When Andrew Bonar died on 30 December 1892, *The Scotsman* commented in its obituary that

> The Rev. Gentleman was one of the most catholic spirited of ministers, and was always willing to hold out the hand of fellowship to brethren to whatever denomination they might belong ... Indeed one who knew him well has summed up his character in a single sentence: 'He had many friends, but not a single enemy'.[44]

It is clear that Andrew Bonar's life and ministry were animated more by evangelical piety than by confessional orthodoxy and this sometimes caused him to move in directions that not everyone in the Free Church was comfortable

---

[44] 'The Late Rev. Dr Andrew A. Bonar, Glasgow', *The Scotsman Digital Archive, December 31st, 1892*, http://archive.scotsman.com/ (accessed 16 May 2009).

with. But while opinions may differ on the wisdom of some of Bonar's broader involvements, what cannot be doubted is that his 'great desire was the salvation of sinners at home and abroad, and this to the glory of God'. [45] Also, it is a testimony to the breadth and strength of the Free Church in the nineteenth century that it was able to embrace a man who held diverse views on some issues.

[45] 'Andrew Bonar', *Banner of Truth Online, http://www.banneroftruth. org/pages/articles/article_detail.php?642* (accessed 14 November 2009).

JOHN DUNCAN, LL.D.

Home & Macdonald. L

9

JOHN DUNCAN
MISSIONARY AND SCHOLAR

'He was at once one of the most profound and versatile
of scholars, one of the humblest of believers, and one of
the most erratic and absentminded of men'.[1]

JOHN 'Rabbi' Duncan is depicted in David Octavious
Hill's picture of the first Free Church General Assembly
as an elderly bearded gentleman, looking rather 'like a character in a fairytale – or maybe a Hebrew patriarch from a
ghetto'. [2] Even though he was not actually present at the
General Assembly in 1843, John Duncan was, nonetheless,
an important figure in the early years of the Free Church.
His ecclesiastical career included a pastorate in Glasgow
and missionary work in Hungary and Italy. He ended his
career as the occupant of the Chair of Hebrew and Oriental
Languages at New College, Edinburgh.

He was a somewhat eccentric figure, well known for
both his brilliant mind and unconventional teaching style.
He was also known as a preacher who deeply touched the
hearts and minds of his hearers. Unlike most of the other
men featured in this book, Duncan's scholarly gifts were
not displayed in print since he published next to nothing

[1] John MacLeod, *Scottish Theology in Relation to Church History*, pp.
282–3.

[2] John Fowler, *Mr Hill's Big Picture: The Day That Changed Scotland
Forever Captured on Canvas* (Edinburgh: St Andrew Press, 2006), p. 10.

during his lifetime. When he was once asked why he hadn't written any books he is said to have replied, 'I cannot write, I'm just a talker'.[3] Following his death, some of his admirers collected and published some of his lectures, sermons and sayings. Therefore we are heavily dependent on these posthumous works and accompanying sympathetic biographical materials to assemble a picture of this unique man. Even David Brown, his lifelong friend and principal biographer, concedes that

> … one who wrote nothing of any general value, whose correspondence was unusually scanty and mostly of a very ordinary nature, and whose private papers consist almost exclusively of mere scraps on the back of letters or printed papers, might yet be one of the most remarkable men of his age is possible; but to attempt, in a Memoir of his life, to give the public any adequate evidence of this is surely a hazardous undertaking.[4]

With the passage of time, the memory of John Duncan has faded and anyone interested in assessing his impact on the church does not have a great deal of material with which to work. Despite this paucity of information, John Duncan is an important figure in the history of the Free Church.

---

[3] John M. Brentnall, *Just a Talker: Sayings of John 'Rabbi' Duncan* (Edinburgh: Banner of Truth, 1997), p. xv.

[4] David Brown, *Life of the Late John Duncan LLD, Professor of Hebrew and Oriental Languages, New College, Edinburgh* (Edinburgh: Edmonston and Douglas, 1872), p. v. In addition to his biography of John Duncan, his books included the six volume *Commentary Critical, Experimental and Practical on the Old and New Testaments* written in conjunction with R. Jamieson and A.R. Fausset. He also wrote the classic nineteenth-century critique of premillennialism and defence of post-millennialism. David Brown served the Free Church as Principal of the Free Church College in Aberdeen.

His passion for missions had a major impact on Eastern Europe and helped to fire the imagination of a generation. His equal passion for the study of the Bible in its original languages demonstrated the Free Church's commitment to taking the Scriptures seriously.

THE EARLY YEARS
1796–1813

John Duncan was born at Gilcomston in the Parish of Old Machar in the city of Aberdeen. It is believed that he was born in 1796, but his birth was not recorded in the parish register. David Brown rather quaintly says in a footnote that

> ... he was born in 1797 was his own impression; but he was far from accurate in such matters, as we shall presently see, and a comparison of certain fixed dates leaves no doubt in my mind that the date [of 1796] ... is the correct one.[5]

His father, John, was a shoemaker and his mother, Ann Mutch, was the daughter of a wealthy father. The Duncans belonged to the Secession Church and it was said of John senior that he was like '... a detached boulder of granite, hard and solitary ... an upright man, walking in the fear of God, strict in his Secession principles, rugged and stern, in family discipline inexorable'.[6] Ann appears to have been a warmer person, someone 'full of human kindness and divine grace'. [7] Another of

---

[5] Ibid., p. 1.

[6] A Moody Stuart, *Recollections of the Late John Duncan LLD. Professor of Hebrew and Oriental Languages, New College, Edinburgh* (Edinburgh: Edmonston and Douglas, 1872), p. 4.

[7] Ibid.

Duncan's biographers, A. Moody Stuart,[8] says of these two very different people that the

> ... extremely opposite characters of John and Ann Duncan throw light on the very peculiar character of their only surviving son: the inflexible determination of the father underlying the tenderness of the mother; and the two elements co-exisiting in a manner rarely paralleled.[9]

Although John and Ann had several children, only their eldest son John survived infancy.

Ann herself died of consumption when John was about six years old. Within a couple of years Duncan's father had married again, this time to Sophia Sutherland, a woman of Episcopalian background. When the couple were married according to the Episcopalian liturgy, Duncan was disciplined by the Secession Church. Despite this inauspicious introduction to the Seceders, Sophia came to embrace the Secession Church after her marriage. She was a good step-mother to John and he reputedly regarded her 'with the utmost gratitude, affection and reverence'.[10] He was considered a 'weakly boy' and while still very young survived an attack of small-pox which 'deprived him of the sight of one eye, a defect that was permanent'.[11]

John Duncan began his education at the local grammar school. There he learned the rudiments of reading through

---

[8] Alexander Moody Stuart was Duncan's Minister at St Luke's Church, Edinburgh. His *Recollections* were published in the same year as David Brown's more detailed biography.

[9] Ibid., pp. 4–5.

[10] Brown, *Life of the Late John Duncan LLD*, p. 7.

[11] James Steven Sinclair, *Rich Gleanings After the Vintage from 'Rabbi' Duncan* (London: Chas. J. Thynne & Jarvis, 1925), p. 10.

a study of the Catechisms and the Bible. His interest in languages and metaphysics developed early and he was once caught reading a copy of Aristotle under his desk. He completed five years of study at the grammar school and in 1810 received a small bursary to attend the University of Aberdeen. He did not display a great deal of promise while pursuing his MA degree; indeed some of his fellow students considered him slow witted. In 1813 he applied and was accepted as a Divinity Student in the Constitutional Associate Presbytery of the Secession Church. He then went on to complete the Arts course in 1814 before turning his attention to being trained for the ministry.

DIVINITY STUDENT AND CONVERSION
1814–30

Little is known of John Duncan's studies between 1814 and 1816 except that in 1816 he decided to transfer from the Secession Church to the Church of Scotland. His father and minister were very concerned about this step but were much more troubled by the fact that Duncan, by his own admission, had become an atheist. At this stage of his life, he is said to have

> ... cast away the Bible; and this ground once lost, he sank down, through unbelief, deism, pantheism, into material atheism, whence there was no longer depth to sink; denying the existence of God, of angelic spirit, of [the] human soul.[12]

In later life, Duncan would look upon atheism as being the great enemy of Christianity and much more damaging than

---

[12] Moody Stuart, *Recollections of the Late John Duncan LLD*, pp. 8–9.

Roman Catholicism. Given the anti-popery feelings of his day, it is somewhat startling to hear a man of Duncan's background saying of the Roman Church that 'no doubt many a devout soul has found spiritual nourishment in that church'.[13]

As he started his studies with the Church of Scotland, he slowly began what would be a long journey toward orthodox Christianity. In Dr Mearn's Divinity class, he gave up atheism and instead embraced a form of Unitarianism. It was during this period of his life that Duncan particularly devoted himself to the study and acquisition of languages. He displayed an enormous facility in several languages, but Hebrew was his 'chief delight', and he was able to support himself by tutoring some of his fellow students.[14] In addition to the private tutoring, he also accepted teaching positions in schools in Darlington in Yorkshire and later in Edinburgh.

Duncan completed the Divinity course in 1821. The next logical step would have been for him to become licensed to preach in the Church of Scotland. However, he chose not to seek licensure since he did not accept the basic doctrines of the Christian faith and could not subscribe to the *Westminster Confession of Faith*. Moody Stuart says of this period of his life that to

> ... an onlooker, his long years as a student seem to present a life of intolerable hardship, which only a will of iron could have passed through...he was often steeped in poverty, badly fed and uncomfortably clothed; with no living faith beyond the grave, and the hope distant, and uncertain, of at last reaching some living in the ministry.[15]

[13] Ibid., p. 11.

[14] Brown, *Life of the Late John Duncan LLD*, p. 82.

[15] Moody Stuart, *Recollections of the Late John Duncan LLD*, p. 18.

Four years later, in 1825, Duncan finally convinced himself that he should proceed to be licensed, although he still did not believe the *Confession's* explicit teachings or much of the Bible either. He took the view that this step was appropriate because he would not preach against any doctrines taught in the *Confession*. That he was able to pass his licensure exams with this extremely low view of what was required says as much about the low standards in the Aberdeen Presbytery as it does the state of Duncan's heart.

In 1826, Aberdeen was visited by Caesar Malan, a minister originally from Switzerland. Malan had been a minister of the State Church in Switzerland but had been deposed because of his evangelical sympathies. He had considered applying for admission to the Church of Scotland but they, in what can only be considered colossal short-sightedness, insisted that he would have to take an extended course of studies at one of the Scottish universities. Recognising his need to be under the jurisdiction and oversight of a church, Malan applied to and was received by the Secession Church which accepted his training and ministerial credentials. Duncan's biographer, David Brown, heard Malan preach in Edinburgh and it had such a powerful effect upon Brown that he insisted that John Duncan meet with Malan. At the meeting, Malan challenged Duncan's unbelief and his clinging to philosophy rather than to the message of the Bible. Under the relentless argumentation of Malan, Duncan's views underwent a dramatic change. He later told a friend that the

> ... next day, as I sat down to study ... I became suddenly the passive recipient of all the truths which I had heard and had been taught in my childhood. I sat there unmoving

for hours, and *they came and preached themselves to me.* There was now no investigation such as I had desired; but presentation of the truth to me passive. And I felt, sitting there, as if in that hour I had got matter for sermons for a lifetime.[16]

Sadly, Duncan's feelings of peace did not last and within two years he spoke of a 'second conversion' which established his faith further. It has been pointed out that he

> ... retained a lifelong dread of superficial Christianity, often entertaining doubts as to the authenticity of his own faith. He never enjoyed a permanent sense of assurance, and although this experience proved painful for himself and his family, it gave him great empathy for others and unusual depth in his evangelistic ministry.[17]

Between 1828 and 1830, Duncan remained in Aberdeen, continuing his private tutoring work and accepting opportunities to preach as they were offered to him. One of the families where he served as tutor was the Towers family, and Duncan became attracted to their daughter Janet. Despite the fact that he was extremely poor and the Towers much wealthier, Duncan proposed marriage, but his proposal was rejected. He did not, however, give up hope and he proposed again two years later and this time was accepted. The engagement was a lengthy one and his biographers state that the surviving letters between John and Janet show him seeking to teach Greek to his fiancée!

---

[16] Brown, *Life of the Late John Duncan LLD*, p. 155.

[17] John S. Ross, 'The Legacy of John Duncan', *International Bulletin of Missionary Research*, v. 29, n. 3 (Jul 2005), p. 150.

Ministry in Perthshire and Glasgow
1830–40

In 1830, Duncan was chosen to be the minister of the Chapel of Persie, in the Parish of Bendochy, Perthshire. It was a small congregation and considered to be a 'poor living'. Because it was only a preaching station rather than a fully fledged parish church, Duncan was not ordained to his work there. Reviews of his labours were somewhat mixed. While

> ... he was much liked by the pious, and also by the intelligent portion of the congregation, but not so well liked by others, as he was rather unsparing in his condemnation of worldly maxims and customs; the morality he inculcated was rather high for some, and on this account they were ready to take advantage of his oddities.[18]

He strongly resisted the establishment of a dancing school in the area which he believed would lower the spiritual tone, particularly among the young. Other accounts indicate that he also got himself into trouble by resisting the inclusion of dances following wedding services. These and other actions lead to the conclusion that in his youthful enthusiasm, he may not have always displayed sufficient pastoral prudence and sensitivity.

In July 1831, Duncan was asked to relocate to Glasgow to take up the position of English assistant to the Rev. Robert Clark at Duke Street Gaelic Chapel. The minister of the chapel was in failing health and welcomed Duncan's assistance. His duties included a lecture on Sabbath afternoon as well as one during the week. Again he received a mixed reception, with some appreciating both the style of

---

[18] Brown, *Life of the Late John Duncan LLD*, p. 241.

his lectures as well as their content, while others thought that his preaching 'was too abstract for most men'. One friend of Duncan's commented that 'he had lived abstractions till they had come to exercise over him the power of concrete realities'. [19] Gradually, however, his preaching improved. Moody Stuart notes that Duncan's

> ... exposition of Scripture, when he did not allow himself to linger over a single verse, but took a psalm or a passage of some length, was eminently of the very highest character, and in its kind quite unequalled by any exposition to be found elsewhere.[20]

As Duncan became more confident in his work, he began to attract a group of people around him who were anxious that he find his own church which would then allow him to be ordained. The church extension movement, which was motivated by the growth of the Evangelical party in the Church of Scotland, was now under way and several of his friends persuaded the publisher William Collins to fund the building of a church for Duncan. Collins' only proviso was that the new parish should be created in one of the poorer areas of the city. While Milton Parish Church was being erected, the congregation met in a Nile Street School. Duncan was ordained on 28 April 1836 with Dr Robert Buchanan presiding. Buchanan later remembered one particular moment during the service. When Duncan was asked the prescribed question

> ... are not zeal for the honour of God, love to Jesus Christ and desire of saving souls, your great motives and chief

---

[19] Moody Stuart, *Recollections of the Late John Duncan LLD,* 39.

[20] Ibid., p. 39–40.

inducements to enter into the functions of the holy ministry and not worldly designs and interests? Instead of simply bowing his head in token of assent, he said slowly with a tremulous voice, 'I hope it is so'. [21]

On January 18, 1837, John Duncan finally married Janet Towers. Mrs. Duncan had an immediate impact on her husband. Several people observed an 'increased punctuality, tidiness and general cheerfulness' in their minister! [22] In March 1838, Janet gave birth to a daughter whom they called Annie.[23] In 1839, even though she was pregnant again, Janet worked hard on raising funds for and distributing coal to some of the poor in the parish. While engaged in this work, she caught a chill and then a baby girl was born prematurely and died almost immediately. A few days later, on 24 January 1839, Janet Duncan also died.

Despite his grief at the loss of his wife and daughter, Duncan continued working. Milton Parish Church began to grow under his leadership and he attracted the attention of the wider church. John Kennedy, while he was still an Aberdeen Divinity student, had the opportunity to hear Duncan preach one evening. He said of the experience that while 'the light was not very good [in the building] the brilliance of the sermon, in close reasoning and soul-stirring power, I'll never forget'. [24]

---

[21] Brown, *Life of the Late John Duncan LLD*, p. 256.

[22] Ibid., p. 259.

[23] Annie married in the summer of 1861 and moved with her husband to the West Indies. They had two children and Annie died in 1864.

[24] Sinclair, *Rich Gleanings After the Vintage from 'Rabbi' Duncan*, p. 7.

MISSIONARY PREPARATION AND SERVICE
1840–3

As has already been noted in the chapter on Andrew Bonar, the Church of Scotland and later the Free Church had a particular interest in missionary work among the Jews. In 1838 The Church of Scotland General Assembly had passed an Act drawing the attention of the wider church to the need to focus on Jewish evangelisation. It established two committees, one in Glasgow and the other in Edinburgh, to carry out the work. In 1839, Duncan received a formal offer from the Glasgow committee 'to be employed as an agent of the Church, either at home or abroad, for the promotion of Christianity among the Jews'. [25] His first task was to look into what special training might be required to properly train missionaries for Jewish evangelism. However, before he could begin this work, another opportunity for service presented itself.

In October 1839, the Chair of Oriental Languages at the University of Glasgow became vacant. After seeking and receiving the permission of the Glasgow Committee, Duncan submitted his application to the university. He began his letter of application in this way:

> Induced by a desire to promote the glory of God, the good of the Church of which I have the honour to be a Minister, the welfare of the house of Israel, and the interests of Eastern learning, I take the liberty of offering myself as a Candidate for the Chair of Oriental Languages ...[26]

Duncan's application went on to describe his knowledge of many languages, his 'daily and delighted study of the

---

[25] Brown, *Life of the Late John Duncan LLD*, p. 281.

[26] Ibid., p. 284.

Hebrew Bible', and an in-depth knowledge of 'the principal Rabbinical writers'. [27] As further evidence of his scholarly gifts, it is also important to note that the previous year he had published a British edition of Edward Robinson's *Lexicon of the Greek and English New Testament*. While there can be little doubt that he had the necessary knowledge, he was ultimately unsuccessful in his application. However, his linguistic gifts were formally recognised when he was awarded the degree of LLD by the University of Aberdeen in 1840.

In July 1840, it was decided to appoint Duncan as the Church of Scotland's first official missionary to the Jews. While Bonar and M'Cheyne's 'Mission of Inquiry' had recommended the establishment of this mission in Palestine, the church decided differently. While many argued that Palestine was the obvious choice, there were a considerable number of people who insisted that the mission should be established in Eastern Europe. So it was agreed that the Rev. Daniel Edward would be sent to Moldavia, and Duncan, with a team of missionaries, would go to Budapest.

There were three reasons for choosing Budapest. First, there was a significant population of educated Jews in Hungary and it was hoped that Duncan's scholarly gifts could be used to reach them. Second, a significant number of Scottish labourers were then working in Hungary, and these workers could form the nucleus of a congregation which would act as a base for missionary work. Third, ministering to the Scottish labourers in Budapest gave the mission legal standing. While the Hapsburg administration were opposed to Roman Catholics converting to Protestantism, and rarely

---

[27] Ibid., pp. 284–5.

allowed people to change their faith, they did not object to a minister from Scotland coming in to provide pastoral care to the Scots who were working there.

In September 1840, Robert Candlish applied to the Glasgow Presbytery of the Church of Scotland, on behalf of the Assembly's Committee for the Conversion of the Jews, to have Duncan released from his pastoral charge in Milton. On 16 May Duncan was installed as a missionary at a special service held at St George's Church, Glasgow. He then left for Budapest in August 1841. Accompanying him were three other student missionaries and his new wife, Janet Douglas-Torrance, who he had married earlier in the year.[28] While the principal objective of the mission was evangelisation of the Jews, Duncan decided that the best approach was to build up and support the local church in Hungary. He was concerned about its weakness and in a letter home he wrote that this was 'the most serious of all impediments ... in the way of Israel's conversion'. [29]

It has been suggested that Duncan's time in Hungary 'was one of the happier periods of his life'.[30] His first task was to acquire the Magyar language and this he was able to do within three months of his arrival. He also reached out to the Hungarian Reformed and Lutheran Churches. Duncan was not narrowly sectarian and was more concerned that the message of Christianity should be disseminated than in the establishment of a particularly Scottish Presbyterian

---

[28] Little is known of Janet Douglas-Torrance's background and of her courtship with Duncan. She had previously been married to a surgeon from Kilmarnock and had two daughters from that marriage.

[29] Brown, *Life of the Late John Duncan LLD*, p. 319.

[30] Brentnall, *Just a Talker: Sayings of John 'Rabbi' Duncan*, p. xxvi.

mission. Another key task was making contact with the Arch-duchess Maria Dorothea, who was a Württemberg pietist and keen supporter of the Protestant cause. David Brown notes that there were several examples of her timely intervention that saved the missionaries from imprisonment and harass-ment and she '... displayed equal promptitude and decision, whenever the mission was imperilled'. [31]

Duncan quickly established English language services for the Scottish workers in Budapest. These services also attracted some Jews who were interested in improving their English. He and the other missionaries also began to attend synagogue services. In this way, Duncan quickly developed cordial friendships within the Jewish community. One of the strongest relationships that he developed was with the Chief Rabbi Low Schwab. Their friendship became so strong that Duncan was invited to the wedding of the Chief Rabbi's daughter. John Ross has noted that 'Duncan was in the habit of spending whole days in receiving visitors and bringing into play his remarkable conversational and persuasive powers'.[32] This gift of hospitality exposed many people to Christianity without having it forced upon them, and slowly but surely conversions began to take place. Among these first converts were the Saphir family, includ-ing the young Adolph Saphir, who would become a highly respected Presbyterian Minister, being ordained by the Presbyterian Church of Ireland in 1854.

After being in Budapest for only little more than a year, Duncan's health broke down and he was sent to recuper-ate in Italy. He and his wife spent a year there where he

---

[31] Brown, *Life of the Late John Duncan LLD*, pp. 310–11.

[32] Ross, 'The Legacy of John Duncan', p. 152.

did some preaching and evangelistic work before returning to Budapest in June 1843. On his way back, he learned of the Disruption when he was given a copy of Hugh Miller's *Witness* newspaper. When he reached Budapest, he received a letter from the Free Church inviting him to take the Hebrew Chair at New College, Edinburgh, which he accepted. Although his time as a missionary was relatively brief, it nevertheless had a lasting impact on the Hungarian Church. John Ross suggests that perhaps

> ... Duncan's major legacy is best understood in terms of the people who, through his witness, though not his alone, embraced Christianity as the fulfilment of Old Testament promise.[33]

Duncan was also responsible for developing better relationships between various branches of the church in Eastern Europe. In fact, some have gone so far as to say that the presence of Duncan and the other Scottish missionaries there was 'the catalyst for the revival of Protestant spiritual life in Hungary'.[34] After his return to Scotland, Duncan continued to correspond with missionaries in Eastern Europe. He was also able to make occasional visits to see how the work was progressing. One contemporary source summed up the ongoing work in this way:

> This favoured station continues to manifest every encouraging appearance: the little church at [Budapest], chiefly gathered out from among the lost sheep of the house of Israel, still gives evidence of its Divine birth

---

[33] Ibid.

[34] Ibid., p. 153.

by its faith, love, zeal and patience in many trials from within and without.[35]

Looking back over Duncan's brief missionary career, there can be little doubt that his linguistic gifts, coupled with the hospitality of his home and even his eccentric personality, left a positive mark in Eastern Europe. It is, therefore, not an exaggeration to suggest that 'few non-Jewish missionaries have had such an impact on missions to Jews'.[36]

PROFESSOR
1843–70

As has already been noted in the chapters on Chalmers, Candlish and Cunningham, the Free Church acted at its very first General Assembly to establish a theological college. When the Education Committee reported their recommendations on Professorial Appointments to the Assembly, they concluded that

> Dr Duncan's unrivalled attainments in Hebrew and Oriental Literature connected with the rare art of kindling to enthusiasm the grateful student, secured him the nomination to the Hebrew Chair.[37]

Duncan arrived back in Scotland and immediately began work at New College. While no one doubted Duncan's

---

[35] The *Jewish Missionary Herald* of November, 1846. Quoted in John S. Ross, 'The Most Fruitful of All Missionary Work' *New Horizons*, http://www.opc.org/nh.html?article_id=459 (accessed 16 June 2009).

[36] Walter Riggans, 'Duncan, John', in Gerald H. Anderson, *Biographical Dictionary of Christian Missions* (Grand Rapids, MI: W.B. Eerdmans, 1999), p. 188.

[37] Baillie, *Proceedings of the General Assembly of the Free Church of Scotland: With a Sketch of the Proceedings of the Residuary Assembly*, p. 77.

scholarly abilities, particularly in the study of languages, even his most complimentary biographers believed that he was not well suited to the role. David Brown says that as Duncan began his work he was required to teach

> ... two Hebrew classes, a junior and a senior; the latter including Exegetical classes in the Old Testament. Those who were familiar with Dr Duncan's mental habits could not help having serious misgivings as to his success in both these departments ... Capable he was beyond most men of kindling enthusiasm ... but he [lacked] the capacity to initiate a large class in the elements of language and to drill them thoroughly, as junior students require to be, in the structure of the language.[38]

A. Moody Stuart echoes these sentiments and goes even further in saying that Duncan's character and personality also made him unfit for this work.

> It was not that he disliked teaching for he was passionately fond of it; nor was it exactly that he disrelished duty merely as such ... But he failed in the ordinary daily round, partly because he was often carried away intellectually with some engrossing mental interest, or carried away spiritually by an absorbing love of God, or a fearful inquiry into his own standing before Him. But that was not all; there was also a singular weakness of purpose in common things. His feebleness of mind was about as marked in this respect as his intellectual vigour otherwise; he has been called, and truly, a giant in intellect and a child in humility; but he was a child also in weakness of will in ordinary matters.[39]

---

[38] Brown, *Life of the Late John Duncan LLD*, pp. 355–6.

[39] Moody Stuart, *Recollections of the Late John Duncan LLD*, p. 84.

Less than a year after the Duncans returned to Scotland, John Duncan's wife gave birth to a daughter who was named Maria Dorothea, after the Austrian Archduchess who had been so helpful to the mission in Budapest. Duncan developed a very close relationship with his daughter and after her marriage to a Lutheran pastor, Albert Spaeth, she and her father actively corresponded until Duncan's death in 1870.[40] These letters show Duncan in a relaxed and tender light, dispensing advice to his daughter as she negotiated life outside of Scotland and within another church tradition.

Duncan remained at New College from 1843 until his death in 1870. So, for twenty-seven years he taught languages and Old Testament to an entire generation of Free Church students. While he wrote little, there are a few hints as to his approach to his task. When the New College building on The Mound in Edinburgh was opened in 1850, each of the Professors gave a lecture laying out their vision for their discipline. Duncan's published lecture 'The Theology of the Old Testament' gives considerable insight into his thought.[41] At the outset he states that as

... the Holy Scriptures are the source and storehouse of all true and saving knowledge of God – the subject about which Christian theology is conversant – it is of extreme importance for all 'who desire the office of a

---

[40] For a selection of this correspondence, see John S. Ross, ed. 'A Family Correspondence: Letters of John Duncan and His Daughter, Maria Dorothea, and Her Husband, Adolph Spaeth, with Extracts from Maria's Diary', *Reformed Theological Journal (Belfast)* 14 (1998).

[41] All of the lectures were published in *Inauguration of the New College of the Free Church, Edinburgh*. References in this chapter to Duncan's lecture are taken from the version published in James Sinclair's *Rich Gleanings After the Vintage from 'Rabbi' Duncan*.

bishop' to become intimately acquainted with them in those languages in which it pleased the inspiring Spirit to communicate them, by which original documents all versions and comments must be tried, all controversies in the last resort determined, and all difficulties and obscurities, as far as possible, removed.[42]

Duncan went on to decry what he called

... the tendency which in other churches and lands has produced the most deleterious effects – I mean the denial of the inspiration and permanent authority of the Old Testament Scriptures ... To surrender the Old Testament is to surrender also the New, nay virtually to deny the Messiahship of Jesus, who by His appeal to these writings, certifies His high claims with their divine authority.[43]

Duncan was keenly aware of the new directions in biblical criticism that were being explored by German scholars. When one of his students was embarking for studies in Germany, Duncan wrote him a lengthy letter. In it he offered the following pastoral advice:

As for your theological studies, I have no suggestions to make but such as are of a very general nature. In German progressionism (real or supposed) take care not to lose Scottish conservatism. Our theology always based on and ever directly recurring for its proof to Holy Scripture has, as a developed system, a venerable back-leaning on the whole history of theology in the Christian Church from the beginning.[44]

---

[42] Sinclair, *Rich Gleanings After the Vintage from 'Rabbi' Duncan*, p. 281.

[43] Ibid., pp. 283–4.

[44] Brown, *Life of the Late John Duncan LLD*, p. 385.

Having sounded this warning, Duncan went on to state that while he was a conservative at heart and believed that this was the best approach to take in biblical studies, he also claimed that he was

> ... progressive also. For we have not exhausted the oracles of God. I have no wish to fetter Christian liberty of thought. We are commanded to prove all things and hold fast that which is good.[45]

The picture that emerges of Duncan the theologian is that he had an extremely high view of the Bible as the inspired Word of God. He was passionate about the Word being studied as much as possible in the original languages and he believed that the Scriptures were authoritative in providing direction to the church.

If this is what he believed, we need to ask what he actually taught, and this is where the picture becomes darker. Certainly his piety was communicated to his students, but he seems to have been unable to teach either Hebrew or the Old Testament coherently. His biographers relate stories of students who were deeply impressed by his obvious piety but who learned little of substance from him. Duncan's erratic behaviour makes for amusing stories but the fact remains that many Free Church students were not properly equipped to deal with the challenges posed by German biblical scholarship that was beginning to make inroads in Scotland at this time.

Worse than this, when the Free Church recognised that Duncan was incapable of delivering the curriculum, they chose to augment his teaching by the appointment of A.B. Davidson. Unlike Duncan, Davidson was a very effective

---

[45] Ibid., p. 386.

teacher, but whose theology was unorthodox. It has been said of Davidson that he was

> ... an overwhelmingly effective teacher [who] initiated a whole generation of Free Church students into the novelties of the critical method [of biblical studies]. He escaped ecclesiastical censure ... probably because of the rather cryptic and undogmatic fashion in which he broached a contentious topic, and because of the immense affection and esteem which as a man he inspired in colleagues and pupils.[46]

John Macleod accurately assessed this appointment when he wrote that Davidson's

> ... teaching, and even more than his positive teaching, his hints and suggestions, became the source of an alien infusion in Old Testament studies in Scotland. Robertson Smith [then] caught the infection and spread the plague.[47]

John Duncan's death in February 1870 marked the end of an era for the Free Church. He was buried in Grange Cemetery close to the graves of Chalmers and Cunningham. His gravestone was inscribed with a tribute which read:

IN MEMORY OF
THE REV JOHN DUNCAN LLD
PROFESSOR OF HEBREW AND OF ORIENTAL LANGUAGES IN THE
FREE CHURCH COLLEGE, EDINBURGH,
AN EMINENT SCHOLAR AND METAPHYSICIAN,
A PROFOUND THEOLOGIAN,
A MAN OF TENDER PIETY, AND OF A LOWLY AND LOVING SPIRIT
BORN 1796 DIED 1870 [48]

---

[46] N.R. Needham, 'Davidson, Andrew Bruce', in *Dictionary of Scottish Church history and Theology*, p. 235.

[47] John MacLeod, *Scottish Theology in Relation to Church History*, p. 288.

[48] Brown, *Life of the Late John Duncan LLD*, p. 491.

After his death, biblical studies took a very different direction of which Duncan would not have approved. As the church continued to drift there were voices raised in protest, but sadly, they went largely unheeded. C.H. Spurgeon watched the decline in the Free Church's colleges with alarm and wrote:

> The Free Church of Scotland must be for the moment regarded as rushing to the front with its new theology, which is no theology but an opposition to the Word of the Lord. That Church ... has entrusted the training of its future ministers to professors who hold other doctrines than those of its Confession. This is the most suicidal act that a church can commit.[49]

While it would be unfair to hold John Duncan solely responsible for the theological drift which followed him, what is unmistakable is that he failed as a teacher to pass on his own faith and theology. It is surely not without significance that so many

> ... of the Free Church liberals who were to spend much of their careers undermining a great deal of what Duncan's admirers held dear, remembered his contribution when they themselves were his students at New College.[50]

That Duncan was a failure as a professor does not detract from his piety, his linguistic abilities, or his missionary and pastoral work. But his life is a helpful reminder to the

---

[49] C.H. Spurgeon quoted in Grant, 'The heirs of the Disruption in crisis and recovery 1893–1920', p. 6.

[50] James Lachlan MacLeod, *The Second Disruption: The Free Church in Victorian Scotland and the Origins of the Free Presbyterian Church. Scottish historical review monographs series, no. 8.* (East Linton, 2000), p. 44.

church and to the academy that it needs to carefully choose those whom they call to teach. The tragedy of John Duncan comes down to this, it 'would have been more serviceable to his Church and the cause of Christianity had he been allowed to remain in Hungary'. [51]

[51] Hew Scott, *Synod of Glasgow and Ayr. Fasti ecclesiae Scoticanae: The succession of ministers in the Church of Scotland from the Reformation. Revised and continued to the present time under the superintendence of a committee* (Edinburgh: Oliver & Boyd, 1920), p. 425.

ALEXANDER DUFF, D.D.

Home & Macdonald

10

ALEXANDER DUFF
PIONEER MISSIONARY

Alexander Duff ... [exercised] an influence upon the
future of India more potent than that of any man of
his time.[1]

O NE of the marks of the early Free Church was a passion
for missionary work. Alexander Duff was in the fore-
front of this movement both at home and abroad. In 1830,
he was sent by the Church of Scotland to India to head up a
mission there and his efforts in India did much to shape the
subsequent educational system in that country. His life also
inspired lively interest in missionary work in the church at
home. After the Disruption in 1843, Duff associated himself
with the Free Church and continued his missionary work. His
furloughs were spent in tireless travel where he sought to raise
the profile of the church's missionary work in Britain, North
America and Europe. He concluded his career as the first Professor of Evangelistic Theology at New College, Edinburgh. It
is important to note at the outset that the foundation of Duff's
life was his passion for preaching the gospel. The sermons
he preached in India were effective in persuading many to
embrace the Christian faith; his speaking and writing while
on furlough did much to persuade many of the necessity of
praying for and supporting the cause of world missions.

---

[1] W. Pakenham Walsh, *Modern Heroes of the Mission Field* (New York:
T. Whittaker, 1882), p. 248.

Early Life
1806–21

Alexander Duff was born at Auchnahyle Farm in the parish of Moulin, Perthshire on 26 April 1806. His parents, James Duff and Jean Rattray, were native Gaelic speakers. However, English was being used increasingly in the parish and services were held in both languages in the church. By the age of three, Alexander could switch back and forth easily between the languages. This early facility in language acquisition served him well later in life.

Alexander began his education at a small school that served the villages of Pitlochry and Moulin where the local schoolmaster is said to have been 'an extremely useless teacher'. [2] The important influences on Duff at this stage were his parents and his church. His early life has been described as being intensely religious. His father seems to have been 'fed … on a strong diet of readings from Foxe's *Book of Martyrs* and Gaelic poetry'. [3] The religious poetry of Dugald Buchanan had a particularly strong impact on the young Duff as some of the poems gave him vivid nightmares about divine judgment. His nineteenth-century biographer claims that these dreams so affected him that they

> … threw him into earnest prayer for pardon, and [this] was followed by what he long after described as something like the assurance of acceptance through the atoning blood of his Lord and Saviour Jesus Christ. [4]

[2] A.A. Millar, *Alexander Duff of India* (Edinburgh: Canongate Press, 1992), p. 5.

[3] Stuart Piggin and John Roxborogh, *The St Andrews Seven: The Finest Flowering of Missionary Zeal in Scottish History* (Edinburgh: Banner of Truth, 1985), p. 15.

[4] George Smith, *The Life of Alexander Duff* (New York: American Tract Society 1880), p. 13.

In 1814, when Duff was eight, he was sent to the school at Kirkmichael. This was further from home, but the teaching was excellent. He was boarded at the school during the week and returned home on the weekends. Duff found himself in a highly competitive environment where the schoolmaster challenged his students to achieve their very best, and all of the twelve pupils in his class would eventually be awarded bursaries to attend St Andrews University.

At the age of fourteen, Duff again changed schools, this time moving to Perth Grammar School where he studied for one year. He excelled particularly in the study of Latin and Greek. When he graduated at the top of his class, he was given a copy of Milton's *Paradise Lost* which would have a significant impact on both his theology and writing style. For much of his life he carried a pocket edition of the book and read from it almost every day.[5]

ST ANDREWS UNIVERSITY
1821—9

Fifteen-year-old Alexander Duff arrived in St Andrews in October 1821. The nearly eight years he would spend there would significantly shape the direction of his life. Duff seems to have been an eager student from the moment he began his studies, although the environment wasn't particularly conducive to learning. The university town has been described as a 'backwater [that had been] by-passed by the industrial development'[6] then revolutionising Scottish society. The university was firmly in the hands of the

---

[5] Ibid., p. 17.

[6] Piggin and Roxborogh, *The St Andrews Seven: The Finest Flowering of Missionary Zeal in Scottish History*, p. 7.

Moderate party in the Church of Scotland and it 'was in dilapidated condition'. [7]

Both the tone and substance of university life at St Andrews changed dramatically in 1823 when Thomas Chalmers was appointed to the Chair of Moral Philosophy. As we saw in chapter two, Chalmers had been a successful minister in Glasgow and came to St Andrews with a desire to impact the lives of young men who were training for pastoral ministry. The effect of Chalmers on his students was a powerful one. A.A. Millar notes that

> ... instead of the dry-as-dust utterances that the aged lec-
> turers read from yellowing pages, here was live creative
> thought, the actual contemporary labours of a great mind
> which riveted the co-operation of others ... It would be
> impossible not to follow where such a leader led the way ...[8]

Duff achieved some significant academic successes during his years at St Andrews. He learned several languages, including Arabic, Chinese, German, Sanskrit, Persian and Russian. In addition, he achieved honours in philosophy and theology and began to develop skills as a public speaker. His academic success was fuelled in part by his heavy usage of the St Andrews University Library. An examination of library records shows that Duff borrowed more books from the library than any of his contemporaries.[9]

During the college session of 1824–5, Duff and several other students founded a Student Missionary Society at

---

[7] Ibid., p. 7.

[8] Millar, *Alexander Duff of India*, p. 12.

[9] Piggin and Roxborogh, *The St Andrews Seven: The Finest Flowering of Missionary Zeal in Scottish History*, p. 35.

St Andrews. A number of the professors were opposed to this move, but the students found an enthusiastic supporter in Thomas Chalmers. Originally confined to Arts students, the membership of the organisation was soon expanded to include Divinity students and by the end of the school year there was an active membership of seventy.[10] Duff's biographer states that the purpose of this organisation was to 'study foreign missions, so as to satisfy themselves of the [needs] of the world outside of Christendom'. [11]

While the Missionary Society provided a forum for academic discussion, its real value was inspiring Alexander Duff and a number of other students to consider missionary work for themselves. It has been said of the society that it '...was the most formidable weapon in the Evangelical armoury, encouraging evangelism ... and challenging all students with the needs of the mission fields'. [12]

The mission field that attracted the most attention was India. In the eighteenth century, the British East India Company, which had a firm grip on the Indian subcontinent, had been unenthusiastic about missionary endeavours. They feared that their profits would be reduced if some of the underlying assumptions and beliefs of the culture were challenged, but gradually they began to allow for the creation of a number of missionary stations. When the Englishman William Carey began work in India in 1793, the pace of change increased. Schools were established and

---

[10] Ibid., p. 42.

[11] Smith, *The Life of Alexander Duff*, v. 1, pp. 24–5.

[12] Piggin and Roxborogh, *The St Andrews Seven: The Finest Flowering of Missionary Zeal in Scottish History*, p. 63.

native preachers were trained. By 1801, Carey had published a New Testament, written in the native tongue and by the 1820s he was considered the patriarch of missionary work in India.

While the Church of Scotland had been slow to embrace missionary work, by 1825 they were beginning to look at the possibilities. The slowness had been caused by a number of factors. One was the belief that in order for a non-Christian culture to embrace the faith it first had to be 'civilized'. Thomas Chalmers responded to this ridiculous notion by saying that it was 'both doctrinally and experimentally untrue that a preparatory civilization is necessary ere the human mind can be in a state of readiness for the reception of the gospel of Jesus Christ'. [13] As Piggin and Roxborough have noted, Chalmers recognised that 'the obligation to believe the gospel belongs to every person by virtue of his humanity rather than his refinement'. [14] Others in the Church of Scotland expressed the concern that the church could not afford foreign mission work for financial reasons. To this the advocates of mission work replied that evangelism was a command, not an option, and that it was central to the work of the church and must go forward.

The Church of Scotland appointed chaplains to the East India Company beginning in the 1820s and then in 1825 a proposal was made to the General Assembly that the church should establish a 'central seminary of education ... under [the direction of] one who ought to be an ordained minister of the church'. [15] Further, the General Assembly's

---

[13] Ibid., p. 44.

[14] Ibid.

[15] Smith, *The Life of Alexander Duff,* v. 1, p. 41.

Committee for the Propagation of the Gospel Abroad issued 'a letter to the people of Scotland' in which they apologised for the church's previous failures to engage in mission work. Pointing to the example of other churches, they called on the people of Scotland to begin to take a more active interest in and display support for missionary work.

While it has been suggested that Duff was stimulated by this renewed interest and may have decided to go to the mission field in India as early as 1827, he did not make a final decision until the conclusion of the 1828–9 academic session. In the spring of 1829, at the age of twenty-three, Duff was proposed as the first official missionary of the Church of Scotland to Calcutta. In a lengthy letter to Thomas Chalmers, Duff indicated that he was prepared to accept the position. In the letter, which reads more like a sermon, he wrote

> I am now prepared to reply to the committee in the words of the prophet, 'Here am I, send me.' The work is most arduous, but is of God and must prosper; many sacrifices painful to 'flesh and blood' must be made, but not any correspondent to the glory of winning souls to Christ. With the thought of this glory I feel myself almost transported with joy; everything else appears to fall out of view as vain and insignificant.[16]

As Duff prepared to leave St Andrews for India he had two events to look forward to: his marriage and his ordination. Little is known of Duff's courtship, but on 9 July, he was married to Anne Scott Drysdale of Edinburgh. Over the course of their 36-year marriage they would have five children, although two of them did not survive

---

[16] Ibid., pp. 48–9.

infancy. Anne Duff played an extremely important role in Duff's missionary work and he would repeatedly state that it had been a very happy marriage.[17] On 12 August, Alexander Duff was ordained and consecrated as a missionary by Thomas Chalmers at St George's Church in Edinburgh.

A PASSAGE TO INDIA
1829–30

Alexander Duff and his bride began the long journey to India on 19 September 1829. The journey to India was an eventful one to say the least. The *Lady Holland* set sail at the end of October and reached the island of Madeira early in November. The plan was to spend about a week there. On the night before the vessel was scheduled to resume its voyage, the Captain gave an on-shore ball for the passengers. This was attended by most of the passengers, but the Duffs had decided to stay on board. During the ball, a massive storm broke which imperilled the ship. Several ships in the harbour were destroyed in the storm. The Duffs, a few other paying passengers and a skeleton crew rode out the storm, but the *Lady Holland* was severely damaged and required three weeks of repairs before the voyage could continue. As they waited for their ship to be made seaworthy, the Duffs and the other passengers spent their time sightseeing.

The voyage finally resumed but only slow progress was made towards the next port of call, which was Cape Town. As it entered Table Bay, another massive storm blew up. Alexander Duff described the ordeal.

---

[17] Ibid., p. 61.

Before, and on every side of us, low dark reefs appeared, amid which the breakers struggled with dashing roar. The vessel had refused to obey the helm, the sails became unmanageable; uplifted by every billow, the ship sunk down again with a shattering crash that made the flesh creak and shiver and the captain in a tone of piercing agony, was heard to exclaim, 'Ah she's gone, she's gone'.[18]

When the order was given to evacuate the ship, there seemed little hope that everyone would survive. Remarkably, after three trips in the longboat to nearby Dassen Island, no lives were lost. The ship's cargo was lost, including most of the passengers' personal possessions. The biggest loss for Duff was his library of 800 books and personal manuscripts. As the travellers slowly began to recover from their ordeal, Duff wrote back to the church in Scotland that

... recent events have made me feel more strongly the vanity of earthly things, the hollowness of earthly hopes; they have taught me the necessity of being 'instant in season and out of season' of 'spending and being spent', in the cause of Christ ... if I am destined to perish in a foreign land, my prayer is to be enabled cheerfully to perish with the song of faith on my lips: 'O death, where is thy sting? O grave, where is thy victory?'[19]

The Duffs renewed their efforts to reach India in March 1830. They searched for another ship to complete the

---

[18] Alexander Duff, *Extract of a Letter Respecting the Wreck of the Lady Holland East Indiaman, from the Rev. Alexander Duff, One of the Passengers in That Ship, Addressed to Dr Inglis, As Convenor of the General Assembly's Committee for the Propagation of the Gospel in India* (Edinburgh: John Waugh, 1830), p. 7.

[19] Ibid., p. 19.

journey, and booked passage on the *Moira* which reached the mouth of the Ganges in May. There it was hit by a cyclone and became stuck in the mud. All of the passengers were forced to disembark in less than ideal conditions, scrambling ashore in waist-deep water. The Duffs could not have endured much worse conditions on their journey, but they were grateful to have arrived safely in India and they began their work with enthusiasm.

INDIA
1830—4

Duff spent the first few months in India becoming acclimatised and working on a strategy for his future labours. Assessing the efforts of other missionaries, he concluded that while there had been a few individual successes, the overall strategy was not working. Most of the missionary energy had been devoted to street preaching and individual evangelism. The problem that he saw was that in India

> ... the evangelist stands up not as a recognised religious teacher, and the doctrinal terms he uses will either seem strange to the ears of his listeners, or will convey a meaning totally at variance to the one he wishes to impart. [20]

Somewhat controversially, Duff decided that the best way to reach India with the gospel was to work from within the culture by means of education. Ten years later he said that through the school system he hoped to

> ... *devote our time and strength to the preparing of a mine, and the getting of a train which shall one day explode and tear up the whole from its lowest depths.*[21]

---

[20] Smith, *The Life of Alexander Duff,* v. 1, p. 108.

[21] Ibid. The emphasis is in the original.

He also believed that education needed to take place in English. His reasoning was that

> ... in the very act of acquiring English, the mind, in grasping the import of new terms, is perpetually brought in contact with the *new ideas*, the *new truths* ... so that, by the time the language has been mastered, the student must be *tenfold less* the child of Pantheism, idolatry and superstition than before.[22]

Duff had been instructed by the Church of Scotland to open a school in the Calcutta area but not within the city itself.[23] However, he believed this was the wrong approach and so opened his school in Calcutta on 12 July 1830. As he began his labours, he was assisted by the Hindu reformer Raja Rammohan Roy. While Roy was not a Christian, he had come to believe in a personal God and was sympathetic to the beliefs taught by Unitarians. He recognised the value of education, and his support for Duff's school was instrumental in overcoming parental suspicion about Duff's missionary motives. Rammohan Roy was particularly helpful in dealing with doubts about the Bible's place in the curriculum. When he was asked about the propriety of Hindus and people of other faiths reading the Bible, he replied that

> Christians, like Dr Horace Hayman Wilson, have studied the 'Hindu Shasters', and you know that he has not become a Hindu. I myself have read all the Koran again and again, and has that made me a Muslim? Nay, I have studied the

[22] Alexander Duff, quoted in Steve Bishop, 'Protestant Missionary Education in British India', *Evangelical Quarterly* 69:3 (1997), p. 248.

[23] The reason for the avoidance of Calcutta is not given in any of the primary sources on Duff. As a result we can only speculate as to why the church should have believed that this was the best way to proceed.

whole Bible, and you know I am not a Christian. Why, then, do you fear to read it? Read and judge for yourself …[24]

The school met with immediate success. Within a week of opening enrolment jumped from 5 students to 200. The curriculum covered a wide variety of subjects including the sciences, but the Bible had a central place and the school unashamedly presented itself as offering Christian religious instruction. It is worth noting that Duff was as opposed to Western secularism as he was to the teaching of Hinduism. As a result,

> Duff's overriding concern was to present the claims of Christianity as the alternative to both of these, at the intellectual as well as the spiritual level. In his school Christianity was not simply one subject to be taught among others: it was an influence which permeated its whole life and work.[25]

While Duff was not the pioneer of Western-style education in India, nor the only one who believed that this was the best path to conversion, he was an articulate proponent of this strategy.

In addition to his educational work, Duff also found time to publish a journal called the *Calcutta Christian Observer*. As an interdenominational journal, its object was 'the exposition of Christian ideals [and] the reviewing of current literature and events'.[26] Duff poured all his

---

[24] Smith, *The Life of Alexander Duff,* v. 1, p. 122.

[25] Michael A. Laird, 'The legacy of Alexander Duff', *Occasional Bulletin of Missionary Research* 3:4 (October 1979), p. 146.

[26] William Paton, *Alexander Duff, Pioneer of Missionary Education* (New York: George H. Doran, 1922), p. 101.

energies into both the school and the journal and by 1834 he was exhausted. When both he and his wife, pregnant with their first child, became sick with dysentery, there was real concern that they might not survive. As they slowly recovered, it was decided to send them home to Scotland to convalesce. Duff was reluctant to leave the work but he came to recognise that he did need a rest. In a letter written while on board the ship home he wrote:

> The very thought of returning home at the commencement of my labours and infancy of the Assembly's mission would have, I verily believe, broken my heart, were it not that God, by successive afflictions, which thrice brought me to the verge of the grave, disciplined me into the belief and conviction, that a change so decided was absolutely indispensable, and that to resist the proposal to leave Calcutta would be tantamount to a resistance of the will of Providence.[27]

FURLOUGH
1834–9

The Duffs arrived back in Scotland on Christmas Day, 1834. Once Alexander had sufficiently recovered his health, he devoted his time to speaking, writing and raising the profile of and support for the church's missionary work. Initially he was met with apathy, but after a lengthy speech at the 1835 General Assembly momentum for mission began to grow. If anything, he was busier during his furlough than he had been in India. He lobbied committees of the church and spoke passionately at General Assemblies. His most impassioned plea was published in a pamphlet entitled *Missions the Chief End of the Christian Church*. It

[27] Smith, *The Life of Alexander Duff*, v. 1, p. 272.

had begun as his charge to Rev. Thomas Smith, who was being ordained as a missionary to India. Twenty thousand copies of this pamphlet sold very quickly and it played a key role in developing enthusiasm for missionary work.

In this work Duff challenged the church to repent. He wrote that after the Reformation of the sixteenth century,

> ... instead of going forth in a progress of *outward* extension, and onward aggression, with a view to consummate the great work which formed at once the eternal design of her Head and the chief end of her being: – the Church seemed mainly intent on turning the whole of her energies *inward* on herself. Her highest ambition and aim seemed to be, to have herself begirt as with a wall of fire that might devour her adversaries – to have her own privileges fenced in by laws and statutes of the realm ...[28]

While Duff did concede that it was appropriate for the church to protect the truth, he went on to argue that this was not enough. He called on the church to

> ... nobly resolve to assume the entire evangelistic character, and implement the Divine condition of preservation and prosperity, by becoming the dispenser of Gospel blessings, not only to the people at home, but as speedily as possible, to all the ... nations of the earth.[29]

Duff recognised that the key to building enthusiasm for missionary work was to develop interest at the local church level. So he set out to establish a missionary organisation

---

[28] Alexander Duff, *Missions the Chief End of the Christian Church: Also the Qualifications, Duties and Trials of an Indian Missionary; Being the Substance of Services Held at the Ordination of the Rev. Thomas Smith* (Edinburgh: Johnstone, 1840), p. 21–2.

[29] Ibid., p. 26.

in each Presbytery to disseminate information about what was taking place on the mission field, collect money for the support of missions work and generally 'form a center round which interest and enthusiasm might gather'. [30]

The Duffs' time in Scotland was notable for two other things. First, in 1835, he was awarded the Degree of Doctor of Divinity by Marischal College, Aberdeen, a remarkable honour for a man who was only twenty-nine. It also indicated just how much of an impact he was having in his homeland. Also during the furlough, Anne Duff gave birth to five children, the first of whom died after only six months. Then, as they prepared to return to India, they made the heart-wrenching decision to leave their children behind in Scotland. Sadly, two of them would die before the Duffs returned from India for their next furlough in 1850.

RETURN TO INDIA
1839—49

The next ten years in India were eventful ones. Duff found himself drawn into a public policy debate when the Governor General Lord Auckland advanced the idea that the education run by the state should be religiously neutral. While Duff was not totally opposed to the recognition of native language and culture in the school system, he was insistent that Christianity was not just another religion to be treated on an equal footing with other belief systems. Educational policy in India would continue to be debated throughout Duff's life, but there is no question that his views kept both the English language and Christianity in the curriculum.

[30] Paton, *Alexander Duff, Pioneer of Missionary Education*, p. 112.

Events leading to the Disruption in the Church of Scotland in 1843 had a major impact on Duff's work. While he was a firmly committed evangelical in his theology, he had not openly taken sides during his furlough in Scotland. In fact, his biographer states that he had been 'so silent regarding his relation to parties and the course he would follow if a rupture took place, that some doubted how he would act'. [31] After the first Free Church General Assembly in May 1843, Duff and the other Church of Scotland missionaries in India were asked by both the Church of Scotland and the Free Church to publicly declare their allegiances. All the missionaries, including Duff, decided to join the Free Church. He explained his decision in this way:

> We were now laid under a double necessity openly to avow our sentiments. Was there any hesitation when the hour of trial came? None whatsoever. So far as concerned my own mind, the simple truth is, that as regards the great principles contended for by the friends and champions of the Free Church, I never was troubled with the crossing of a doubt or the shadow of a suspicion ... But though there was not a moment's hesitation as to the rectitude of the principles, and consequent obligation in determining the path of duty, there was a sore conflict of natural feeling, – a desperate struggle of opposing natural interests. Many of my dearest and most devoted personal friends still adhered to the Establishment; and I could not but foresee how ecclesiastical separation might lead to coolness, coolness to indifference, and indifference to eventual alienation.[32]

---

[31] Smith, *The Life of Alexander Duff*, v. 2, pp. 2–3.

[32] Smith, *The Life of Alexander Duff*, v. 2, pp. 13–14.

Initially, Duff had hoped that it might be possible for the newly founded Free Church to purchase the school proper-ties, library and equipment from the Church of Scotland, but after some debate this idea was rejected. Instead, Duff and his fellow missionaries began the work of rebuild-ing. With significant financial support from the church in Scotland, they made speedy progress. Such was the repu-tation of Duff's educational colleges that money was also raised among other Christian denominations in India as well as from wealthy Hindus and from places as far away as America and Asia.[33] Remarkably, within a year, new premises had been secured and the schools were up and running once again.

The death of Thomas Chalmers in June 1847 shook Duff. In a letter to James Buchannan dated 7 August 1847, he paid tribute to Chalmers as a mentor and prominent sup-porter of missionary work in the church. As the Free Church considered a replacement for Chalmers, a proposal was made that the Theology Chair at New College should be offered to Duff. He, however, was convinced that he was not the right man for the job and declined the offer, stating that while he appreciated the honour of being considered, he must remain and 'die as he had lived – the missionary'. [34]

SCOTLAND, THE UNITED STATES AND CANADA 1850—5

By 1849, Duff's strength and energies were running out. When news of his decline reached his friends in Scotland, they encouraged him to return home to rest. Once recov-

---

[33] Millar, *Alexander Duff of India*, p. 129

[34] Smith, *The Life of Alexander Duff*, v. 2, p. 117.

ered, he again turned his attention to raising interest in and funds for missionary work. In May 1851, Duff was chosen to be the Moderator of the General Assembly of the Free Church. He viewed this distinction as more a recognition of the place of missions in the life of the Free Church than any particular honour accorded to him.

Duff was invited to give evidence before a parliamentary select committee in 1853 that was examining the renewal of the East India Company's charter. This invitation recognised that Duff was 'undoubtedly the most prominent missionary to India'. [35] His evidence on how education should be structured resulted in a system which recognised

> ... that it was the duty of the British government to provide India with 'improved European knowledge' by means of the English language to the higher branches of education, and by that of the vernacular languages to the great mass of the people.[36]

In practical terms, this meant that Indian universities were to be based on the English model. The plan provided government grants to schools that met accepted standards, which meant mission schools would benefit significantly, as they were best placed to meet the standards.

In 1854, Duff was off on his travels again, this time to the United States and Canada. He arrived in New York City on 13 February 1854. During the three-month tour, he preached to thousands of people in numerous places including New York, Washington, Philadelphia and as far west as St Louis.

---

[35] W.G. Blaikie, *Rev. David W. Savage*, 'Duff, Alexander', in *Oxford Dictionary of National Biography* (Oxford: Oxford University Press, 2004), v. 17, p. 122.

[36] Ibid.

When Duff reached Canada, he was ill with a severe cold, but continued his public engagements despite the concern of many friends who were worried about his health. His visit to Toronto was greeted with great anticipation. *The Globe* newspaper enthused that

> Toronto has never enjoyed the opportunity of paying respect to one whose services have been so eminently useful in promoting the cause of our common Christianity; and it is believed that members of every evangelical denomination will have pleasure in listening to the interesting accounts … Dr Duff will be able to give and also in paying respect to one who has shown himself so able and devoted a follower of his Divine Master.[37]

While in Toronto he preached in one of the city's biggest churches 'crammed to suffocation with 3,000 people'.[38] At another church service one of his hearers was William Lyon Mackenzie who had led a notoriously rebellious life, fighting for more democratic government for Canada. He had been a journalist, politician and had served time in prison for leading an ill-fated rebellion in 1837.[39] When Mackenzie appeared at the service, Duff was suspicious that he was only there to collect material for a newspaper article which would poke fun at the church. However, the next day, one of Duff's friends received a letter from Mackenzie which stated that as he listened to Duff, he had been 'arrested in a way he never was before by Divine

---

[37] 'Rev. Dr Duff', *The Globe* (20 March 1854).

[38] Smith, *The Life of Alexander Duff*, v. 2, p. 285.

[39] For more information on the eventful life of Mackenzie, see 'Mackenzie, William Lyon'. *Dictionary of Canadian Biography Online*, http://www.biographi.ca/ (accessed 9 July 2009).

truth'. [40] Whether or not this service had any lasting impact on Mackenzie is unclear, but what it does show is the power of the Holy Spirit and Duff's ability to draw, hold and inspire an audience.

The North American tour was a major success. Although it had not been designed as a fund-raising trip, it did bring in a significant amount of money that was used for building schools in Calcutta. Among the honours paid to Duff during his time in North America, he was awarded the LLD from New York University. What is most striking is Duff's self-effacing response to all of the adulation he received. Again and again his diary records his hope that this trip would be used by God for the furtherance of the missionary enterprise.

INDIA
1856—63

Alexander and Anne Duff returned to India for the final time in 1856. By this time, the church in India was enjoying slow but steady growth. Native pastors were now serving in many locations and it is estimated that there were 150,000 Christians worshipping regularly. The Duffs returned to India at a tumultuous time in its history. Tensions had been building for some time between the administration of the British East India Company and many parts of the native population. A punitive tax system and the seizure of lands were among the contentious issues. False rumours that the British East India Company was conspiring with the church to forcibly convert all of the population to Christianity were

---

[40] Ibid., p. 284.

also being circulated, and this increased tensions significantly. What provoked the outbreak of the Indian Mutiny in May 1857 was the introduction by the British army of the Enfield rifle, which had cartridges greased with pig and cow fat. This caused offence to both Muslim and Hindu soldiers and tensions exploded in armed rebellion.[41]

Throughout this time the Duffs were concerned about the impact the mutiny would have on their work. They also had a very personal concern, as their son Alexander was serving as a surgeon in the British army stationed in India. Duff recorded his response to the year-long mutiny in a series of twenty-five letters that were published in *The Witness* and subsequently as *The Indian Rebellion; Its Causes and Results*.[42] Not surprisingly, he offered a spirited defence of the church in Indian society and made the point that the church was not at all interested in forced conversions. He also argued that it would only be as the gospel was spread that true peace would persist in India.

The highlight of Duff's remaining time in India was the founding of the University of Calcutta in 1859. He was among those who drew up the university's constitution, was appointed Vice Chancellor and effectively ran the institution. He was responsible for the addition of the physical sciences to the curriculum and did more than anyone else to establish the reputation of the school.

By 1863, both Anne and Alexander were again suffering from ill health and the church decided that they should return home. They left India with regret, but could look

[41] Millar, *Alexander Duff of India*, p. 182.

[42] Alexander Duff, *The Indian Rebellion; Its Causes and Results* (New York: R. Carter, 1858).

back on significant successes as their vision for education had been firmly established.

LAST YEARS
1865–78

Alexander reached Scotland in December 1865 and only a month later his wife died. Characteristically, Duff buried himself in his work. His first objective was to endow a missions chair at New College. He believed that giving missions work prominence in the college curriculum would result in it receiving greater prominence in the life of the church. He successfully raised funds for and was elected as the first occupant of the Chair of Evangelistic Theology in 1867. One of Duff's biographers comments that he was far from successful in this role.

> Duff was out of his métier as a lecturer to theological students ... He was getting old, and with age ... he had not the ability ... to lay out the kind of lecture scheme which would attract the keener minds of the younger generation.[43]

Perhaps his declining powers also caused him to vacillate during the Robertson Smith case. During the first stages of the debate, Duff sought to maintain the church's historic position on the inspiration of Scripture, but he seems to have believed that Smith was being misunderstood and not being read generously enough by his critics. How Duff would have voted on Smith's removal from office is unknown since the final decision did not occur until after his death.

In 1871, the 65-year-old missionary statesman was again travelling. This time he toured through Europe and reached Russia seeking to stir up missionary interest wherever he

---

[43] Paton, *Alexander Duff, Pioneer of Missionary Education*, p. 187.

went. His schedule was a punishing one and he may have deliberately kept busy so as to not have to deal with his grief over his wife's death.

Back in Scotland, the 'union controversy' was raging and Duff initially took the side of the pro-unionists, believing that a united Scottish church would help to further missionary work. He was again appointed Moderator of the General Assembly in 1873. When it appeared that the Free Church might divide over union, he was instrumental in persuading James Begg and his followers to agree to the mutual eligibility scheme between the Free Church and the United Presbyterians which prevented schism.

Despite declining health, Duff continued to work. One of his last acts was his enthusiastic support for the founding of the Alliance of Reformed Churches. Just before its first meeting at the end of 1877, his health broke down completely and he died in Edinburgh on 12 February 1878 at the age of seventy-two.

Some modern missiologists have suggested that Duff's legacy is ambiguous because he did not accept the view that all religions are equal. And indeed it is true that he "shared in the 'wholesale condemnation of the non-Christian religions that virtually all missionaries at that period expressed'."[44] Three things need to be said in response to this. First, in advancing orthodox Christianity as the only way of salvation, Duff was simply being faithful to the words of Christ when Jesus said that he was 'the way, the truth and the life'. Second, Duff's work in India and his efforts while on furlough significantly increased interest in and support for missionary work both in Scotland and in

[44] Laird, 'The legacy of Alexander Duff', p. 148.

North America. Finally, there is no ambiguity about the fact that without Duff's championing of education in India and his visionary leadership, it is unlikely that India would ever have been ready for self-government in the twentieth century.

JOHN KENNEDY, D.D.

Home & Macdonald.

11

JOHN KENNEDY
HIGHLAND PREACHER AND
CONFESSIONAL DEFENDER

More than any other single figure, he deserves to be
called the Father of the Free Church as we know it
today.[1]

JOHN Kennedy was Minister of Dingwall Free Church
from his ordination in February of 1844 until his death
forty years later. During this time, he gained a reputation
as the best Highland preacher of his day. He was also a
resolute defender of the reformed faith, particularly as it is
defined in the *Westminster Confession of Faith, Catechisms
and Directory for Public Worship*. Kennedy exercised faithful
pastoral ministry throughout his life and fought a number
of battles within the Free Church to preserve what he perceived to be the best of Scottish Presbyterianism in the face
of modern encroachments. In light of some of the controversies in which he found himself, it has rightly been noted that
'John Kennedy knew where he stood, and why. He followed
the old paths out of intellectual and moral conviction'.[2] His
writings included tracts, sermons and ecclesiastical history,
some of which continue to shape Scottish Presbyterianism.

---

[1] Donald Macleod, 'Our Fathers: Where are They?' *Monthly Record of
the Free Church of Scotland* (May 1984), p. 99.

[2] Alan P.F. Sell, *Defending and Declaring the faith: Some Scottish
Examples 1860–1920* (Exeter: Paternoster Press, 1987), p. 13.

This is particularly true of his most famous work, *The Days of the Fathers in Ross-Shire,* which has been called 'a warm and sometimes sentimental look at a bygone age'. [3]

Kennedy was described by C.H. Spurgeon as being 'true as steel and firm as a rock'. [4] This strength of character equipped Kennedy to wage his campaigns, but it also resulted in accusations that he was an obscurantist who was only interested in the past. While he would receive a great deal of criticism during his life, one of his critics recognised that he was

> ... in many ways, a noble man. He was a man of quite remarkable personal charm in private conversation. He had literary culture, and read through Shakespeare every year and knew the poets as intimately as he knew the Puritans. [5]

And, in addition to his literary interests, he was something of an expert on English cricket!

Highland Roots and Preparation for Ministry 1819–43

John Kennedy was born in the Manse at Killearnan on 15 August 1819. He was the fourth son of the Rev. John Kennedy, the minister of the parish. The chief source of information on 'the Minister of Killearnan' comes from his son in a lengthy chapter in his book *The Days of the*

---

[3] Iain D. Campbell, 'Resolutions of a Preacher' *Loch a Tuath News (January 2001),* http://www.backfreechurch.co.uk/studies/latn/latn_0008.jsp (accessed 19 May 2009).

[4] Quoted in James Barron, 'Memoir of Rev. John Kennedy D.D., of Dingwall', *Inverness Courier, 1893,* http://kennedy.nesher.org.uk/Memoir_of_Dr_Kennedy.html (accessed 19 May 2009).

[5] Simpson, *The Life of Principal Rainy,* p. 442.

Fathers in Ross-Shire. Kennedy makes no apology for the fact that he was painting a very positive portrait. In the introduction he writes:

> ... I can by no means keep down the son in my heart as I write or when I think of him. This accounts for the frequency with which 'I' and 'my' appear on the following pages ... [The] effort to hide the son in the writer [required] an indifference that was far from my feeling, both my heart and my conscience revolted against it.[6]

The picture that emerges of his father is of a saintly man who was deeply loved by the people he served and whose 'labours were much blessed for the winning of souls to Christ'. While John Kennedy did not embrace Christianity while he lived with his parents, his biographer comments that the fact 'that silent impressions were left, is evident from his later poignant regret at not having improved these privileges while they lasted'. [7] *The Days of the Fathers in Ross-Shire* not only demonstrates Kennedy's affection for his family, but it also clearly indicates his devotion to the distinct version of Highland Protestant spirituality it embodies. It has been suggested that what emerges is a 'clear distinction between the religion of the Lowlands and that of the Highlands'. [8] To balance this view it should

---

[6] John Kennedy, *The Days of the Fathers in Ross-Shire* 5th edition (Inverness: Northern Chronicle Office, 1897), p. 164.

[7] Alexander Auld, *Life of John Kennedy, D.D.* (London: T. Nelson and Sons, 1887), p. 1. Alexander Auld's life of Kennedy is typical of nineteenth-century ecclesiastical biographies, in that it is rich in detail and is very sympathetic to its subject.

[8] Allan W. MacColl, *Land, Faith and the Crofting Community: Christianity and Social Criticism in the Highlands of Scotland, 1843–93* (Edinburgh: Edinburgh University Press, 2006), p. 85.

be noted that there were ministers in the Lowlands who were concerned about many of the same things as Kennedy, and not all Highland ministers had a monolithic view of theology and the church either.

It is clear that Kennedy believed that the particular character of Christianity that existed in the Highlands took spiritual matters with much more seriousness than was common in the Lowlands. This seriousness was often caricatured as gloominess, but Kennedy disagreed. He does concede that Highlanders were 'free from frivolity' and then goes on to say that they

> ... were grave, but not gloomy. They had not the light cheerfulness of unbroken hearts. They did not, like others, take it for granted that they were 'the Lord's', they could not like others speak peace to themselves; but unlike many others, they were dependent on the Lord for their hope and their joy.[9]

John Kennedy's education began at the parish grammar school where he excelled, particularly in the study of Latin. One of his biographers states that 'he was able to conjugate a Latin verb at six years of age'.[10] When he was seventeen he enrolled at King's College, Aberdeen for studies in Arts and Divinity. Another of his biographers states that it

> ... does not appear that he gave any special diligence in his studies in the early part of his curriculum, but even then his undoubted gifts enabled him to give a most creditable account of himself in Classics and Mathematics. Towards the close of his literary course, when he really began to

---

[9] Kennedy, *The Days of the Fathers in Ross-Shire*, p. 129.
[10] Ibid., p. 2.

apply himself ... his superior powers easily gained for him several prizes.[11]

Kennedy graduated with an MA in 1840 and then enrolled in the Divinity School. It would appear that his choice of vocation was made 'to please his parents, [more] than to gratify any inclination of his own'.[12] One of his fellow students later remarked that

> ... there was not much in his conversation to give any special promise of that high-toned personal piety and power as a preacher by which he afterwards became distinguished. Indeed, the stage was then believed to possess nearly as great attractions for him as the pulpit.[13]

In January of 1841, John Kennedy's father died unexpectedly after a brief illness. This death affected him profoundly, bringing about 'a [spiritual] crisis in his life'.[14] After his father's funeral, his friends noted that his demeanour had changed. 'His former indifference to Divine things had given place in his mind to deep seriousness, his self-sufficiency to self-abasement, the things of time to the things of eternity.'[15] We don't have to take Kennedy's biographer's word for the significant change that took place in his life at this stage. The surviving fragments from his own diary depict a man who is now consciously preparing for

---

[11] John Noble, 'Memoir of the Rev. John Kennedy, D.D.', in John Kennedy, *The Days of the Fathers in Ross-Shire*, pp. xxxiii–xxxiv.

[12] Ibid., p. xxxiv.

[13] Auld, *Life of John Kennedy, D.D.*, p. 4.

[14] John Noble, 'Memoir of the Rev. John Kennedy, D.D.', in John Kennedy, *The Days of the Fathers in Ross-Shire*, p. xxxiv.

[15] Auld, *Life of John Kennedy, D.D.*, p. 6.

his chosen vocation. His father's death also placed him in a precarious financial situation, so he had to take on tutoring in order to finance his education.

The period of his theological studies coincided with the growing crisis within the Church of Scotland which led to the Disruption. In fact, when the Disruption occurred, he abandoned his studies in pursuit of full-time ministry in the church, because 'promising students who were well through their courses were encouraged to present themselves for license'. [16] He was duly licensed by the Presbytery of Chanonry in September of 1843 and delivered his first public sermon the following month in the Killearnan churchyard, where his brother Donald was now the minister. This first sermon was very well received, although Kennedy himself never looked upon it with any great satisfaction.

MINISTER OF DINGWALL FREE CHURCH
1844–84

Dingwall is located near the head of Cromarty Firth and was made a Royal Burgh in 1226. Its location, roughly equidistant from the northern and southern points of the Highlands, has always granted it a certain prominence. At the Disruption, Dingwall had been one of a minority of Highland parishes whose minister remained within the Church of Scotland along with some of the more wealthy members of the community. There was nonetheless a significant number of people whose sympathies were with the newly created Free Church, and so they began their search for a minister. Kennedy's call to the Dingwall congregation 'resembled in its leading steps a pre-Disruption

---

[16] Ibid., p. 42.

rather than a post-Disruption settlement'. [17] First, the Kirk Session petitioned the Presbytery to hear Kennedy preach. After he preached for the congregation, the Presbytery were then asked to moderate a call that was addressed to Kennedy 'from the Magistrates, Councillors, Heritors, of the royal burgh of Dingwall and from the Elders, Communicants and Adherents of the Free Church of said burgh and parish'. [18] Kennedy accepted the call and was ordained and inducted in February of 1844. At a number of different points during his life, he would receive many calls to other churches in Scotland and from as far away as Australia. But he declined all of them, choosing to remain where he had been ordained.

Four years after his induction, Kennedy married Mary Mackenzie, the daughter of Major Forbes Mackenzie. Mary, who lived from 1819 to 1896, gave birth to four children but only twin daughters survived infancy. The fifth edition of Kennedy's *Days of the Fathers in Ross-Shire* includes a portrait of Mary Mackenzie that says 'she was truly a "helpmeet" to her ... husband who well knew and appreciated all her admirable qualities'. [19]

HIGHLAND PREACHER AND PASTOR

Kennedy's lasting reputation has been secured first and foremost by his work as preacher and pastor in Dingwall. While few of his sermons were printed in his

---

[17] Ibid., p. 46.

[18] Ibid.

[19] John Kennedy, 'Memoir of Mrs. Kennedy', in John Kennedy, *The Days of the Fathers in Ross-Shire*, p. clxxxii.

lifetime,[20] contemporary accounts of his preaching give us a picture of his gifts and abilities. We do not have the text of many of his sermons because Kennedy did not usually write them out before they were preached. When he was finally persuaded to publish a volume of his sermons in 1883, he wrote that

> ... on the day in which I was licensed, the late Mr Stewart of Cromarty said to me 'John ... take one advice from me. Don't write your sermons. Spend your time in thinking, for be assured that if you do not express clearly it will be because you have not thought sufficiently.' [21]

He goes on to say that he followed this advice '... because of the pressure of work that came upon me ... [during] the busy year of the Disruption, and which certainly did not become less, as years were passing by'. [22]

There is some dispute among Kennedy's biographers about how he went about the task of preparing his sermons. John H. Fraser, who wrote the sketch of Kennedy that is included in *Disruption Worthies of the Highlands,* commented that with

> ... his mental resources, his large experience, and his extemporaneous gifts, he could preach well without the trouble of much writing and severe study ... No character-istic of his mind is more marked than his reliance on his

---

[20] A collection of John Kennedy's sermons was published in 1883 the year before he died and a second expanded edition of this volume was published in 1888, to coincide with the holding of the Free Church General Assembly in Inverness. In more recent times, two volumes of Kennedy's sermon notes were published in 2007 and 2008 by The James Begg Society.

[21] John Noble, 'Memoir of the Rev. John Kennedy, D.D.', p. xlix.

[22] Ibid.

own resources in all his mental efforts. He seems to place little reliance on books, or on the thoughts and labours of others. He is not a learned man in the broad sense of that term; at least, with his many pulpit duties, he had no time to become an extensively read man, and, we believe, he lays no claim to this distinction. He works out his numerous discourses with little beside his Bible and Concordance to aid him. They all bear the impress of his own mind and characteristics, and hence their freshness, depth of experience, and eminently Scriptural character.[23]

While this makes for pious hagiography, a more plausible description is given by Alexander Auld. He drew attention to Kennedy's intimate knowledge and use of Greek and Hebrew and mentions his library that contained 'the standard authors on systematic theology'. He then concludes that 'there is no ground for thinking that his researches with a view to the exhibition of the truth were less scholarly and profound than those of any of the foremost preachers of his day'. [24]

Kennedy's preaching focused on God's greatness and his free grace offered to sinners. From the notes of his sermons, taken down by his hearers and recently published, a picture emerges of a man whose preaching was

> ... determined by his profound sense of the majesty and sovereignty of God, [by] his wholehearted acceptance of the authority of Scripture, his firm grasp of the system of doctrine revealed in Scripture, and his personal experience of the power of Scripture truth when applied by the Spirit of God.[25]

[23] John H. Fraser, 'Rev. John Kennedy D.D., Free Church, Dingwall', in *Disruption Worthies of the Highlands, a Memorial of 1843*, p. 258.

[24] Auld, *Life of John Kennedy, D.D.*, p. 73.

[25] Hugh Cartwright, 'Dr John Kennedy', *Monthly Record of the Free Church of Scotland* (October 1983), p. 211.

Kennedy particularly enjoyed the Wednesday evening prayer meeting. Although it was conducted in English, many Gaelic-speaking people from other parishes attended. Soon after he arrived in Dingwall, Kennedy began an exposition of the Book of Psalms at the English prayer meeting. As he began this series he said to a friend, 'I think not until I have gone over the Book of Psalms will my ministry be ended in Dingwall'. His biographer then goes on to say that to

> ... those who knew that this was his impression, it was a coincidence that filled them with misgivings that on the very week before he left Dingwall for Rome, whence he did not return in life, he had reached in course the last Psalm the 150th.[26]

He was also responsible for the pastoral care and catechising of his parish. Catechising was the practice of examining the people of his parish, particularly the children, on their knowledge of the Bible and the *Westminster Shorter Catechism*. He freely admitted that his early attempts to instruct children were not particularly successful, since he 'shot quite over their heads', but he continued working on this and eventually he was able to make this teaching both 'suitable and attractive to children and to older people'. [27]

A glimpse at Kennedy's diary gives an indication of just how busy he was. On Sundays he conducted a service (which included both a lecture and a sermon) in Gaelic from 11:00 a.m. to 1:30 p.m. Then at 1:45 p.m. an English service was held. This was followed by another service in the evening, which alternated between English and Gaelic each week.

---

[26] Auld, *Life of John Kennedy, D.D.*, p. 54.
[27] Ibid.

In addition, separate Gaelic and English prayer meetings were held during the week. As his ministry developed, he became a very popular preacher and was in high demand in other churches around the country. At various points he was forced to take recuperative breaks from his punishing schedule, but these were often used for travel and writing.

Kennedy's workload would cause some twenty-first-century Christians to gasp, and to wonder how he managed to do it all. To be sure, he had gifted elders who helped him with pastoral work, and when he was away, students and other ministers filled his pulpit. But he must have been a man of considerable energy, to say the least! Another striking thing about Kennedy's ministry is the high value placed on preaching in his church. While times have changed and conditions are very different now, one can't help but wonder if the church in our own day might not be more vital if we placed the same value on the Word of God preached as was the case in the nineteenth-century Free Church in Dingwall.

CONFESSIONAL DEFENDER

Although John Kennedy has been called 'a reluctant controversialist',[28] he was no stranger to controversy. He had been too young to be involved in the events leading up to the Disruption in 1843, but he was nonetheless a firm believer in the principles which had brought about the establishment of the Free Church. He was convinced that the 'establishment principle' was biblical, and that the theology taught in the *Westminster Confession of Faith, Catechisms,* and *Directory for Public Worship* accurately reflected the

---

[28] Alan P.F. Sell, 'Kennedy, John', in *Oxford Dictionary of National Biography*, v. 31 (Oxford, 2004), p. 256.

teaching of Scripture. He was also firmly convinced that the Free Church's practice of worship was correct. When these convictions and others were challenged, he believed that it was his duty to speak. Over the course of his lifetime, there were a series of important issues in which Kennedy found himself in open and marked disagreement with others in the Free Church. We saw in chapter eight how Kennedy had clashed with the Bonar brothers over their involvement in the evangelistic campaigns of Moody and Sankey and, as was noted in the chapter on James Begg, Kennedy was actively involved in the discussions over union with the United Presbyterian Church.

When the movement toward closer union began in 1863, Kennedy was one of those appointed by the Free Church to consult with the United Presbyterian Church. As the process began, it 'was hailed with satisfaction by many and with hope by all'.[29] However, disagreements soon surfaced on at least two key issues. First, it emerged that there were different views on Christ's atonement. Second, it became very clear that there were divergent understandings of the relationship between the civil magistrate and the church as expressed in the establishment principle.

As the discussions continued, Kennedy began to have serious doubts about the whole process and began to speak and write openly about the problems. On the issue of the atonement, Kennedy did not dispute that 'the death of Christ is sufficient for all, is adapted to all and is offered to all'.[30] However, some in the United Presbyterian Church had gone quite a bit further. In 1869, Kennedy released

[29] Auld, *Life of John Kennedy, D.D.*, p. 134.
[30] Ibid., p. 135.

a book on the doctrine of adoption entitled *Man's Relations to God Traced in Light of the Present Truth*. In it he sought to defend the scriptural and confessional teaching regarding Christ's death against the double reference, or Amyraldian view of the atonement. He summarised the problem in this way:

> There are some who, Calvinists in their vows and Arminians in their tendencies, teach the doctrine of a *double reference* of the atonement; representing the atonement as offered in one sense for the elect, and in another sense for all. These maintain that there was a special atonement securing a certainty of salvation to some, and a universal atonement securing a possibility of salvation to all.[31]

Kennedy goes on to say that if

> ... it be objected, that unless the salvation of all who are called is possible there is no hope for them, it is enough to reply, that just as surely as salvation is not possible without atonement, neither is it so without faith; and that instead of tracing the possibility of a universal salvation to a universal reference of the atonement, the wise and the right thing would be, to insist on the ability of Christ to save *all* who come to Him; on the certainty of salvation through faith; and on the impossibility of salvation without it. But this universal reference, of which so much is made, is after all no reference of *the atonement*. There was no atonement that does not imply satisfaction to divine justice. There was no satisfaction of justice that did not avail to the purchase of redemption. Is there a universal reference of such an atonement to all? If not, of what atonement? And

---

[31] John Kennedy, *Man's Relations to God Traced in Light of the Present Truth* (Edinburgh: John Maclaren, 1869), pp. 100–1.

if of another, how can it avail to make salvation possible? To say that the atonement, being of infinite value, is sufficient for all, is beside the mark, for the question is as to the divine intention. To say, that, if the atonement was of infinite value, it was intended to be so, is to rhapsodize considerably: for, surely, the value of the atonement does not flow from the intention of God the Father, but from the dignity of God the Son, who offered it.[32]

One of the things that most troubled Kennedy in this discussion was that a false view of the atonement undermined the preaching of the gospel which he was passionate about. He wanted to preach and teach that Christ's death actually saved people from their sins, and not just that it made salvation possible. Kennedy was also concerned that this view was gaining ground in the United Presbyterian Church and that it had not been condemned by their General Assembly.

On the relationship between the civil magistrate and the church, the United Presbyterians had rejected the establishment principle and wanted no connection between the church and the state. They had even gone so far as to appeal to the Parliament in London in 1869 to abolish all forms of patronage in the church. When they made a submission to Prime Minster Gladstone, he directed their attention back to the events of 1843. He rather pointedly told them that

... you have borrowed clothes which were fabricated some twenty-five years ago by other brethren of yours for which they suffered, and, most undoubtedly, justice requires that in any change, I should consult the original donors.[33]

---

[32] Ibid., pp. 102–3.

[33] Sell, *Defending and Declaring the faith: Some Scottish Examples 1860–1920*, p. 26.

We may well suspect that Gladstone was playing politics with the United Presbyterians and having some fun at their expense, but he did have a point!

Kennedy was convinced that the state had a duty to support the work of the church while at the same time allowing the church spiritual independence, the very issues which had brought about the Disruption in 1843. He remarked in one pamphlet that the 'Free Church was set on a hill, before the eyes of Christendom, to shed light on the twin truths of the Church's right to be established and the Church's right to be free'. [34]

By 1870 opinion in the Free Church had changed, at least in part through the efforts of Kennedy's writing on the subject. Momentum for church union had certainly been slowed if not altogether stopped. When those who had been pushing for union recognised that there was not enough support for the cause, they proposed instead the idea of mutual eligibility of ministers between the two churches. This plan, as we noted in the chapter on James Begg, was ultimately accepted by the Free Church. Throughout this stage of the debate, Kennedy remained very concerned that desire for unity of the churches was taking precedence over both biblical truth and the Free Church's confessional commitments.[35]

For the rest of his life Kennedy continued to write and speak about these matters as they were persistently debated

---

[34] John Kennedy quoted in Sell, *Defending and Declaring the faith: Some Scottish Examples 1860–1920*, p. 24.

[35] It is also possible that compromise on the issue came about partly because of fear that the minority would have claimed to be *The Free Church*, which could have resulted in lengthy legal battles over property.

in the church. In one of a series of articles written for the *Perthshire Courier* in 1879 he argued that there had been

> ... a time when the leaders of the Free Church clearly saw, that zeal for the crown-rights of Christ, as Governor among the nations, demanded a firm maintenance of the principle of Establishment, and that a wise regard to the best interest of Scotland also required this at our hand. But this state of opinion and feeling has now passed away. Coldness of heart has caused dimness of eye; and the proposal now is finally to remove from Scotland all the testimony for Christ, and all the advantage to the community, implied in a well constituted Establishment.[36]

Alan Sell has pointed out that this was not just an academic discussion for Kennedy. As the union talks were proceeding, and as the country debated the question of disestablishment, there were also discussions taking place on how education should be delivered. Those holding to the Voluntarist position argued that the government should not legislate the delivery of religious education in schools. For Kennedy '... this was tantamount to practical atheism; it would [ultimately] preclude all legislation based upon the moral law of God'. [37]

Kennedy was equally perturbed by those who wanted to make changes to the way in which the Free Church worshipped. In 1865, the Free Church General Assembly was asked to allow the use of hymns in public worship. Some,

---

[36] John Kennedy, *The Present Cast and Tendency of Religions Thought and Feeling in Scotland: Eight Articles Contributed to the 'Inverness Courier' from 4th February to 1st April 1879* (Inverness: Northern Counties Newspaper and Printing and Publishing Company, 1955), p. 38.

[37] Sell, *Defending and Declaring the faith: Some Scottish Examples 1860–1920*, p. 25.

like the Bonars, were firmly in support of this movement, and others, like Robert Candlish, were prepared to allow a few hymns 'but not so much as to distract the church'. [38] John Kennedy was vehemently opposed to the introduction of any hymns and made common cause with James Begg in an attempt to block this change. When a *Free Church Hymn Book* was eventually presented to the Assembly for approval, Kennedy made an impassioned speech in which he argued that the Psalms were more than sufficient for the worship of the church. By 1883, when the Free Church was discussing the introduction of instrumental worship into worship, Kennedy presented a petition signed by 53,000 people objecting to the innovation. He also released a pamphlet entitled, *The Introduction of Instrumental Music into the Worship of the Free Church*. In this pamphlet he argued that the use of instrumental music was part of the worship of the Old Testament and could not be supported in the New Testament era. He reiterated the argument that he had advanced a few years earlier in his articles in the *Inverness Courier* where he wrote that Scripture taught that '... the fruit of the lips, unaccompanied by sounds from musical instruments, was the offering prescribed as the service of praise'. Then after stating that the church must not deviate from scriptural directions for worship he stated that there

> ... can be no justification of a change that it is not in express terms forbidden – enough to condemn it is the fact of its being unauthorized. Nothing *in* worship is lawful which is 'not appointed in the Word'. [With respect to the] parts of

[38] Wilson, *Memorials of Robert Smith Candlish DD*, p. 544.

worship, and their relative importance, and the manner in which they are to be performed, the Church has no alternative but to adhere to the rule which the Lord has given.[39]

During his lifetime, he became increasingly concerned that many in the Lowland Free Church were seeking to take the church in unbiblical directions, so the list of causes in which John Kennedy was involved was a long one. It is not that he sought conflict, but rather he believed it was his duty to defend the gospel and the practice of the Free Church which he loved so much.

One of the things that is very striking about all of Kennedy's writings on controversial issues is his desire to accurately reflect the Scriptures and the *Westminster Confession of Faith*. Unlike some of his opponents, who at times seemed more concerned about what might work on a pragmatic level, Kennedy tried his best to ask first what was right from a biblical perspective. Some may argue he didn't always get the right answer to this question, but he was certainly starting from the right place.

It is also important to note that Kennedy's opposition to some trends in the Free Church did not mean that he lived a life isolated from other Christians. He was an ecumenically spirited man who enjoyed a particularly good relationship with C.H. Spurgeon. Spurgeon was invited to preach at the opening of the new Free Church building in Dingwall in May of 1870 and when he returned to England, he wrote this in a letter to Kennedy:

---

[39] Kennedy, *The Present Cast and Tendency of Religions Thought and Feeling in Scotland: Eight Articles Contributed to the 'Inverness Courier' from 4th February to 1st April 1879*, p. 57.

You are very kind to express the pleasure my visit gave you, but rest assured mine was quite equal to yours. It was a sunny spot in a very sunny life when I saw you ... I shall always look back on it with unfeigned joy, and we will even talk of it in heaven, for the Lord was there.[40]

THEOLOGIAN OF THE HIGHLANDS

As has already been noted, Kennedy was proud of his Highland heritage and he saw it as part of his ministry to proclaim, defend and maintain some of the distinctive features of Highland Presbyterianism. *The Days of the Fathers in Ross-Shire* is both a defence of the religion of the Highlands and attempt to explain it to those from the Lowlands. The book can also be viewed as a plea for understanding. Kennedy's hope was that if people didn't fully understand the spiritual life that he depicted, they would at least respect it.

One of the foundational arguments of the book is that the Highland Christian experience was based on a desire 'to raise a godly seed'. The leaders of the church or 'the fathers' also saw it as their duty to cultivate deep piety in the church. Kennedy notes that

... personal Christianity was the great object on which their attention and their labour were bestowed. They were not anxious merely to spread a layer of religion thinly over the face of society, but to obtain, from the Lord's hand, living specimens of the power of His Grace. [41]

As a result of this desire for sincere faith, the Highland church guarded admission to the Sacrament of Lord's Supper very

---

[40] Spurgeon. *Autobiography v. 2: The Full Harvest*, p. 255.

[41] Kennedy, *The Days of the Fathers in Ross-Shire*, p. 136.

carefully. Kennedy explains this position in the following way. He says that the fathers

> ... regarded the guests at the table as having the most conspicuous connection with the cause and glory of Christ. They saw the Church pointing the eye of the world to a Communion table, to inform them whom she accredited as the true people of God. On all these accounts they felt that they were specially called to guard the passage to the table of the Lord, and to subject to the closest scrutiny all who would approach it.[42]

John Macleod has noted that this policy resulted in 'no one [being] admitted to the Lord's Table without a clear conversion narrative'. In addition, intending communicants were expected to be able to 'answer questions on their [conversion] experience'.[43] Macleod also notes that this strict standard for participation in the Sacrament was actually against the official policy of the church which directed ministers and elders to examine people before admitting them to the Lord's Table, but this was to be done 'without any inquisitorial minuteness'.[44] It is not surprising therefore that the number of people who received the Sacrament was relatively low in some congregations and that there was real reluctance on the part of many people to submit to examination by the church.

If the standard for admission to the Lord's Table was unduly high, the same cannot be said for the way in which the Highland church typically dispensed baptism. The Free

---

[42] Ibid., p. 149.

[43] MacLeod, *Banner in the West: A Spiritual History of Lewis and Harris*, p. 316.

[44] Ibid.

Church's position on who should receive baptism was spelled out in the *Westminster Larger Catechism* question 166.

> *Question 166:* Unto whom is Baptism to be administered?
>
> *Answer:* Baptism is not to be administered to any that are out of the visible church, and so strangers from the covenant of promise, till they profess their faith in Christ, and obedience to him, but infants descending from parents, either both, or but one of them, professing faith in Christ, and obedience to him, are in that respect within the covenant, and to be baptized.[45]

Baptism was to be administered to all who professed saving faith and to their children. Kennedy, however, inherited and endorsed the practice of allowing children of adherents to be baptised. Adherents were those who themselves had been baptised but who had not professed faith so as to be allowed to receive the Lord's Supper.[46] Kennedy's argument was that because those who had themselves been baptised were members of the 'visible church', their children, as a result, were entitled to receive the Sacrament. That this was not the plain teaching of the Westminster Standards did not seem to concern him.

It is unfortunate that the overly strict guarding of the Lord's Supper stopped many worthy Christians from enjoying the blessing that comes from receiving the Sacrament. Also, the looser administration of baptism created situations where Kirk Sessions were faced with people who

---

[45] *Westminster Larger Catechism*, http://www.reformed.org/documents/ index.html?mainframe=http://www.reformed.org/documents/larger1 (accessed 5 June 2009).

[46] For a discussion on the development of the concept of the adherent in Scottish Presbyterianism, see A. Herron, 'Adherent', in *Dictionary of Scottish Church History and Theology*, p. 5.

requested baptism for their children when they were not living consistent Christian lives. It is important to note that one of the important principles of the Reformation was that the Sacraments should be properly administered and it is difficult to fully embrace Kennedy's arguments as being consistent with this. While there is no doubt that Kennedy and other Highland churchmen were seeking to build the church in a way that they believed pleased and glorified God, their distinctive views on who should receive the Sacraments were problematic.

Travels, Honours and Legacy

In 1873, Kennedy was persuaded to take a break from his labours. Although he had enjoyed good health for most of his life, his friends became concerned that he could not maintain the pace of his life. His time away from work was spent on a trip to North America. The trip had a twofold purpose. First, Kennedy wanted to visit with Highlanders who had emigrated to Canada; second, he was also anxious to attend the meeting of the Evangelical Alliance in New York. His lasting memories of the trip were of seeing Niagara Falls and meeting with Charles Hodge in Princeton. Also in 1873, Kennedy was awarded a Doctor of Divinity Degree by the University of Aberdeen, his *alma mater*. He accepted this degree with a mixture of pride and humility.

By the early 1880s Kennedy was beginning to lose some of his vigour due to the effects of diabetes. In 1884 he was again persuaded to take some time off and this time travelled to Italy. He died on his way home, on 29 April 1884. There was a massive outpouring of grief at his death with thousands of people attending his funeral in Dingwall Free Church. *The Scotsman* said of him in their obituary that the

... position which Dr Kennedy held in the Highlands among his Free Church countryman was unique. Like his greater friend Dr Begg, he has left a place vacant which it is not likely any man will ever occupy with like authority.[47]

Kennedy's claim to be called a father of the Free Church rests with the fact that he was, during his lifetime, able to serve as an articulate spokesman for those who wished to maintain traditional views on issues of worship and confessional orthodoxy within the church, and he played no small part in slowing union with the United Presbyterian Church. Further, the Free Church which survived into the twentieth century was largely a Highland denomination that closely reflected the values that Kennedy held dear. Most importantly, he set an example for those who would seek to 'proclaim the truth positively and thereby to glorify God'. [48]

---

[47] 'The Late Rev. Dr John Kennedy of Dingwall', *The Scotsman Digital Archive, April 29th 1884*, http://archive.scotsman.com/ (accessed 5 June 2009).

[48] Sell, *Defending and Declaring the faith: Some Scottish Examples 1860–1920*, p. 37.

DISRUPTION WORTHIES

A Memorial of 1843.

With an Historical Sketch of the Free Church of Scotland
from 1843 down to the Present Time

By the REV. JAMES A. WYLIE, LL.D.

AUTHOR OF THE "HISTORY OF PROTESTANTISM"

LEAVING THE MANSE: A MEMORIAL OF THE DISRUPTION

VOLUME I.

EDINBURGH
THOMAS C. JACK, GRANGE PUBLISHING WORKS
(Successor to A. Fullarton & Co.)
LONDON: 45 LUDGATE HILL

12

THE CHURCH IN THE TWENTY-FIRST CENTURY

*The [Free] Church still looks to its sole King and Head
and prosecutes its various enterprises in reliance upon
His grace, provision and guidance – still jealous of the
Crown Rights of Jesus.*[1]

*A*S we examined the lives of ten key figures in the life
of the Free Church of Scotland, we encountered men
who were committed to the proclamation of the gospel and
to meeting the needs of the world in which they lived. All
of them were extremely gifted but nevertheless displayed
lapses of judgment and made missteps at various points
in their lives. They were not perfect men, but from the
vantage point of the twenty-first century, it is important
that we understand their common commitments, where
they differed, and most importantly why their lives still
have something to say to the contemporary church.

COMMON COMMITMENTS

The first thing to note about these men is that they had
a high regard for the church of Christ. For them commitment to and involvement in the life of the church was not
an option; it was a command. They all believed that the
message of the gospel had been given to the church to

---

[1] Clement Graham, 'Introduction', in C. Graham, *Crown Him Lord of
All: essays on the life and witness of the Free Church of Scotland*, p. vii.

proclaim to a needy world and that it was also their duty to defend the truth when it was challenged. This call to commitment was certainly expressed by preaching the gospel, but it also encompassed education, evangelism and various forms of social action.

Second, they were men of principle. The principle they were called upon most to defend in their day was the spiritual independence of the church. If they had not believed in this, they would never have joined the Free Church. It must be remembered that by leaving the established church in Scotland, Free Church ministers lost their livelihoods, their homes and their church buildings. They took this step because they wholeheartedly believed that God was calling them to defend the church from the encroachment of the state into the affairs of the church. It is also important to remember that many of them could have stayed in the established church, but they recognised that to do so was to compromise the truth. They could not step away from their principles no matter what the consequences might be.

Third, the first generation of leaders in the Free Church were all committed to an extremely high view of Scripture. A careful reading of the early theologians of the Free Church displays general agreement that Scripture is 'fully and equally God's word and man's', [2] and all of them accepted that it was inerrant. They therefore devoted themselves to the study of the Bible and to teaching its message as clearly as they could.

A fourth common element in the first years of the Free Church was a commitment to the Calvinism expressed

[2] Nicholas R. Needham, *The Doctrine of Holy Scripture in the Free Church Fathers* (Edinburgh: Rutherford House Books, 1991), p. 152.

in the *Westminster Confession of Faith* and *Catechisms*. While there were some points of difference over what might be considered smaller matters, there was broad agreement on a statement of faith that provided a foundation upon which to live and work. In writing about James Begg, James W. Campbell commented that Begg believed that in its *Confession* '...the church possessed a foundation which was above the whims of the moment [and] that was superior to the demands of the age'. [3] This view was shared by the founders of the Free Church, although it has to be admitted that toward the end of Begg's life, many were beginning to question this and were in fact putting their faith in the programmes and institutions of the church rather than in what the church confessed. As a result, the basis for unity became what the church was doing rather than what it believed and taught.

Finally, the founders of the Free Church all believed that the church should reach out to the world. This commitment was evident in the Free Church from its earliest days. Thomas Chalmers sought to bring about a godly commonwealth through his parish model and through his vision that the Free Church should become a truly national church. James Begg and Thomas Guthrie worked hard for improvements in housing and education, recognising that the church should not remain aloof from the problems of the world. Alexander Duff devoted his life to the belief that the chief purpose of the church was missionary work. While these men took different approaches, all of them

---

[3] Campbell, *Trembling for the Ark of God: James Begg and the Free Church of Scotland*, p. 111.

were animated by a desire to see the 'Great Commission' put into action both at home and abroad.

Divergent Views and Approaches

While these men had much in common, they also had some divergent views. As we have seen, the church was able to peacefully coexist when some held different opinions on issues such as the interpretation of prophecy and, to a lesser extent, the understanding of what properly constituted worship.

The Free Church also encompassed men who believed in different approaches to ministry. Ministers like Andrew Bonar endorsed the usage of mass evangelism to reach the lost, while at the same time those like John Kennedy believed that the gospel was best presented through preaching, catechising and pastoral care in the local church. The fact that men like James Begg and Thomas Guthrie, who in contemporary terms might be called social radicals, could live peacefully with more pietistic men like Andrew Bonar, speaks well of the health of the church. The Free Church at its best provides a reminder that it is possible to have unity without absolute uniformity.

Initially, the church's diversity could be viewed as strength, but there came a point when this was no longer the case. When the Free Church began to give way on core commitments, decline was inevitable. By the early 1890s, as the issue of church union was being hotly debated, the Free Church took the disastrous step of passing a 'Declaratory Act' which allowed much looser subscription to the *Westminster Confession*. While this act made union with the United Presbyterians possible, it also meant division since it resulted in the creation of the Free Presbyterian Church of Scotland.[4]

The changes that took place in the Free Church at the end of the nineteenth century were motivated, at least in part, by a desire to appear 'enlightened and forward looking', [5] but the final result shows that principles were replaced by pragmatism, and faithfulness exchanged for expediency. The doctrinal slide of the Free Church at the end of the nineteenth century provides a clear warning that still needs to be heeded. A church that puts a priority on pragmatics rather than principle has lost its way and ultimately will become irrelevant.

LESSONS FOR THE TWENTY-FIRST CENTURY

The Free Church which survived the convulsions of the church union movement in Scotland was a much-reduced body which some viewed as an anachronism.[6] After 1900, there were even predictions that it would die within five

---

[4] The sad saga of the Declaratory Act and the church union question has been given extensive study. For an academic treatment, see James Lachlan MacLeod's *The Second Disruption: The Free Church in Victorian Scotland and the Origins of the Free Presbyterian Church. Scottish historical review monographs series, no. 8.* For the Free Church of Scotland's perspective, see Maurice Grant, 'The heirs of the Disruption in crisis and recovery 1893–1920', in C. Graham, *Crown Him Lord of All: essays on the life and witness of the Free Church of Scotland*, pp. 1–36. For the views of the Free Presbyterian Church see that denomination's official history. Free Presbyterian Church of Scotland, *History of the Free Presbyterian Church of Scotland 1893–1970* (Glasgow: Publications Committee, Free Presbyterian Church of Scotland, 1975), pp. 59–69.

[5] Grant, 'The heirs of the Disruption in crisis and recovery 1893–1920', p. 6.

[6] Those wishing to read a brief summary of the history of Free Church in the first part of the twentieth century, particularly with respect to the issues of church union, should consult G.N.M. Collins, *The Heritage of Our Fathers*, chapters 19 and 20.

years, but it has survived and continues to minister in the United Kingdom, in North America and through connections with various missionary endeavours in other parts of the world.

Both the history of the Free Church and its contemporary existence are reminders that God honours faithfulness. The stand taken by Thomas Chalmers and his supporters in 1843 was an important moment in church history. These men embraced principles that still have relevance for the contemporary church. The Disruption in the Church of Scotland and the creation of the Free Church was, first and foremost, about the spiritual independence of the church. The leaders of the Disruption-era Free Church were committed to the belief that 'Christ is Head and Lord of the Church and has appointed a structure of government and godly administration within it'. [7] There was also broad consensus that the state was a divinely appointed institution and that church and state must work cooperatively for the public good. It followed from this that 'the two structures were obligated to help and nurture one another without interference by either in the province of the other'. [8]

It is stating the obvious to say that this view of the relationship between church and state has altered dramatically since the Free Church came into existence. The church has become weaker and is now just one voice among many. Further, the 'American ideal of government "of the people, by the people and for the people" is generally accepted', at

---

[7] Clement Graham, 'The Headship of Christ in a Pluralistic Society', in C. Graham, *Crown Him Lord of All: essays on the life and witness of the Free Church of Scotland*, p. 136.

[8] Ibid.

least in the Western world.[9] This means that most people no longer see government as a divine institution. Rather, they believe that government only has legitimacy when it operates with the consent of the people. It has been pointed out that in 'an ideal situation the Church would be united and pure and the state would be just'. [10] Sadly, in our day, the church is divided and prone to faults, and the state far from just. So, what is to be done?

Surely we can say at least this much. It is appropriate for the church to encourage her members to be both politically aware and active. While the church as an institution should not be setting up political parties nor taking direct political action, it is her duty to educate her members to think wisely and biblically about the issues of the day. The founders of the Free Church believed that they had a right to speak publicly and this duty has not changed. It is time again for the church to be speaking with a clear voice to those in authority and reminding them of the 'demands and implications of [God's] Word for the conduct of public life'. [11] More than this, it is appropriate to note that if we are going to emulate their vision and be faithful to the message of the Scriptures we

> ...must widen our vision, open our mouths and work with our hands, for a just and peaceful society in which the Gospel is freely proclaimed to all men and people are

---

[9] Ibid., p. 137.

[10] David A. Robertson, 'Church and State: Good Neighbours and Good Friends', in C. Graham, Crown Him Lord of All: essays on the life and witness of the Free Church of Scotland, p. 54.

[11] Campbell, Trembling for the Ark of God: James Begg and the Free Church of Scotland, p. 108.

able to 'live peaceful and quiet lives in all godliness and holiness. This is good and pleases God our Saviour, who wants all men to be saved and to come to knowledge of the truth' (I Timothy 2:2). [12]

Clearly, the members of the nineteenth-century Free Church made a difference where they lived. They were not afraid to speak out and take action when they saw social injustice. Contrary to this view, some American Presbyterians developed the concept of 'the spirituality of the church'. One articulation of this view came from the pen of Charles Hodge, the nineteenth-century Princeton theologian. He wrote that

...the state has no authority in matters purely spiritual and that the church [has] no authority in matters purely secular or civil. To be sure, in some cases their spheres of responsibility overlapped. Still, the two institutions are distinct, and their respective duties are different. [13]

While few in the reformed tradition would disagree with this, in practice the spirituality of the church has often come to mean something quite different and much more radical. Sean Michael Lucas has described the modern manifestation of this concept in these terms. It means that

...the church, especially in its ministerial and declarative functions, has no authority or power granted to it by the resurrected and ascended Christ to teach on moral matters that may be issues under consideration in the broader

---

[12] Robertson, *'Church and State: Good Neighbours and Good Friends'*, p. 54.

[13] Charles Hodge, 'The General Assembly', *Biblical Repertory and Princeton Review*, v. 33, n. 3 (1861), p. 557.

public realm. This would be evidenced in comments that the church should not preach or teach on issues related to poverty, systemic injustice, or racism because those are 'public' issues.[14]

The ministers, elders and laity who made up the early Free Church would not have recognised this as biblical and it is good that they did not. Had they accepted this view, they would not have spoken about issues such as the housing conditions of the poor, abuse of alcohol and the urgent requirement to do something about the education of poor children. It is also worth noting that the social activism of the early Free Church was not just a concern of the church's ministers. Hugh Miller's *Witness* newspaper frequently addressed the social and political issues of the day. Many of the church's laity were actively involved in their communities seeking to put the gospel into practice.

Another key component of the early Free Church was a passion for missions. The church in Scotland may have been a little slow to embrace the concept of world missions, but by the end of the nineteenth-century, the Free Church had seven different fields of missionary endeavour, encompassing Aden in modern day Yemen, India, Natal, what is now known as Malawi, the New Hebrides, South Africa and Syria. In addition there was missionary work focused on Jewish evangelism.[15]

---

[14] Sean Michael Lucas, *The Spirituality of the Church*, http:// seanmichaellucas.blogspot.com/2007/03/spirituality-of-church.html (accessed 23 July 2009).

[15] W.D. Graham, 'Beyond the Borders of Scotland: The Church's Missionary Enterprise', in C. Graham, *Crown Him Lord of All: essays on the life and witness of the Free Church of Scotland*, p. 101.

The Free Church's missionary work was motivated principally by two things. First and foremost, there was the firm 'belief in the Divine Sovereignty and the Kingship of Christ over all nations which [gave] an authority to Christian missions'.[16] God had created the world, sent his Son to redeem it from sin and now called upon the church to tell the good news to those who had not as yet heard it. Secondly, the church's missionary endeavour was animated by an optimistic eschatology. W.D. Graham has noted that with a

> ... few (but notable) exceptions the eschatology of Scottish evangelicalism, as represented by the Disruption Church, was post-millennialism.[17] This put a very distinct stamp upon the whole missionary movement of the church. The missionaries viewed the future with enthusiasm – the Christian optimism that, having been placed in the world to be lights for Christ and to work for the coming of His kingdom, they could concentrate upon those activities which would not only convert individuals but Christianise nations.[18]

As we reflect on this optimism, it is tempting to assert that it is just outdated romanticism from a bygone age. After

---

[16] Ibid., p. 94.

[17] It is important to note here that the post-millennialism of the nineteenth-century Free Church should not be confused with modern-day theonomy or Christian Reconstructionism. The Disruption era Free Church was not interested in a Christianity that was forced on the society through the radical imposition of Old Testament civil law. Rather, it believed that the gospel had the power to transform nations and cultures just as it does people who have come to faith in Christ. For a contemporary treatment of post-millennialism, see John Jefferson Davis, *Christ's Victorious Kingdom: Postmillennialism Reconsidered* (Grand Rapids, Mich.: Baker Book House, 1986).

[18] Graham, 'Beyond the Borders of Scotland: The Church's Missionary Enterprise', p. 95.

all, despite the significant missionary successes in the first fifty years of the Free Church, the grand vision has not been fully realised. Further, by the beginning of the twentieth century the impetus for missions had changed. The biblical eschatology of the nascent Free Church had been supplanted by liberal Protestantism's version of the social gospel, and by evangelicalism's almost total embrace of premillennialism, which no longer believed that the nations could be brought to Christ. Put very bluntly, the evangelical missionary agenda was now believed to be, in G.W. Brooke's inelegant and condescending phrase, 'giving the simple gospel message to the greatest number possible of ignorant heathen, in the shortest possible time'. [19]

As the church considers missionary strategy in the twenty-first century, a number of key factors must be kept in mind. First, immigration to Western countries from other parts of the world has placed the mission field at the front door of the Western church. Not only are there many people representing all of the world's major faiths living in the West, but the secularisation of Western culture means that there are large numbers of people who have not embraced Christianity. Indeed, as Jesus said, 'the fields are white for harvest' (John 4:35). Being a missionary in the nineteenth century usually meant making significant personal sacrifices, leaving the comforts of home and travelling to exotic parts of the world. In the twenty-first century, the mission field is everywhere and it is the calling of all Christians to be ambassadors for Christ wherever we are placed.

A second factor in developing mission strategy is the continuing population shift from rural to urban. Men like

---

[19] Ibid.

Thomas Chalmers, James Begg, Thomas Guthrie and Andrew Bonar were city pastors and sought to find ways to reach city populations. If anything, the population shift to the cities has become even more pronounced. As a result, Roger Greenway has correctly noted that the church must

> build an urban strategy on the more solid foundations of a Calvinist world and life view. The Biblical Gospel is far larger than either the liberal social activists or the traditional fundamentalists imagine. It is a gospel which includes winning disciples to Christ, and establishing churches, and building a Christian community with all its facets and areas of concern. The whole city, from top to bottom, must be called to repentance toward God and faith in the Lord Jesus Christ. This is the full gospel which requires the total renewal of man and his society, and it is the only Gospel which offers any genuine hope for today's urban world.[20]

As the modern church contemplates its missionary strategy and programme for evangelism one might be tempted to think that the message needs to change in order to be attractive to a modern world. While appropriate contextualisation should always be welcomed, what the church really needs is renewed confidence in the historic message of the gospel. The church also should reaffirm the truth that

> ... Christ [is] ... Saviour [and] Lord of the universe as well as Head of his Church. This delivers [us] ... from frustration and pessimism and provides a beacon of hope no matter how grim and difficult and hostile the material prospect may be.[21]

---

[20] Roger S. Greenway, *Calling Our Cities to Christ* (Nutley, N.J.: Presbyterian and Reformed, 1973), pp. 111–12.

[21] Graham, 'The Headship of Christ in a Pluralistic Society', p. 152.

As the church worships, witnesses and cares for the world, it should do so with the confident expectation that the message of the gospel has the power to transform the lives of individuals and nations. The church needs to be reminded that

> Christ the mighty King reigns *now*, and his invincible power is available to the church. It is in this hope that Christ's disciples can labour confidently and perseveringly for the extension of his kingdom in the world.[22]

We have already quoted Thomas Chalmers' vision for the Free Church, but it is worth repeating. It was right for the Free Church in his day and it is still true for all the church.

> Jesus Christ died, the just for the unjust to bring us unto God. This is a truth, which, when all the world shall receive it, all the world will be renovated ... It is this doctrine which is the lone instrument of God for the transformation of our species.[23]

---

[22] Davis, *Christ's Victorious Kingdom: Postmillennialism Reconsidered*, p. 134.

[23] Chalmers, *The Works of Thomas Chalmers*, v. 6, p. 261.

Bibliography

In addition to the books, journal articles and internet sites cited in this bibliography, extensive use has been made of *The Scotsman Digital Archive*, http://archive.scotsman.com/ which makes available the contents of *The Scotsman* newspaper from 1817–1950. The *New York Times Digital Archives*, http://select.nytimes.com/mem/archive which covers the years 1850–1980 has also been used.

Aird, Andrew, *Glimpses of Old Glasgow* (Glasgow: Aird & Coghill, 1894).

Anderson, Gerald H., *Biographical Dictionary of Christian Missions* (Grand Rapids, MI: W.B. Eerdmans, 1999).

Anderson, William, *A Guide to the Free Church of Scotland College and Offices* (Edinburgh: Knox Press, 1994).

'Andrew Bonar', *Banner of Truth Online*, http://www.banneroftruth.org/pages/articles/article_detail.php?642

Auld, Alexander, *Life of John Kennedy, D.D.* (London: T. Nelson and Sons, 1887).

Baillie, John (ed.), *Proceedings of the General Assembly of the Free Church of Scotland: With a Sketch of the Proceedings of the Residuary Assembly, 1843* (Edinburgh: W.P. Kennedy, 1843).

Barron, James, *Memoir of Rev. John Kennedy D.D., of Dingwall* (Inverness Courier, 1893), http://kennedy.nesher.org.uk/Memoir_of_Dr_Kennedy.html

Bayne, Peter, *The Life and Letters of Hugh Miller* (London: Strahan & Co., 1871).

Begg, James, *The Hand of God in the Disruption and the Vital Importance of Free Church Principles. Being an Address delivered at the Opening of the General Assembly of the Free Church of Scotland on the 18th of May 1865*, http://nesher.org.uk/JBS/ebooks/begg_presbyterianism/begg_presbyterianism_01.html

Begg, James, *Happy Homes for Working Men, And How to Get Them* (London: Cassell, Petter, & Galpin, 1866).

Beith, Alexander, *A Highland Tour: Three Weeks with Dr Candlish (2nd edition)* (Edinburgh: Adam and Charles Black, 1874).

Bishop, Steve, 'Protestant Missionary Education in British India' *Evangelical Quarterly* 69:3 (1997).

Bonar, Andrew A., *Memoir and Remains of Robert Murray M'Cheyne* (Edinburgh: Oliphant, Anderson and Ferrier, n.d.).

Bonar, Andrew A. and Robert Murray M'Cheyne, *Narrative of a Mission of Inquiry to the Jews from the Church of Scotland in 1839* (Philadelphia: Presbyterian Board of Publication, 1842).

Bonar, Horatius, *The Old Gospel: Not 'Another Gospel', but the Power of God Unto Salvation : a Reply to Dr Kennedy's Pamphlet, 'Hyper-Evangelism'* (Edinburgh: Andrew Elliot, 1874).

Bonar, Marjorie, *Andrew A Bonar, DD, Diary and Letters, transcribed and edited by his daughter* (London: Hodder and Stoughton, 1894).

Bonar, Marjorie, *Reminiscences of Andrew A. Bonar, DD* (London: Hodder & Stoughton, 1895).

Brentnall, John M., *Just a Talker: Sayings of John 'Rabbi' Duncan* (Edinburgh: Banner of Truth, 1997).

Brown, David, *Life of the Late John Duncan LLD, Professor of Hebrew and Oriental Languages, New College, Edinburgh* (Edinburgh: Edmonston and Douglas, 1872).

Brown, Stewart J., 'The Making of New College: 1843–6', *New College Bulletin* (2006).

Brown, Stewart J. *Thomas Chalmers and the Godly Commonwealth in Scotland*. Oxford: Oxford University Press, 1982.

Brown, Thomas, *Annals of the Disruption: with extracts from the narratives of Ministers who left the Scottish establishment in 1843* (Edinburgh: Macnivan and Wallace, 1890).

Campbell, Iain D., 'The Church in Scotland 1840–1940: An Overview, *Quodlibet Journal*, v.1, no. 8 (December 1999), http://www.quodlibet.net/articles/campbell-scotland.shtml

Campbell, Iain D, 'Resolutions of a Preacher', *Loch a Tuath News* (January 2001), http://www.backfreechurch.co.uk/studies/latn/latn_0008.jsp

Campbell, James W., *Trembling for the Ark of God: James Begg and the Free Church of Scotland*, Thesis (Th. M.) – Westminster Theological Seminary (1980).

Candlish, Robert, S., The Fatherhood of God: *Being the First Course of the Cunningham Lectures Delivered Before the New College, Edinburgh, in March 1864* (Edinburgh: Adam and Charles Black, 1865).

Candlish, Robert, S. (ed.), *The Organ Question: Statements of Dr Ritchie, and Dr Porteous, for and against the use of the organ in public worship, in the proceedings of the Presbytery of Glasgow 1807–08 with an Introductory notice by Robert S. Candlish, D.D.* (Edinburgh: Johnstone and Hunter, 1856).

Candlish, Robert, *Sermons by the Late Robert S. Candlish. Minister of Free St George's and Principal of the New College, Edinburgh* (Edinburgh: A & C . Black, 1874).

The Carlyle Letters Online, http://carlyleletters.dukejournals.org

Carlyle, Thomas, and R. Brimley Johnson, *Pen Portraits by Thomas Carlyle; Found in His Works and Correspondence* (London: G. Allen, 1896).

Cartwright, Hugh, 'Dr John Kennedy', *Monthly Record of the Free Church of Scotland* (October 1983).

Chalmers, Thomas, *Sermons and Discourses of Thomas Chalmers, D.D., L.L.D., Now Completed by the Introduction of his Posthumous Sermons* (New York: Robert Carter & Brothers, 1853).

Chalmers, Thomas, *The Works of Thomas Chalmers* (Glasgow: William Collins, 1836–42).

Cheyne, A.C., *The Transforming of the Kirk: Victorian Scotland's Religious Revolution* (Edinburgh: Saint Andrew Press, 1983).

Clark, E.A.G., 'The Superiority of the "Scotch System": Scottish Ragged Schools and Their Influence', *Scottish Educational Studies*, v. 9, no 1 (May 1977).

Collins, G.N.M., T*he Heritage of Our Fathers* (Edinburgh: John Knox Press, 1976).

The Confession of Faith Agreed upon by the Assembly of Divines at Westminster: Examined and approved, Anno 1647, by the General Assembly of the Church of Scotland; and ratified by Acts of Parliament 1649 and 1690, http://www.freechurch.org/resources/confessions/westminster.htm

Corbett, Steve, and Brian Fikkert, *When Helping Hurts: How to Alleviate Poverty Without Hurting the Poor – and Yourself* (Chicago, IL: Moody Press, 2009).

A Course of Lectures on the Jews by Ministers of the Established Church in Glasgow (Philadelphia: Presbyterian Board of Publication, 1840).

Cowan, Charles, *Reminiscences* (Edinburgh: Printed for Private Circulation, 1878).

Cunningham, William, *The Reformers and the Theology of the Reformation* (Edinburgh: T and T Clark, 1862).

Cunningham, William (J.J. Bonar ed.), *Sermons from 1825 to 1860* (Edinburgh: T & T Clark, 1872).

Davis, John Jefferson, *Christ's Victorious Kingdom: Postmillennialism Reconsidered* (Grand Rapids, Mich.: Baker Book House, 1986).

Dictionary of Canadian Biography Online, http://www.biographi.ca

The Directory for the Public Worship of God, http://www.reformed.org/documents/wcf_standards/index.html?mainframe=/documents/wcf_standards/p369-direct_pub_worship.html

Disruption Worthies: A Memorial of 1843 (Edinburgh: J. Greig & Son, 1876).

Disruption Worthies of the Highlands, a Memorial of 1843 (Edinburgh: John Grant, 1886).

Dow, Colin, 'Andrew Bonar – Joshua of the Disruption', Streams of Living Water: *Sermons and Writings of Rev. Colin Dow*. http://www.greekthomsonchurch.com/dowblog/2007/09/03/andrew-bonar-joshua-of-the-disruption/

'Dr Guthrie', *Free Church of Scotland Monthly Record* (1 Nov. 1864).

Duff, Alexander, *Extract of a Letter Respecting the Wreck of the Lady Holland East Indiaman, from the Rev. Alexander Duff, One of the Passengers in That Ship, Addressed to Dr Inglis, As Convenor of the General Assembly's Committee for the Propagation of the Gospel in India* (Edinburgh: John Waugh, 1830).

Duff, Alexander, *The Indian Rebellion; Its Causes and Results* (New York: R. Carter, 1858).

Duff, Alexander, *Missions the Chief End of the Christian Church: Also the Qualifications, Duties and Trials of an Indian Missionary; Being the Substance of Services Held at the Ordination of the Rev. Thomas Smith* (Edinburgh: Johnstone, 1840).

Duncan, John and William Angus Knight, *Colloquia Peripatetica* (Edinburgh: Edmonston & Douglas, 1873).

Fowler, John, *Mr Hill's Big Picture: The Day That Changed Scotland Forever Captured on Canvas* (Edinburgh: St Andrew Press, 2006).

Free Presbyterian Church of Scotland, *History of the Free Presbyterian Church of Scotland 1893–1970* (Glasgow: Publications Committee, Free Presbyterian Church of Scotland, 1975).

Geneva Bible Notes, http://www.reformedreader.org/gbn/gbnromans.htm

Gillies, James B. (ed.), *Disruption Worthies: A Memorial of 1843; with a Historical Sketch of the Free Church of Scotland from 1843 Down to the Present Time* (Edinburgh: T.C. Jack, 1881).

Graham, Clement (ed.), *Crown Him Lord of All: essays on the life and witness of the Free Church of Scotland* (Edinburgh: Knox Press, 1993).

Greenway, Roger S, *Calling Our Cities to Christ* (Nutley, N.J.: Presbyterian and Reformed, 1973).

Gribben, Crawford and Timothy C.F. Stunt (eds), *Prisoners of Hope? Aspects of Evangelical Millennialism in Britain and Ireland* (Carlisle: Paternoster Press, 2004).

'Guthrie, Thomas 1803–73', *Literate Lifetime*, http://literatelifetime.com/browse/author/Thomas_Guthrie

Guthrie, Thomas, David Kelly Guthrie and Charles John Guthrie, *Autobiography of Thomas Guthrie. D. D.: And Memoir by His Sons* (Detroit: Craig and Taylor, 1878).

Guthrie, Thomas, *A Plea for Ragged Schools or Prevention Better than Cure* (Edinburgh: John Elder, 1847).

Hanna, William, *Memoirs of the Life and Writings of Thomas Chalmers* (Edinburgh: Edmonston and Douglas, 1867).

Harman, Allan M., 'Introduction', in Andrew A Bonar and Robert Murray McCheyne, *Mission of Discovery* (Fearn, Ross-shire: Christian Focus, 1996).

Hodge, Charles, 'The General Assembly', *Biblical Repertory and Princeton Review*, v. 33, n. 3 (1861).

Honeycutt, Michael W., *William Cunningham: His Life, Thought, and Controversies*, Thesis (Ph. D.) – University of Edinburgh (2002).

Inauguration of the New College of the Free Church, Edinburgh (Edinburgh: Johnstone and Hunter, 1851).

Kennedy, John, *The Days of the Fathers in Ross-Shire. (5th edition)* (Inverness: Northern Chronicle Office, 1897).

Kennedy, John, *Hyper-Evangelism 'another Gospel', Though a Mighty Power: A Review of the Recent Religious Movement in Scotland* (Edinburgh: Duncan Grant & Co, 1874).

Kennedy, John, *Man's Relations to God Traced in Light of the Present Truth* (Edinburgh: John Maclaren, 1869).

Kennedy, John, *Memoir of Mrs Kennedy*, in Kennedy, John, *The Days of the Fathers in Ross-Shire (5th edition)* (Inverness: Northern Chronicle Office, 1897).

Kennedy, John, *The Present Cast and Tendency of Religions Thought and Feeling in Scotland: Eight Articles Contributed to the Inverness Courier from 4th February to 1st April 1879* (Inverness: Northern Counties Newspaper and Printing and Publishing Company, 1955).

Kennedy, John, *Sermons by the late Rev. Dr Kennedy, Dingwall* (Inverness: Northern Chronicle Office, 1888).

Lachman, D.C. and D.E. Meek (eds), *Dictionary of Scottish Church History and Theology* (Downers Grove Ill: InterVarsity Press, 1993).

Laird, Michael A, 'The legacy of Alexander Duff', *Occasional Bulletin of Missionary Research* 3:4 (October 1979).

Larsen, Timothy, D.W. Bebbington and Mark A. Noll (eds) *Biographical Dictionary of Evangelicals* (Leicester, England: InterVarsity Press, 2003).

Lucas, Sean Michael, *The Spirituality of the Church*, http://seanmichaellucas.blogspot.com/2007/03/spirituality-of-church.html

MacColl, Allan W., *Land, Faith and the Crofting Community: Christianity and Social Criticism in the Highlands of Scotland, 1843–93* (Edinburgh: Edinburgh University Press, 2006).

McIntosh, John, 'The Events of 1900', *The Monthly Record of the Free Church of Scotland* (October 2000).

Mackay, William M., *Thomas Chalmers: A Short Appreciation* (Edinburgh: Knox Press, 1980).

Mackay, William M., *Thomas Chalmers And His Vision Of The Church Of Scotland*, (Edinburgh: Free Church of Scotland), http://www.freechurch.org/resources/history/chalmers2.htm

Macleod, Donald, 'Footnotes', *West Highland Free Press*, 26 April 2002, http://www.hughmiller.org/controversies_g.asp

Macleod, Donald, 'Macleod on Miller', *Monthly Record of the Free Church of Scotland* (January 2003).

Macleod, Donald, 'Our Fathers: Where are They?' *Monthly Record of the Free Church of Scotland* (May 1984).

MacLeod, James Lachlan, *The Second Disruption: The Free Church in Victorian Scotland and the Origins of the Free Presbyterian Church*, Scottish historical review monographs series, no. 8 (East Linton, Scotland: Tuckwell Press, 2000).

Macleod, John, *Banner in the West: A Spiritual History of Lewis and Harris* (Edinburgh: Birlinn, 2008).

MacLeod, John, *Scottish Theology in Relation to Church History Since the Reformation: Lectures delivered in Westminster Theological Seminary, Philadelphia, USA* (Edinburgh: Publications Committee of the Free Church of Scotland, 1943).

Marx, Karl, *Capital: A Critique of Political Economy* (New York: Modern Library, 1936).

Matthew, H.C.G., and Brian Howard Harrison, *Oxford Dictionary of National Biography: In Association with the British Academy: from the Earliest Times to the Year 2000* (Oxford: Oxford University Press, 2004).

Millar, A.A., *Alexander Duff of India* (Edinburgh: Canongate Press, 1992).

Miller, Hugh, *Headship of Christ and the Rights of the Christian People* (Boston: Gould and Lincoln, 1863).

Miller, Hugh, *My Schools and Schoolmasters*; or, *the Story of my Education* (Edinburgh: William P. Nimmo & Co., 1879).

Miller, Hugh, *The Testimony of the Rocks*; or, *Geology in its Bearings on the Two Theologies, Natural and Revealed* (Boston: Gould and Lincoln, 1857).

Moody Stuart, A., *Recollections of the Late John Duncan LLD. Professor of Hebrew and Oriental Languages, New College, Edinburgh* (Edinburgh: Edmonston and Douglas, 1872).

Moody Stuart, A., *The Life of John Duncan* (Edinburgh: Banner of Truth, 1991).

Moody, William Revell, *The Life of Dwight L. Moody* (New York: Fleming H. Revell, 1900).

Murray, John and William Young, *Minority Report of the Committee on Song in the Public Worship of God Submitted to the Fourteenth General Assembly of the Orthodox Presbyterian Church*, http://www.opc.org/GA/song.html#Minority

Needham, Nicholas R., *The Doctrine of Holy Scripture in the Free Church Fathers* (Edinburgh: Rutherford House Books, 1991).

Noble, John, 'Memoir of John Kennedy', in Kennedy, John, *The Days of the Fathers in Ross-Shire (5th edition)* (Inverness: Northern Chronicle Office, 1897).

Old, Hughes Oliphant, *The Reading and Preaching of the Scriptures in the Worship of the Christian Church, vol. 6* (Grand Rapids, Mich.: Eerdmans, 2004).

Paton, William, *Alexander Duff, Pioneer of Missionary Education* (New York: George H. Doran, 1922).

'A Plea For Ragged Schools or Prevention Better than Cure', *Edinburgh Review or Critical Journal*, v. 85 (January–April 1847).

Piggin, Stuart and John Roxborogh, *The St Andrews Seven: The Finest Flowering of Missionary Zeal in Scottish History* (Edinburgh: Banner of Truth Trust, 1985).

Price, John, *Old Light on New Worship: Musical Instruments and the Worship of God, a Theological, Historical and Psychological Study* (Avinger, Tex: Simpson Pub, 2005).

Rainy, Robert and James Mackenzie, *Life of William Cunningham, DD* (London: T. Nelson and Sons, 1871).

'Rev. Dr Duff', *The Globe* (20 March 1854).

Richardson, Alexander, *The Future Church of Scotland by 'Freelance'* (Edinburgh: Maclachlan & Stewart, 1870).

Robertson, James, *Observations on the Veto Act* (Edinburgh: W. Blackwood, 1840).

Rodger, Richard, *The Transformation of Edinburgh: Land, Property, and Trust in the Nineteenth Century* (New York , N.Y.: Cambridge University Press, 2001).

Ross, Kenneth R., 'Calvinists in Controversy: John Kennedy, Horatius Bonar and the Moody Mission of 1873–4', in *Scottish Bulletin of Evangelical Theology*, v. 9, no. 1 (Spring 1991).

Simpson, Patrick Carnegie, *The Life of Principal Rainy* (London: Hodder and Stoughton, 1909).

Rosie, George, *Hugh Miller: Outrage and Order: a Biography and Selected Writings* (Edinburgh: Mainstream Pub., 1981).

Ross, John S. (ed.), 'A Family Correspondence: Letters of John Duncan and His Daughter, Maria Dorothea, and Her Husband, Adolph Spaeth, with Extracts from Maria's Diary'. *Reformed Theological Journal (Belfast)* 14 (1998).

Ross, John S., 'The Legacy of John Duncan', *International Bulletin of Missionary Research*, v. 29, no. 3 (Jul 2005).

Ross, John S., 'The Most Fruitful of All Missionary Work', *New Horizons*, http://www.opc.org/nh.html?article_id=459

Roxborough, John, 'The Legacy of Thomas Chalmers', *International Bulletin of Missionary Research*, v. 23, no. 4 (October 1999).

Scott, Hew, *Synod of Glasgow and Ayr. Fasti Ecclesiae Scoticanae: The succession of ministers in the Church of Scotland from the Reformation. Revised and continued to the present time under the superintendence of a committee*, vol. 3 (Edinburgh: Oliver & Boyd, 1920).

Sell, Alan P.F., *Defending and Declaring the faith: Some Scottish Examples 1860–1920* (Exeter: Paternoster Press, 1987).

Sinclair, James Steven, *Rich Gleanings After the Vintage from 'Rabbi' Duncan* (London: Chas. J. Thynne & Jarvis, 1925).

Smith, George, *The Life of Alexander Duff* (two volumes in one) (New York: American Tract Society, 1880).

Smith, Thomas, *Memoirs of James Begg, D.D.: Minister of Newington Free Church, Edinburgh* (Edinburgh: J. Gemmell, 1885).

Spurgeon, C.H., *C.H. Spurgeon Autobiography. Volume 2: The Full Harvest, 1860–92* (Edinburgh: Banner of Truth Trust, 1973).

Stroup, Herbert Hewitt, *Social Welfare Pioneers* (Chicago: Nelson-Hall, 1986).

Sutherland, Elizabeth, *Lydia, Wife of Hugh Miller of Cromarty* (East Linton: Tuckwell Press, 2003).

Taylor, Michael A., *Hugh Miller, Stonemason, Geologist, Writer* (Edinburgh: National Museums of Scotland, 2007).

Vaudry, Richard W., *The Free Church in Victorian Canada: 1844–61* (Waterloo, Ontario: Wilfred Laurier University Press, 1989).

Walker, Norman L., *Chapters from the History of the Free Church of Scotland* (Edinburgh: Oliphant, Anderson and Ferrier, 1895).

Walsh, W. Pakenham, *Modern Heroes of the Mission Field* (New York: T. Whittaker, 1882).

Ward, Rowland S., *Psalm-Singing in Scripture and History: A Study in History and Doctrine.* (Victoria, Australia: R.S. Ward, 1985).

Ward, Rowland S., *The Psalms in Christian Worship: A Doctrinal, Historical and Expository Guide* (Melbourne: Presbyterian Church of Eastern Australia, 1992).

Webber, Frederick R., 'Thomas Guthrie, Apostle to the Slums'. In *Concordia Theological Monthly*, v. 20, no. 6 (June 1949).

Westminster Larger Catechism, http://www.reformed.org/documents/ index.html?mainframe=http://www.reformed.org/documents/larger1

Wilson, William, *Memorials of Robert Smith Candlish D.D.* (Edinburgh: Adam and Charles Black, 1880).

Wright, D.F. and Badcock, G.D. (eds), *Disruption to Diversity: Edinburgh Divinity 1846–1996* (Edinburgh: T&T Clark, 1996).

"...a fine and fresh account of a great and godly minister of the gospel."
Eric Alexander

AWAKENING
THE LIFE & MINISTRY OF ROBERT MURRAY McCHEYNE
David Robertson

AWAKENING

The Life and Ministry of Robert Murray McCheyne

David Robertson

"Was Mccheyne for real?"; "Was he just famous because he died so young?"; "Does he have anything to teach us today?"

In this book, David Robertson, the present-day minister of McCheyne's church, St Peter's in Dundee, Scotland, seeks to answer these and other questions. Through the use of published sermons, private papers and historical material, this contemporary devotional biography traces McCheyne's life and influence from his upbringing, conversion and training for the ministry to the revival that occurred in St Peter's in 1839 and his early death. The contemporary relevance of McCheyne for today's church is demonstrated and the glory of God is seen in this wonderful story of what He can do with one 'consecrated sinner'.

The freshest presentation of McCheyne available
Ligon Duncan,
Senior Minister, First Presbyterian Church, Jackson, Mississippi

Having used Robert Murray McCheyne's 1842 Bible Reading Calendar for many years, and having admired his hunger for holiness, I am very glad that David Robertson has written this new biography.

John Stott,
Rector Emeritus, All Souls Church, Langham Place, London

...a fine and fresh account of a great and godly minister of the gospel. David Robertson gives us new insight into McCheyne's personal life, and his preparation for preaching, his deep social concern and his absolute devotion to the glory of God as the ultimate motive of everything he did.

Eric Alexander
formerly minister of St George's Tron Church, Glasgow

ISBN 978-1-84550-542-4

Constrained
by his
Love

*A New Biography
on
Robert Murray McCheyne*

LJ Van Valen

CONSTRAINED BY HIS LOVE

A New Biography of of Robert Murray McCheyne

LJ Van Valen

Robert Murray McCheyne was born in 1813 and died in 1843. His life, was nothing short of extraordinary. Given the charge of St Peter's Church, Dundee at the age of 23, even his trial sermon was blessed, with two people being saved. The church saw astonishing growth, overflowing with 1,100 hearers.

He stands today as one of the outstanding preachers in the history of Scotland. His spirituality, and focus on the work of Christ was immediately apparent – with hostile crowds melting as they realised the sincerity of the man and the power of his message.

His life is a lesson to us all, that when we submit to our Sovereign Lord and his plan, he can and will use our bodies, no matter how weak, our gifts, no matter how limited and our lives, no matter how short.

Finally – a definitive, contemporary biography on Robert Murray McCheyne abounding with historical detail, sterling illustrations, and spiritual warmth.

Joel R Beeke,
President, Puritan Reformed Theological Seminary,
Grand Rapids, Michigan

He was an outstanding man of God, and his life story, here told in fullest detail and with fullest sympathy, should on no account be missed.

J I Packer,
Board of Governors' Professor of Theology, Regent College,
Vancouver, Canada

ISBN 978-1-85792-793-1

THE
DAYS OF THE FATHERS
IN ROSS-SHIRE

John Kennedy D.D.

Days of the Fathers in Ross-shire

John Kennedy

Dr Kennedy was the pastor of Dingwall Free Church congregation from 1844 until his death in 1884 at the age of 65. He was renowned and powerful preacher whose services were in much demand by congregations throughout the the highlands and much of scotland. He was also a staunch defender of the reformed faith who as his friend describe him 'true as steel and firm as rock'. He has an honoured place among the chroniclers of the religious history and biography of the Highlands of Scotland.

ISBN 978-0-90673-100-0

Tom Lennie

"Just as Pentecost was desperately needed at the beginning of the Christian era, so another season of God-sent revival is the urgent need of this hour. A careful reading of "Glory in the Glen" will help in many ways."

Richard Owen Roberts
International Awakening Ministries

Glory in the Glen

A History of Evangelical Revivals in Scotland

1880–1940

GLORY IN THE GLEN

A History of Evangelical Revivals in Scotland 1880-1940

Tom Lennie

No nation on earth has a richer, more colourful, and more long-standing heritage of evangelical awakenings than Scotland - yet most people are unfamiliar with its dramatic legacy. Most historical studies stop at, or before, the Moody & Sankey Revival of 1873-74. It is commonly assumed that very few genuine revivals occurred since that date until the Lewis Revival of 1949-53. Tom Lennie thoroughly debunks this idea – showing that religious awakenings were relatively common in Scotland between these dates – and provides a comprehensive account of the many exciting revivals that have taken place throughout Scotland.

Extensively researched and engagingly written Tom Lennie is to be commended for bringing to life an element of Scottish church history that has not received the attention it deserves

Sandy Finlayson,
Westminster, Theological Seminary, Philadelphia, Pennsylvania

...a welcome addition to the literature on the evangelical history of Scotland. He has researched the sources – both oral and written – thoroughly, and has assessed the evidence thoughtfully...

Iain D Campbell,
Point Free Church of Scotland, Isle of Lewis

the awesome God of holiness himself drawing near to his people and setting mind and heart ablaze with glorious light. Read – and pray!

Michael A. G. Haykin,
The Southern Baptist Theological Seminary,
Louisville, Kentucky

ISBN 978-1-84550-377-2

Christian Focus Publications

publishes books for all ages

Our mission statement –
STAYING FAITHFUL

In dependence upon God we seek to impact the world through literature faithful to His infallible Word, the Bible. Our aim is to ensure that the LORD Jesus Christ is presented as the only hope to obtain forgiveness of sin, live a useful life and look forward to heaven with Him.

REACHING OUT

Christ's last command requires us to reach out to our world with His gospel. We seek to help fulfil that by publishing books that point people towards Jesus and help them develop a Christ-like maturity. We aim to equip all levels of readers for life, work, ministry and mission.

Books in our adult range are published in three imprints:

Christian Focus contains popular works including biographies, commentaries, basic doctrine and Christian living. Our children's books are also published in this imprint.

Mentor focuses on books written at a level suitable for Bible College and seminary students, pastors, and other serious readers. The imprint includes commentaries, doctrinal studies, examination of current issues and church history.

Christian Heritage contains classic writings from the past.

Christian Focus Publications Ltd
Geanies House, Fearn,
Ross-shire, IV20 1TW, Scotland, United Kingdom
info@christianfocus.com

Our titles are available from quality bookstores and
www.christianfocus.com